IMAGES
of America

ATLANTA

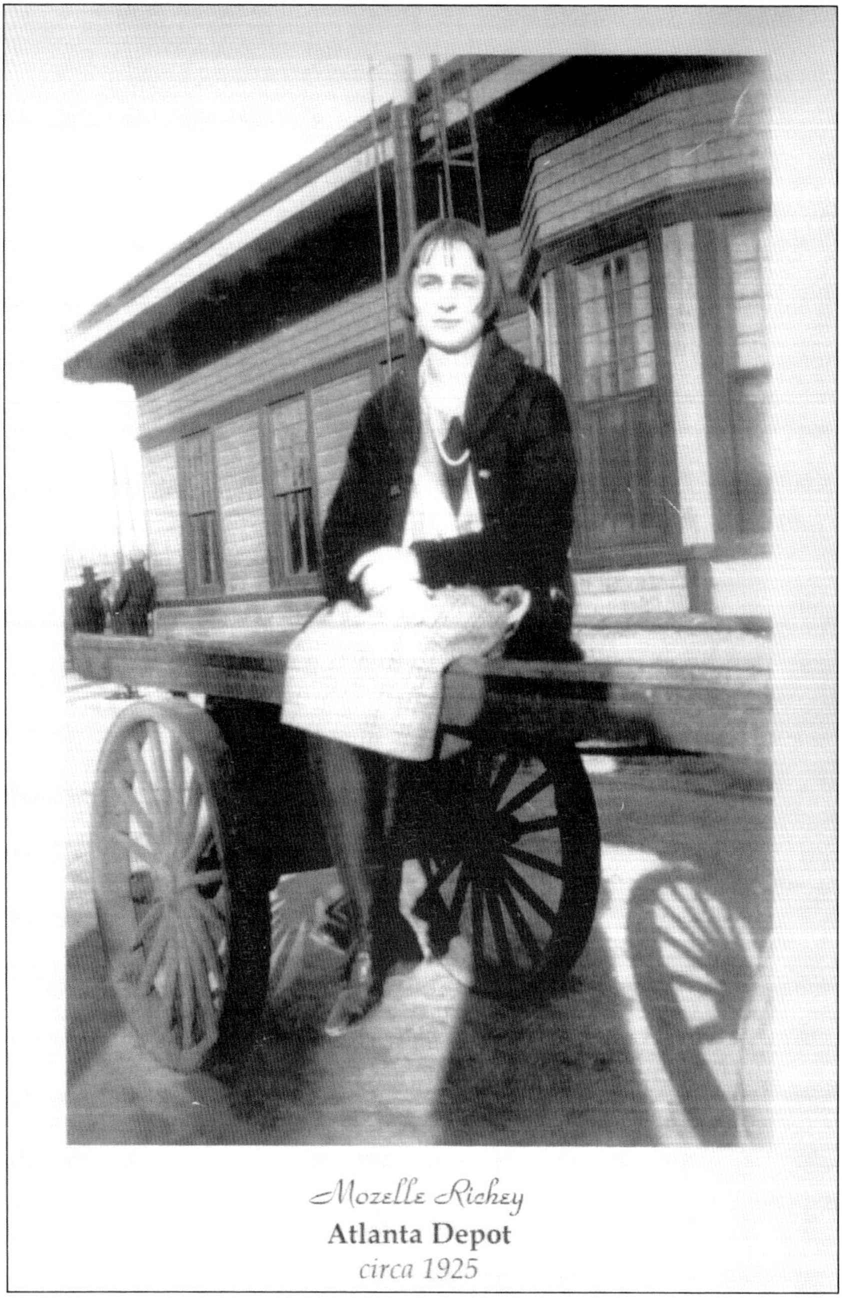

Mozelle Richey is pictured sitting in front of the Atlanta train depot on a dray wagon around 1925. Dray wagons were once a familiar site at train depots in the 1800s and early 1900s. These wagons were used to haul and deliver the freight that came in on the trains. (Courtesy of Cass County Genealogical Society.)

ON THE COVER: This photograph of Atlanta High School's marching band on a class trip was taken around 1937. The young boy standing in front holding the baton is Roy Price, the current owner of Price's Hardware Store. (Courtesy of Mark and Julia Mays.)

IMAGES
of America

ATLANTA

Heather Ridpath Pilcher
and Sarah L. Ridpath

ARCADIA
PUBLISHING

ISBN 978-0-7385-8485-0

Published by Arcadia Publishing
Charleston, South Carolina

Printed in the United States of America

Library of Congress Control Number: 2011922350

For all general information, please contact Arcadia Publishing:
Telephone 843-853-2070
Fax 843-853-0044
E-mail sales@arcadiapublishing.com
For customer service and orders:
Toll-Free 1-888-313-2665

Visit us on the Internet at www.arcadiapublishing.com

In loving memory of Roger W. Ridpath, father

CONTENTS

ACKNOWLEDGMENTS

This book was a group project and ultimately belongs to the residents of Atlanta, Texas. I could not have completed this task without much help. Everyone who contributed, no matter how little, shares in this book's completion. The Atlanta community can take pride in its rich heritage. I want this book to help preserve the memories of our past for generations to come.

I would like to thank my sister and coauthor of this book, Sarah. She was very helpful in organizing the initial gathering of information and photographs. My father in-law, Charles "Boots" Pilcher Sr., helped narrow down the dates of some of the photographs by identifying car makes and models. Patricia Pyle Ridpath contributed family photographs and information. I would also like to thank Beth Griffin and the staff at the Atlanta Public Library, who continually brought me resources and pictures and were very accommodating in sharing their limited space. I would like to give special thanks to Kathy Peacock and the Cass County Genealogical Society for giving me access and assisting me in acquiring a large number of photographs for this project.

My former teacher Julia Mays and her husband, Mark, loaned me several family photographs and identified locations of former building sites. Irene Bradley, known to me and many others as Granny Irene, shared her personal photographs. Also, most captions for the scanned newspaper photographs that appear in this book came directly from the centennial issues of the *Citizens Journal*. The public library and my friend Pearl Brown loaned me a stack of centennial *Citizens Journal* issues to cull through.

INTRODUCTION

Atlanta is located in Cass County in East Texas. According to local historic resources, the Caddo Indians occupied the area until the late 1700s. Disease and the threat from other Indian tribes necessitated the Caddo tribe's move elsewhere. Cass County was named for Lewis Cass, a Michigan senator who was in favor of the annexation of Texas. However, during the Civil War, Cass fell out of favor with the locals because he was against Texas seceding from the Union. As a result, Cass County was temporarily renamed Davis County in honor of the Confederate president, Jefferson Davis. Soon after the Civil War, Atlanta was named; it became an official town in 1872. The name Atlanta was chosen because many settlers to this area came from Atlanta, Georgia.

East Texas is an agricultural area that focuses on livestock and timber. Some families also currently have stock in local oil wells. Residents who are not locally employed commute to Texarkana, Shreveport, or other areas for work. The plentiful woods and beautiful lakes in the area draw many people to retire and vacation in Cass County. In 1954, Texas acquired 1,475 acres of land that would become the Atlanta State Park. Another area of local pride for Atlantans is the 3A Atlanta High School football team. Football is a large part of life in Atlanta, second only to hunting and fishing. The school mascot is the rabbit, a play on the name of William Edward Rabb, the school's first football coach. In 1966, the Rabbits had an undefeated season under coach James Moffatt.

Atlanta also has had its share of residents who became famous. Bessie Coleman was the world's first licensed African American aviator. The local museum has a display featuring Coleman and a children's book about her. Roscoe Beck is a famous jazz bass guitarist who pioneered the five-string bass. Country musician Tracy Lawrence was born in Atlanta, and Ted Thompson, the general manager of the NFL's Green Bay Packers, graduated from Atlanta High School in 1971.

One

Downtown

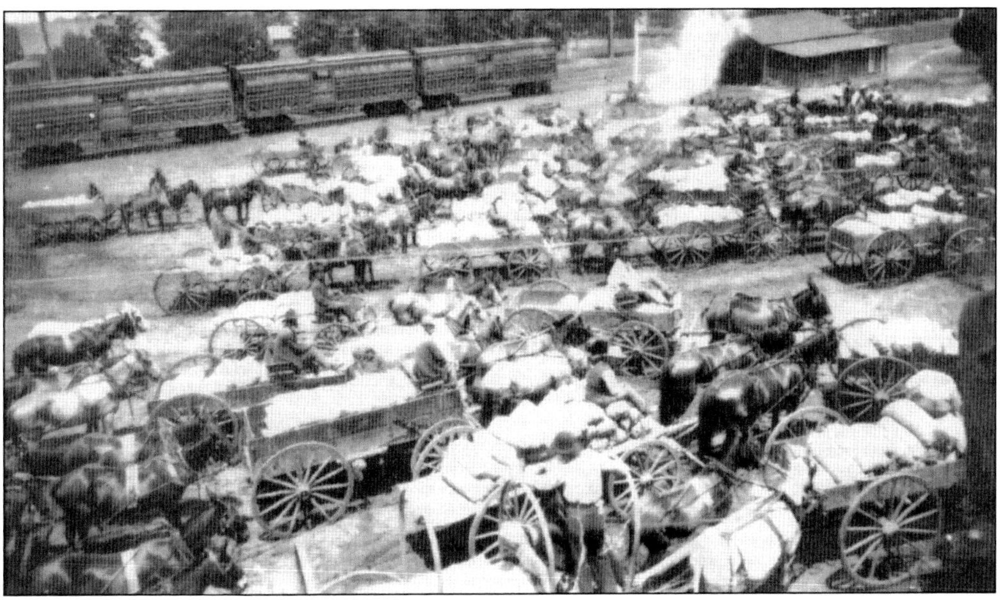

This 1185 view of North East Street shows wagonloads of potatoes lined up for shipping on the Texas & Pacific Railway Company (T&P). The picture was taken from the second floor of Hughes Brothers General Store on the corner of Hiram Street. The second floor was also used as the telephone office. In the background to the right are John Harvey's icehouse and bottling works, which later became the parking lot in front of Grogan's Store. (Courtesy of Pearl Brown.)

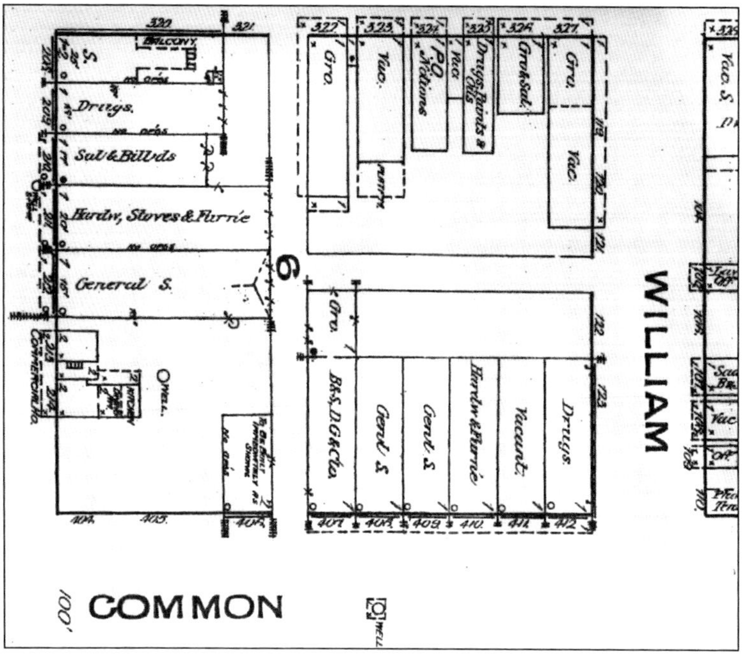

This schematic from Sanborn Map Company shows a section of downtown Atlanta in 1885. Common Street is now Main Street. (Courtesy of Cass County Genealogical Society.)

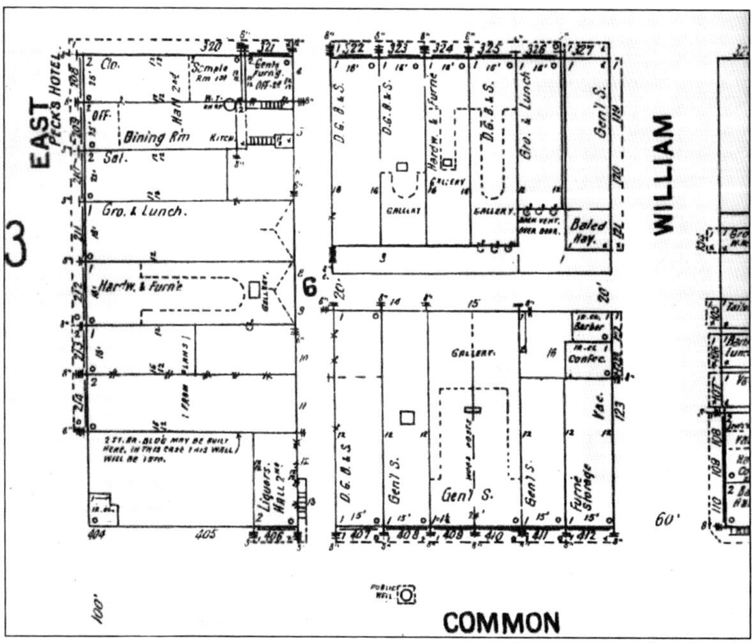

This schematic shows the same section of downtown in 1901. While the name of Common Street has not yet changed, some new shops seem to have been established. (Courtesy of Cass County Genealogical Society.)

Another schematic shows the section again in 1911. Each drawing is carefully detailed. The types of businesses and vacancies within the buildings are identified; the dotted lines inside the businesses represent the second-floor gallery areas. (Courtesy of Cass County Genealogical Society.)

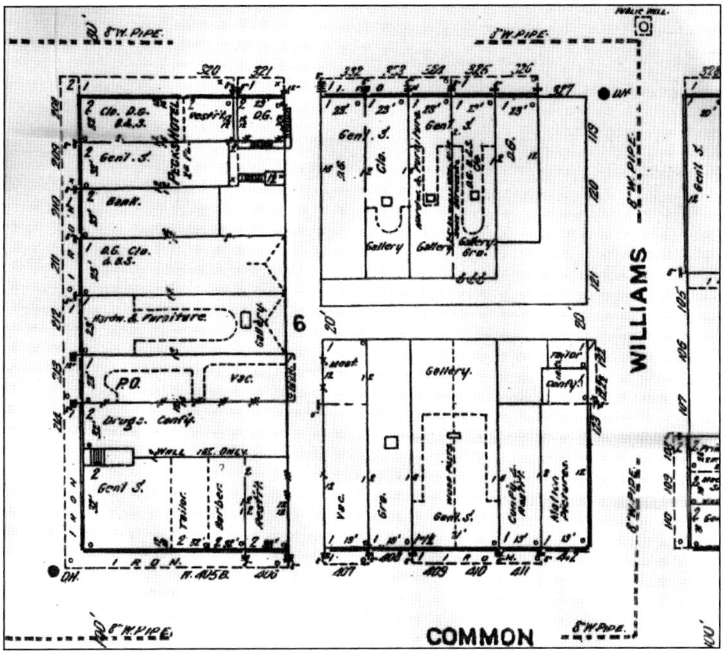

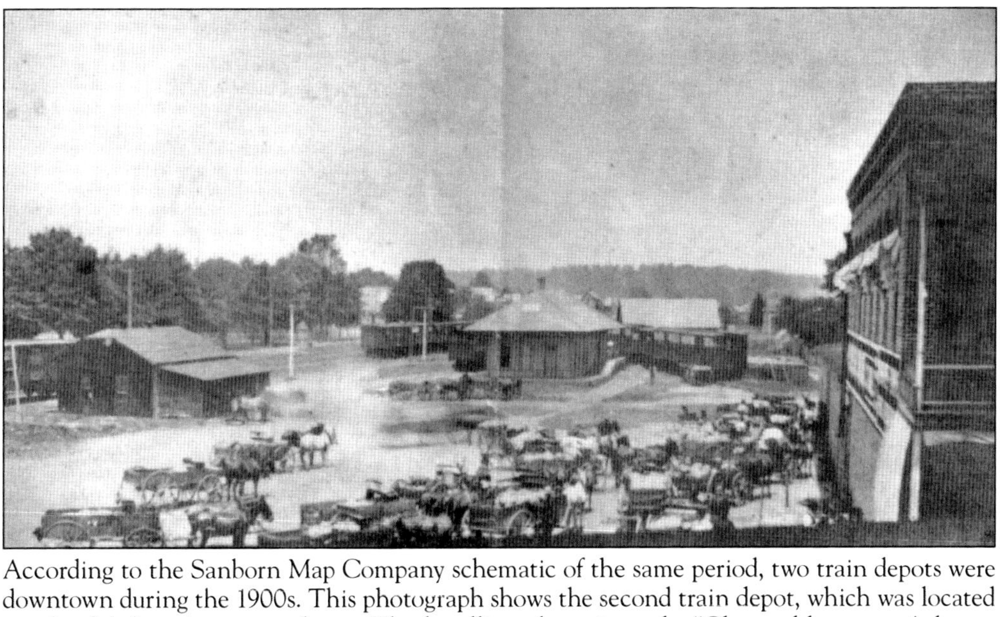

According to the Sanborn Map Company schematic of the same period, two train depots were downtown during the 1900s. This photograph shows the second train depot, which was located north of Atlanta's current depot. The headline above it reads, "Chugged between Atlanta, Bloomburg." Hughes Brothers General Store is believed to be the building on the right. (Courtesy of Cass County Genealogical Society.)

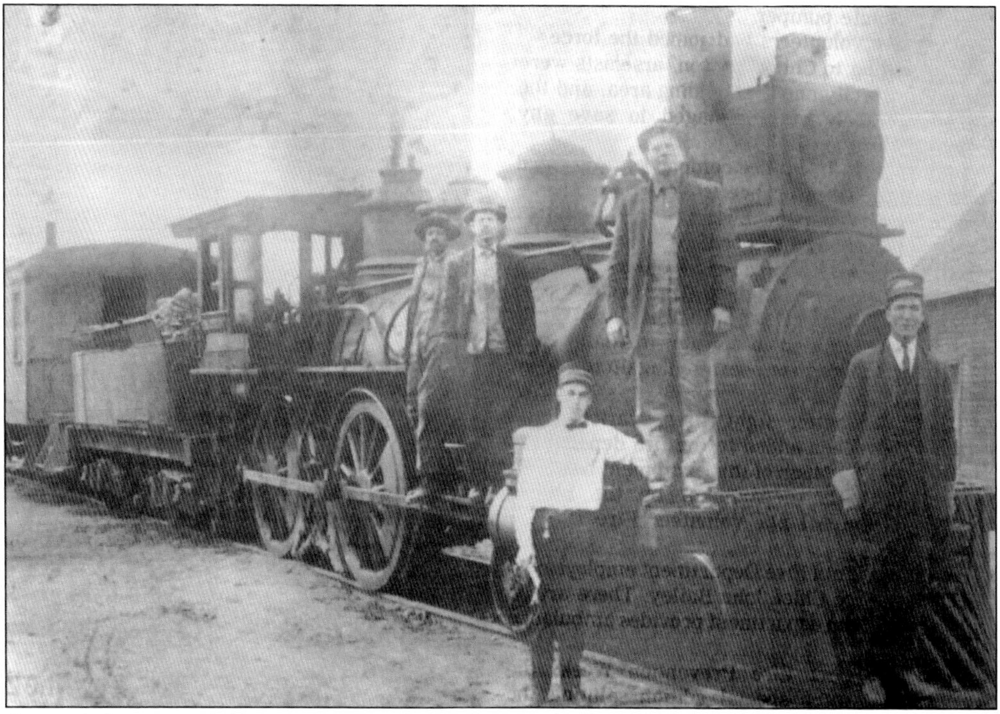

Around the turn of the century, a train nicknamed "the Dummy" ran between Atlanta and Bloomburg. Posing in front of the train are, from left to right, (first row) an unidentified agent and Rube Simmons; (second row) an unidentified workman, V.T. Parker, and Noah Parker. The train made its last run in 1918. (Courtesy of Cass County Genealogical Society.)

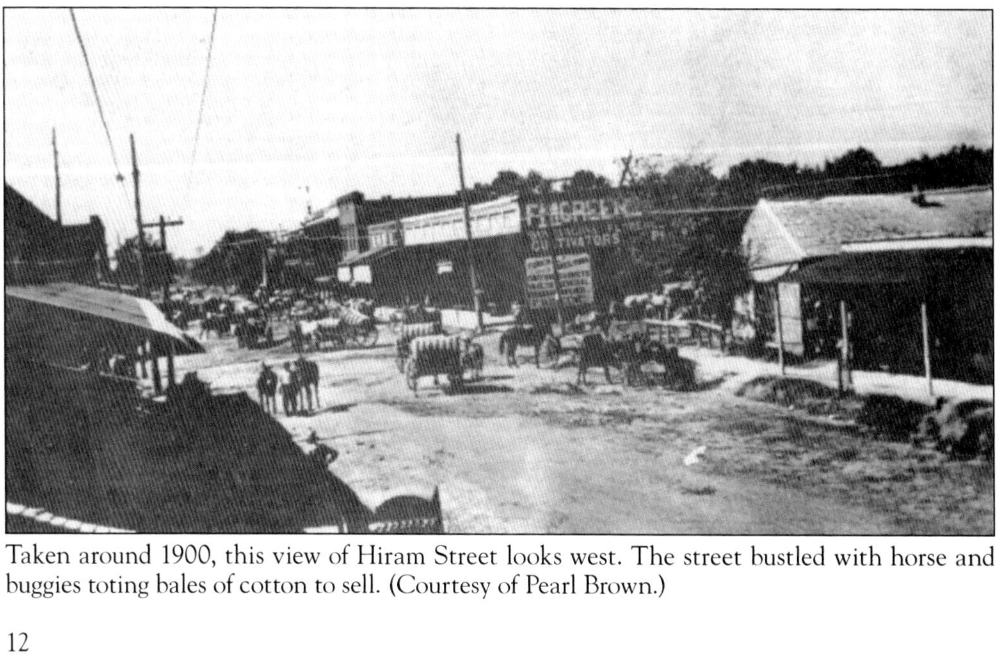

Taken around 1900, this view of Hiram Street looks west. The street bustled with horse and buggies toting bales of cotton to sell. (Courtesy of Pearl Brown.)

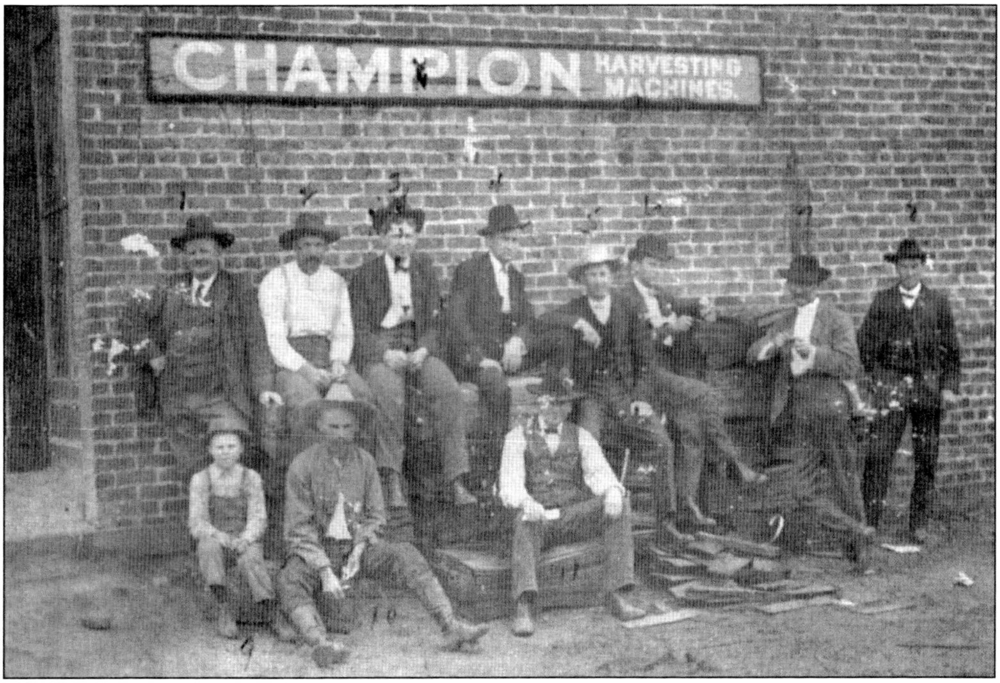

This street scene was taken in 1902 beside the old A.C. Smith Store at 100 East Main Street (the current location of Roark Auto Parts). Those pictured include, from left to right, (first row) Rowe Curtright, Nat S. Curtright Sr., and Noah S. Spearman; (second row) George Hughes, unidentified (possibly one of the four Hughes brothers), Jim A.B. Jett, L.W. Willis, R.P. Dunklin, John J. Ellington Sr., L.F. Allday, and William F. Cameron. (Courtesy of Pearl Brown.)

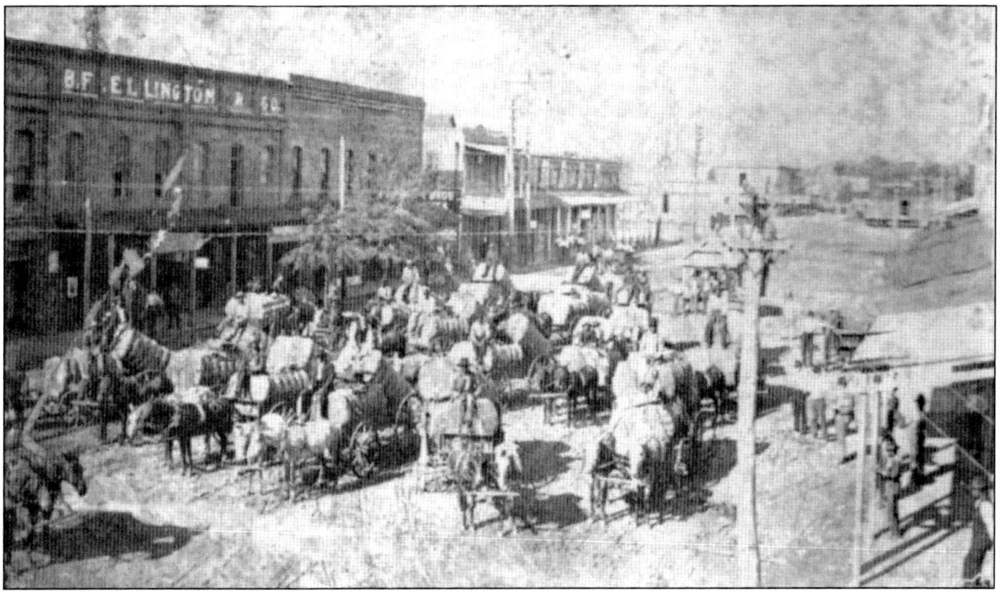

Ben F. Ellington and nephew John Ellington were early cotton buyers in Atlanta. Farmers sold their bales to the Ellington Company. This picture looks west toward the railroad and was taken in front of the Ellingtons' business in 1905. The company was located on the corner of Main and Williams Streets, and the structure still stands there today. (Courtesy of Pearl Brown.)

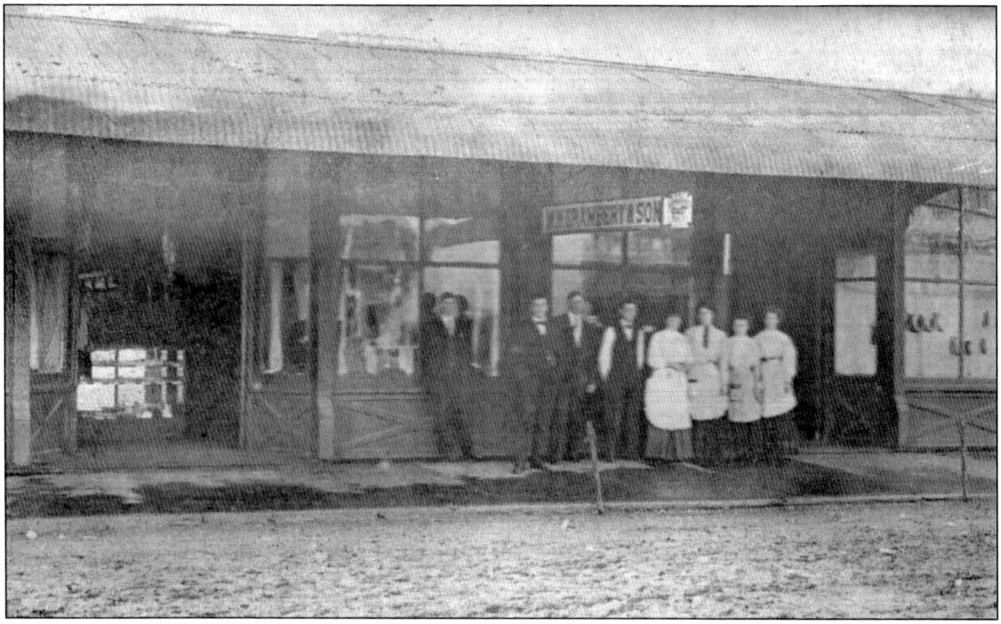

W.H. Erambert owned and operated a general merchandise store in early Atlanta for 10 years. This picture, taken in 1908, shows the store employees. They are, from left to right, an unidentified man, W.H. Erambert, O.C. McClung, Totsy Pitts, the wife of Luther Johnson, Nannie Erambert, ? Lovelady, and Beulah Scott. According to a 1970s centennial edition of the *Citizens Journal*, Erambert's business was located where Perry Brothers Store is currently located. (Courtesy of Pearl Brown.)

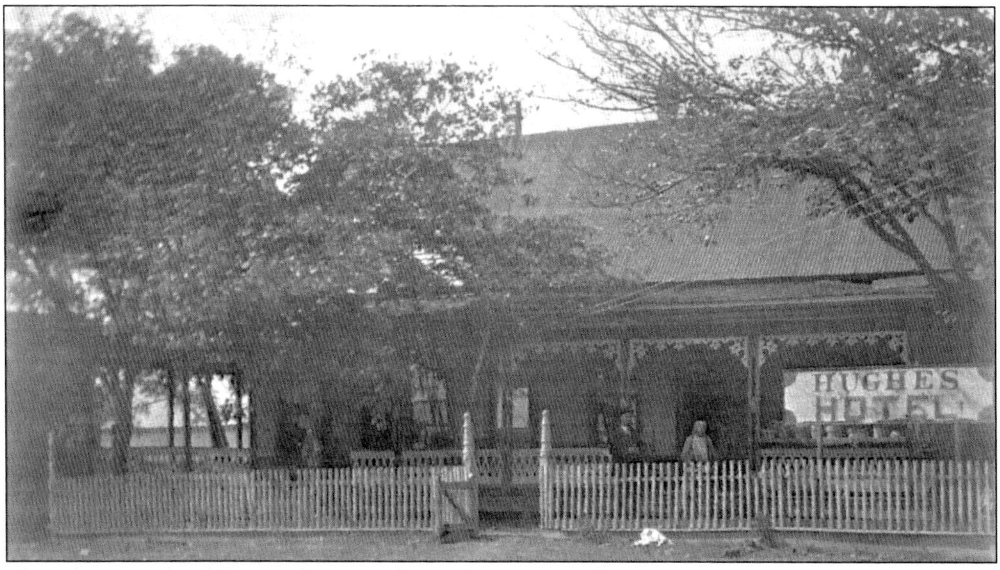

This photograph of the Hughes Hotel in Atlanta was taken in November 1912. In addition to the hotel, members of the Hughes family ran a livery stable, a general store, and other businesses around town. (Courtesy of Cass County Genealogical Society.)

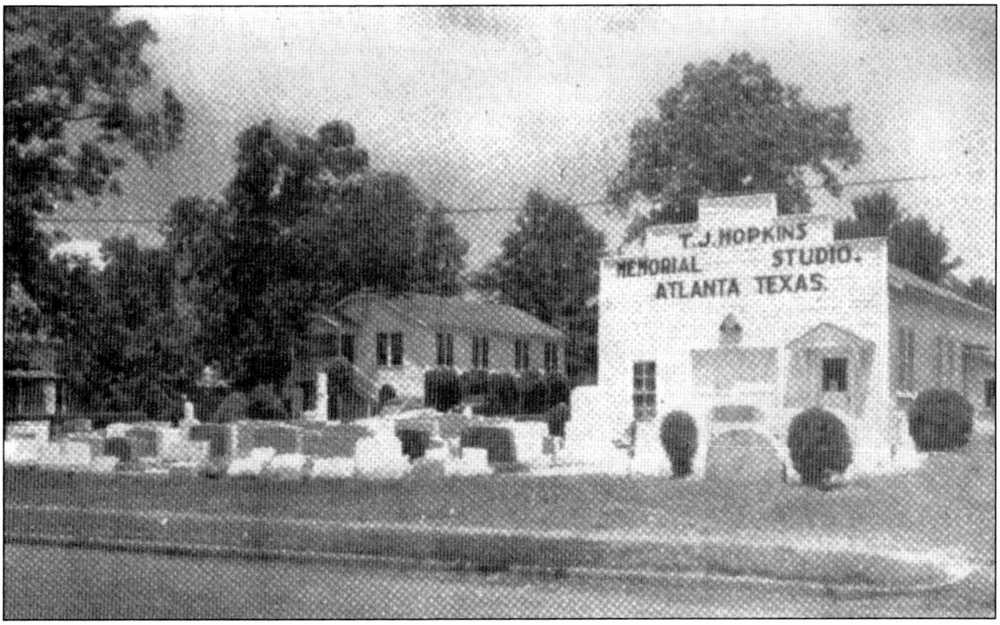

This view of the T.J. Hopkins Memorial Studio was taken in 1939. The business was located on South West Street in this 1962 yearbook advertisement. The Annie Green-Willis building can be seen to the left in the background. This building still exists today, but the front has been altered. Hopkins has been in business since 1910 and is now located on South Louise Street. (Courtesy of Cass County Genealogical Society.)

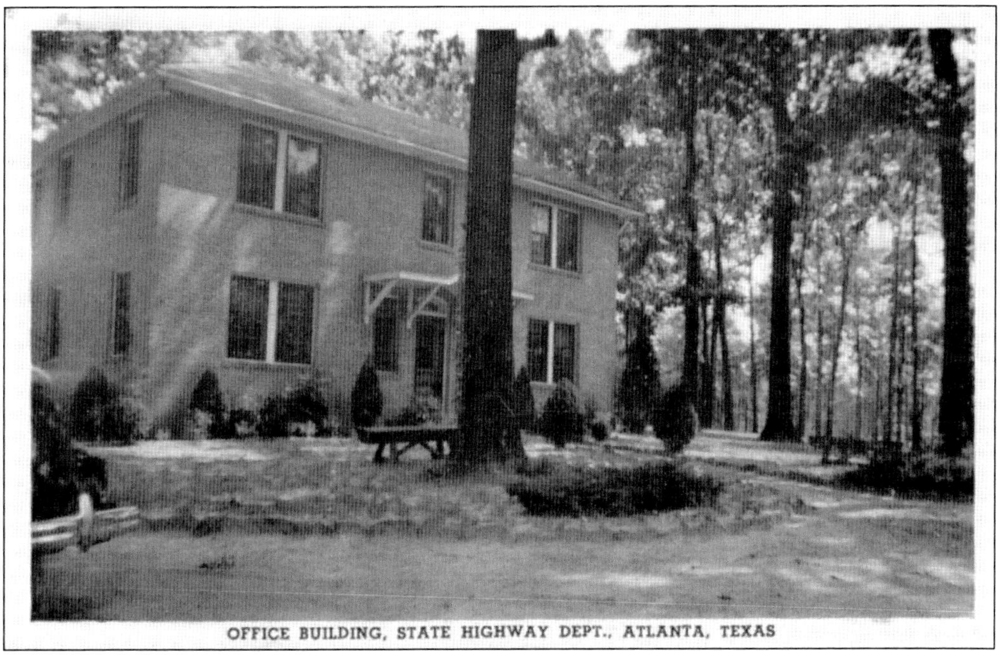

A postcard from the 1930s shows the Texas Highway Department office building located on East Main Street. Before the office building was erected, this site was home to the city park and goldfish pond. The building pictured has since been replaced with a new highway department building. (Courtesy of Russ Harrison.)

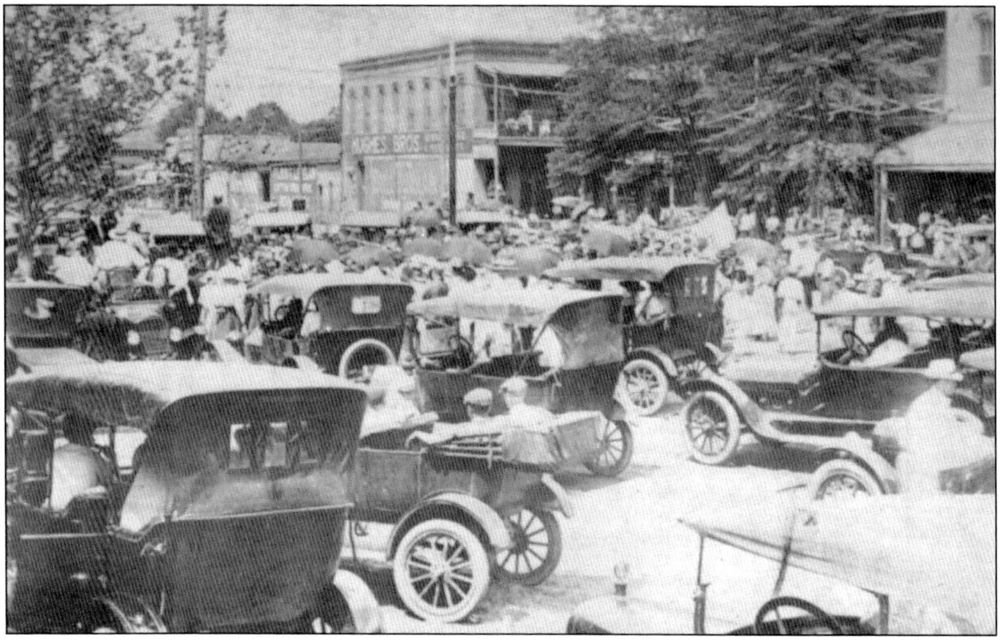

Residents have come to town to buy Liberty Bonds during World War I. The picture was taken in June 1917 from the location of the present Atlanta depot, which now houses the Atlanta Chamber of Commerce. Hughes Brothers General Store can be seen in the background. (Courtesy of Cass County Genealogical Society.)

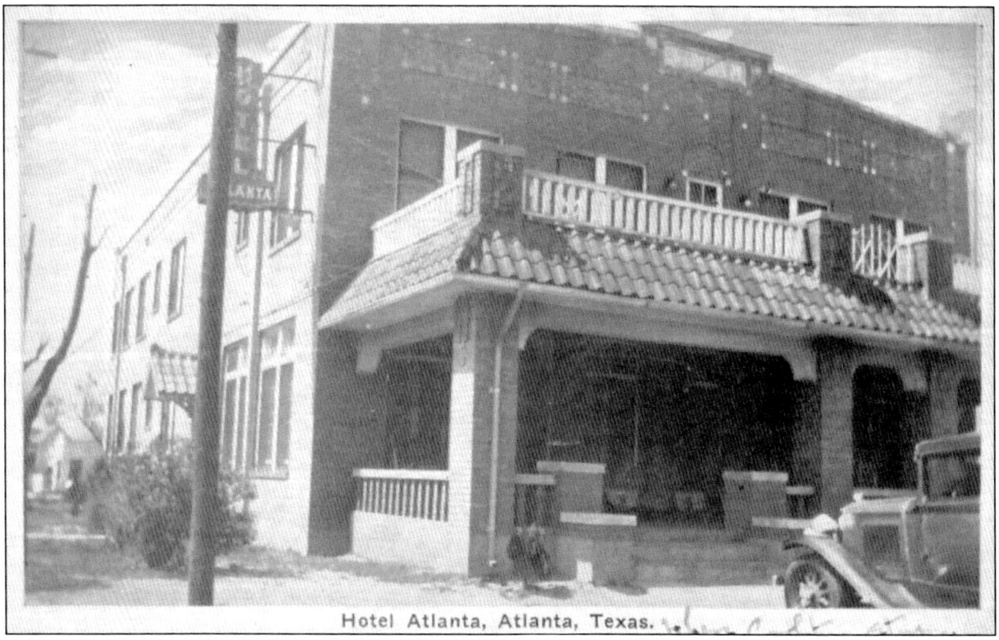

This postcard of the Hotel Atlanta dates to around 1925. According to local realtor Mark Mays, the hotel used to be located on the northwest corner of West Main and North West Streets. According to local history, the hotel was built within walking distance of the train depot, and many travelers stayed there. Hotels on the loop around Atlanta have replaced the Hotel Atlanta and others like it. The Hotel Atlanta lot is now vacant. (Courtesy of Heather Ridpath Pilcher.)

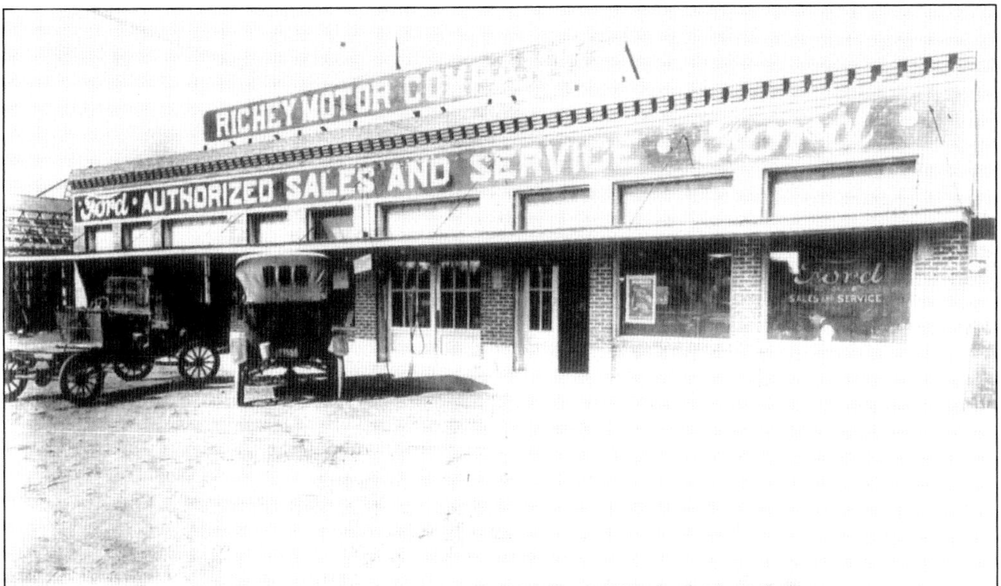

T.R. Ritchey, Owner. Note: He is seated inside window on right end under sign stating Ford Sales and Service. This building located at Main and So. West Grand Street. Building wax extended 10-12 feet wider and constructed into a Two-story building. The Texas State Guard (National) was upstairs.

Also according to Mark Mays, Richey Motors was once located on the corner of South West and Main Streets. An old water tower was also located on the property, which later became home to thousands of bats. The Hotel Atlanta was located across the street. The owner, T.R. Richey, can be seen sitting at his desk in the front window. (Courtesy of Cass County Genealogical Society.)

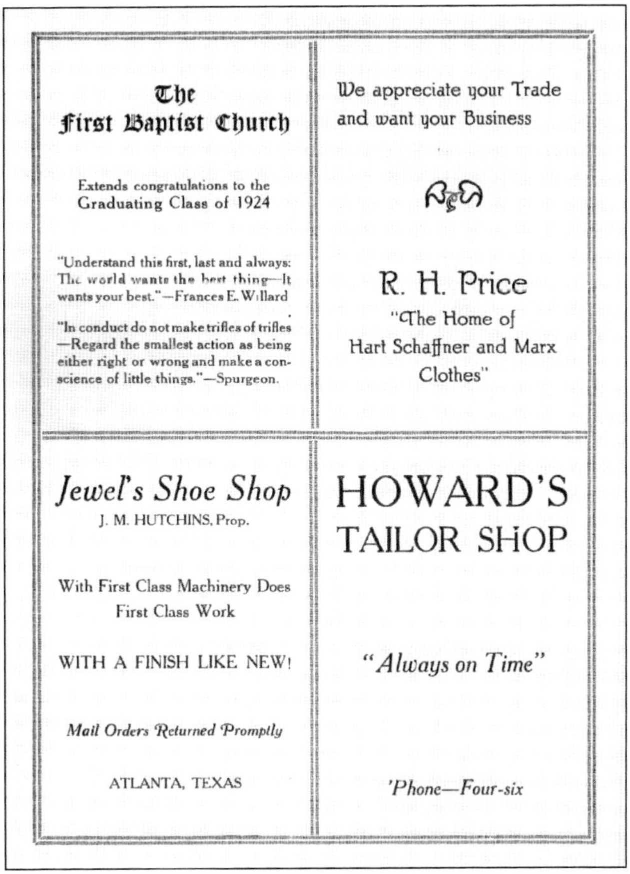

Several local businesses and the local Baptist church took out advertisements in 1924. Howard's Tailor shop is the only business on this page with a telephone number listed; customers simply had to dial 46. (Courtesy of Cass County Genealogical Society.)

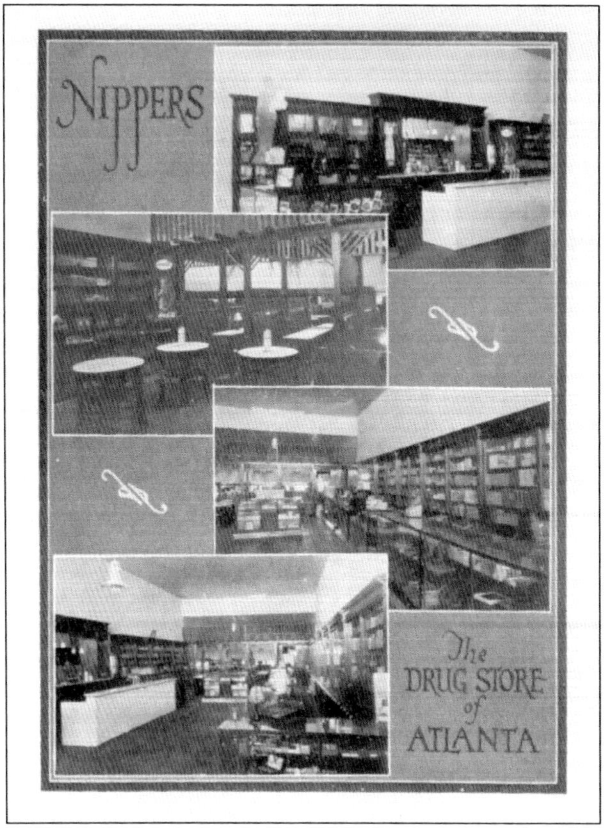

An early advertisement from 1924 shows the inside of Nippers Drug Store in Atlanta. (Courtesy of Cass County Genealogical Society.)

In 1929, a shipment of 4,361 peach trees and several hundred paper-shell pecan trees were delivered to Atlanta to be planted in home orchards around town. This photograph was taken at the corner of South East and Hiram Streets looking south. (Courtesy of Cass County Genealogical Society.)

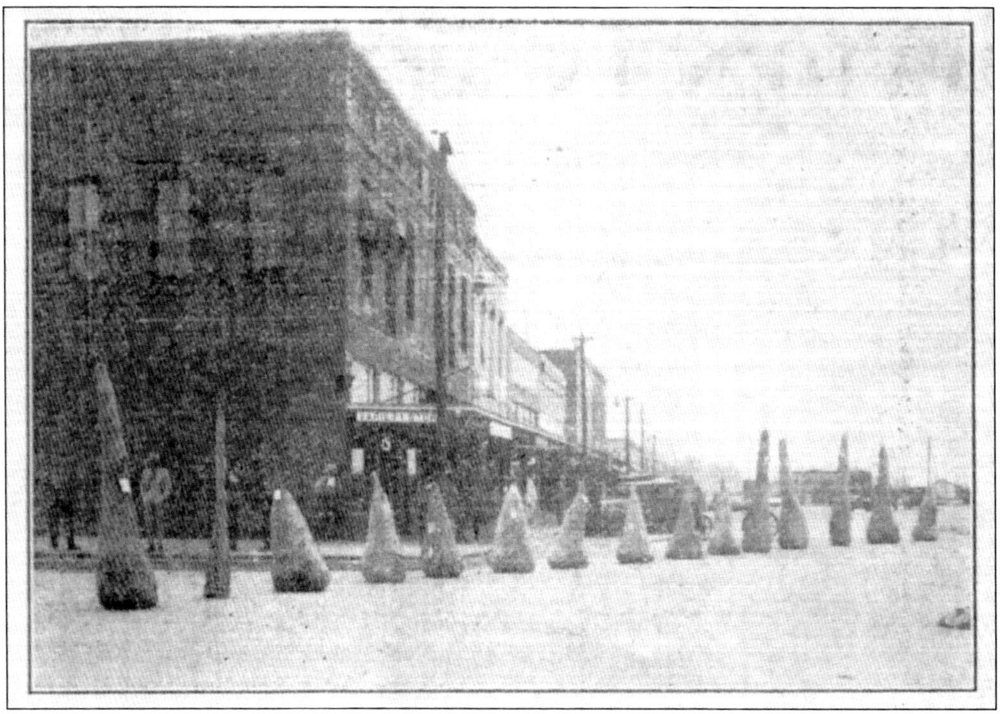

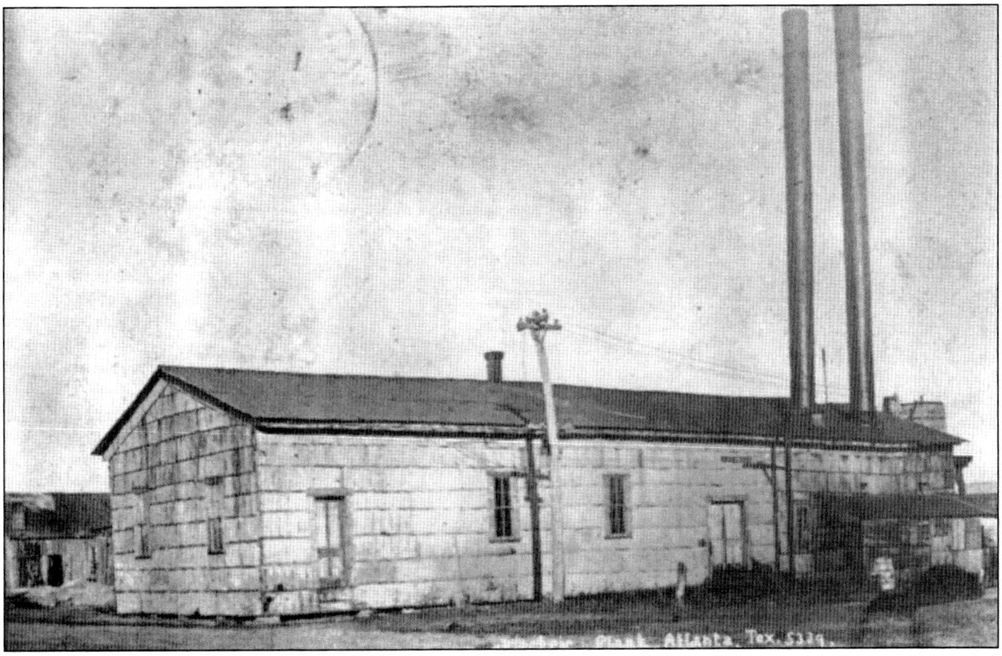

Atlanta's first electric power plant was built by John T. Chamblee on the site that was occupied by the old icehouse on North West Street. The franchise for bringing electricity to the area was granted in December 1902, less than 25 years after Thomas Edison lit the first incandescent lamp. (Courtesy of Pearl Brown.)

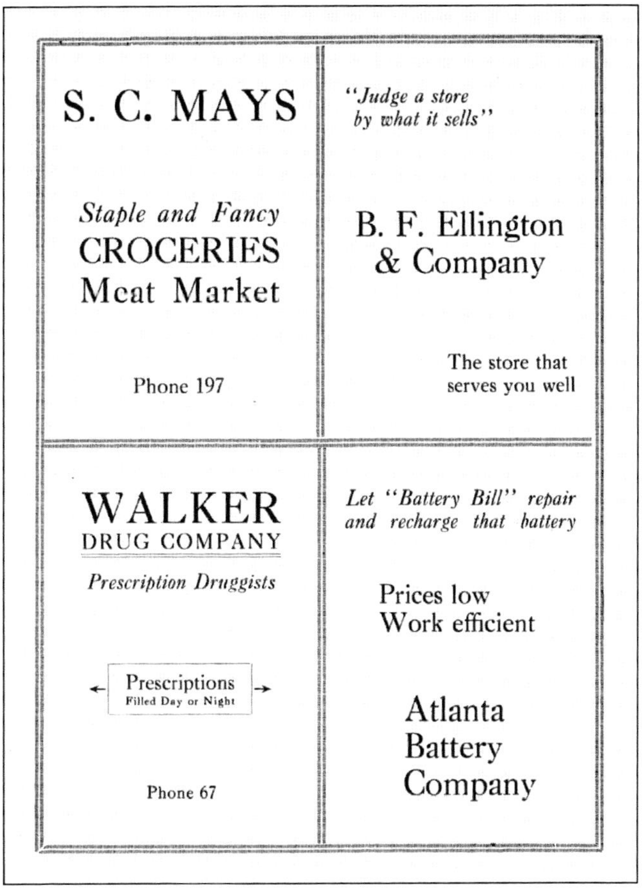

Pictured are more business advertisements from 1924. S.C. Mays, Walker Drug Company, and presumably at least 195 other folks in town (if Mays's telephone number, 197, is any indication) had telephone lines at the time. (Courtesy of Cass County Genealogical Society.)

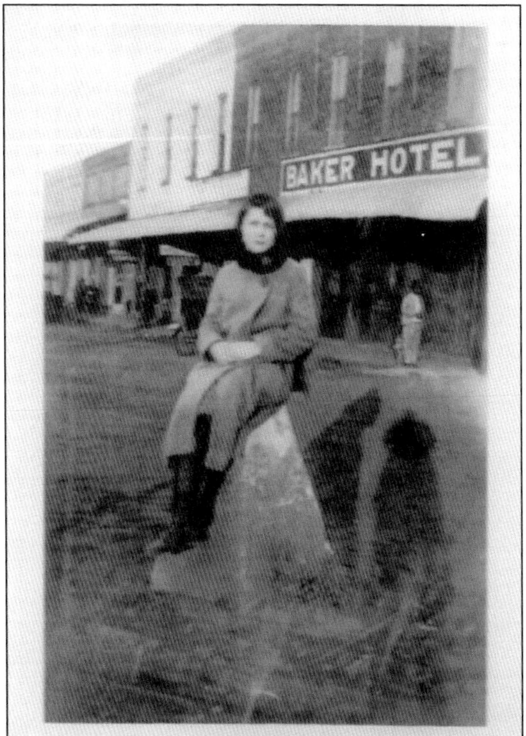

Otis Ford Oden
Downtown Atlanta
circa 1925

Otis Ford Oden is sitting in front of the Baker Hotel in downtown Atlanta. The photograph was taken around 1925. Oden died in her early 20s, having never been married; she is buried in the Pine Crest Cemetery. (Courtesy of Cass County Genealogical Society.)

The first mail service in Atlanta was established in 1871. The former US Post Office building was constructed on West Hiram Street in 1931 and opened to the public in 1932. The building currently houses the Atlanta Public Library. Atlanta's current post office building is located on Holly Street. (Courtesy of Pearl Brown.)

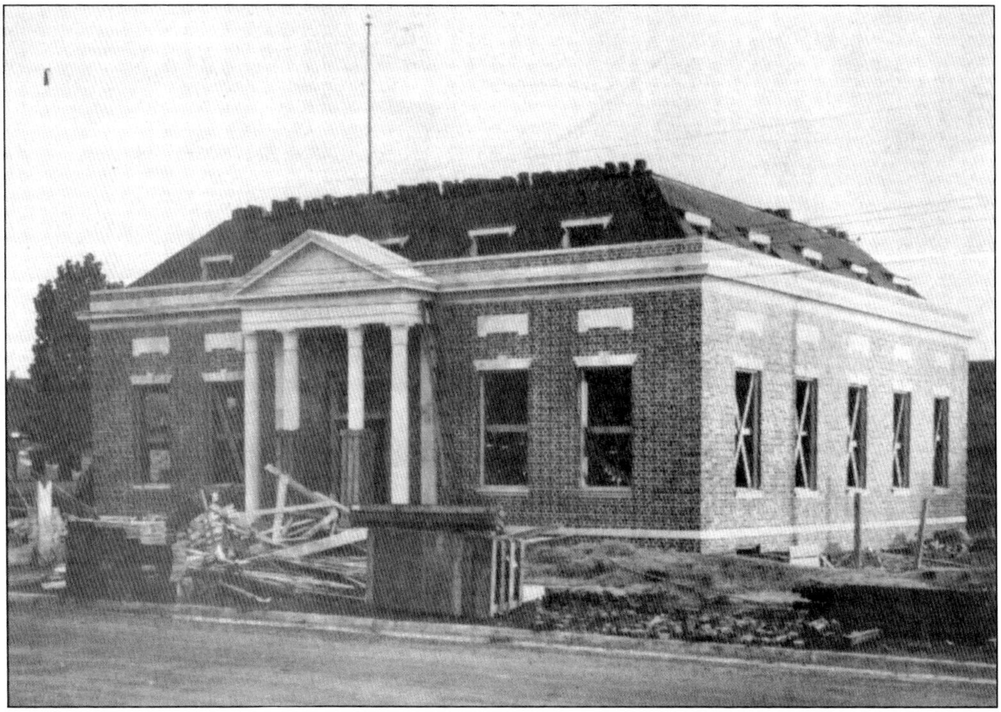

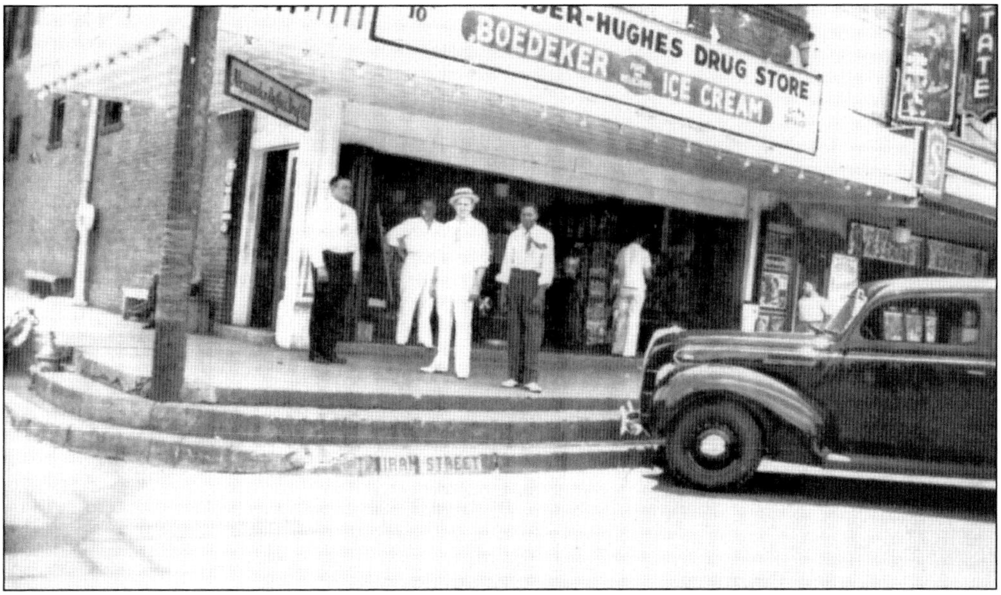

The Alexander Hughes Drug Store was located on Hiram Street when this photograph was taken around 1935. (Courtesy of Cass County Genealogical Society.)

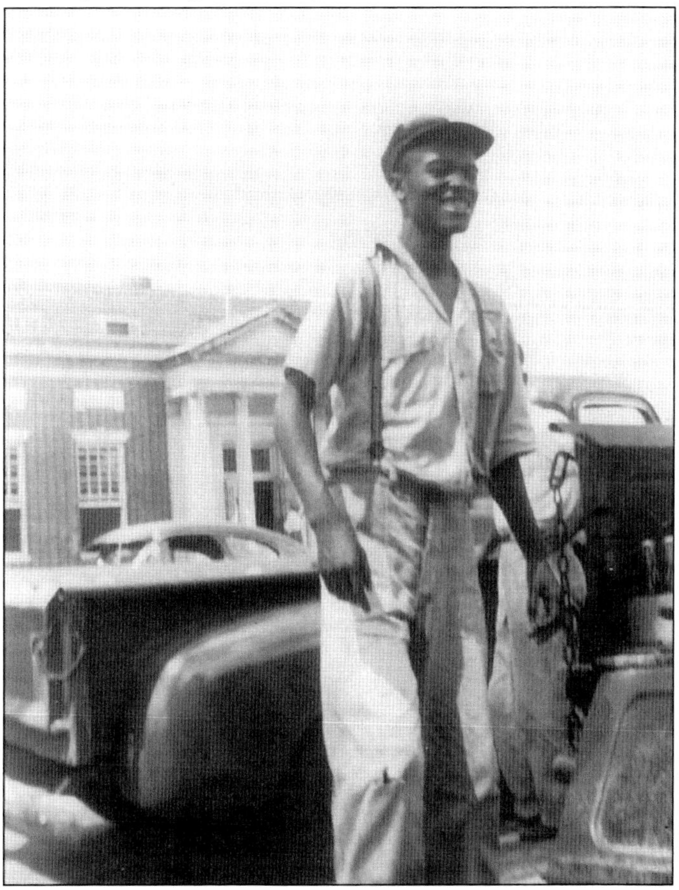

This photograph of Bubby Johnson standing across the street from the old post office was taken in the 1950s. Johnson worked at Cameron's Grocery Store. (Courtesy of Cass County Genealogical Society.)

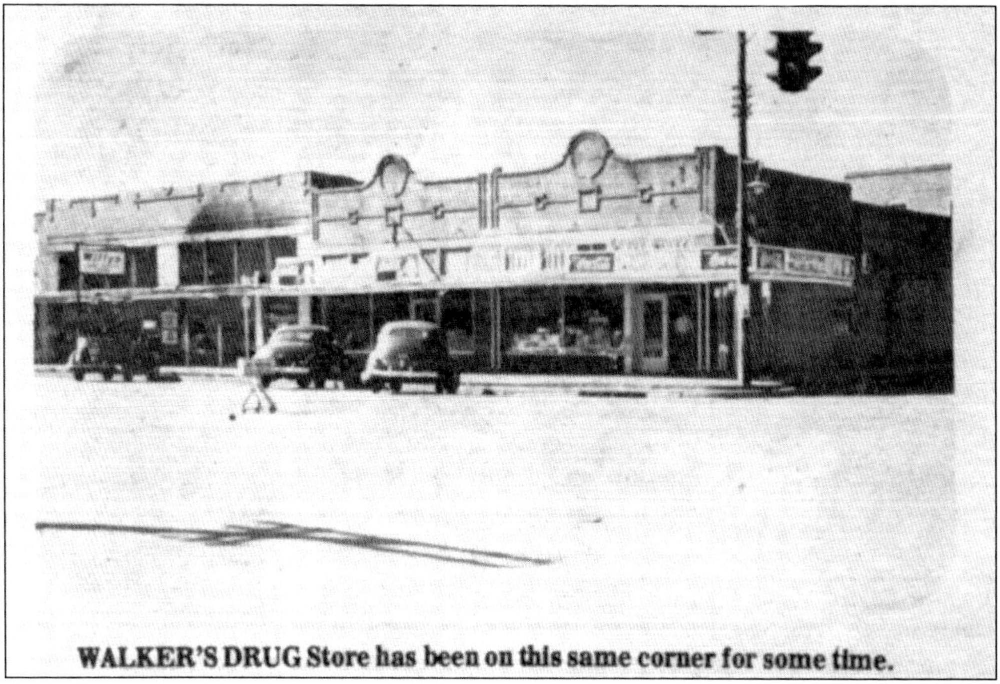

This photograph of Walker's Drug Store was taken around 1940. The Walker's pictured was located on the corner of Hiram and Williams Streets. (Courtesy of Cass County Genealogical Society.)

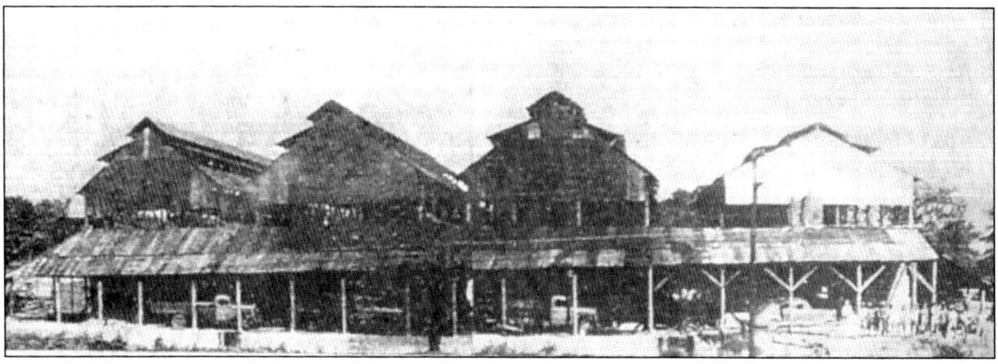

Pictured in a newspaper advertisement from 1939 is the Atlanta Brick Company. Employees can be seen standing in the lower right corner. The small house just behind them to the right may have been a rental house for some of the workers. The view looks toward the west from the rail lines just north of downtown. (Courtesy of Cass County Genealogical Society.)

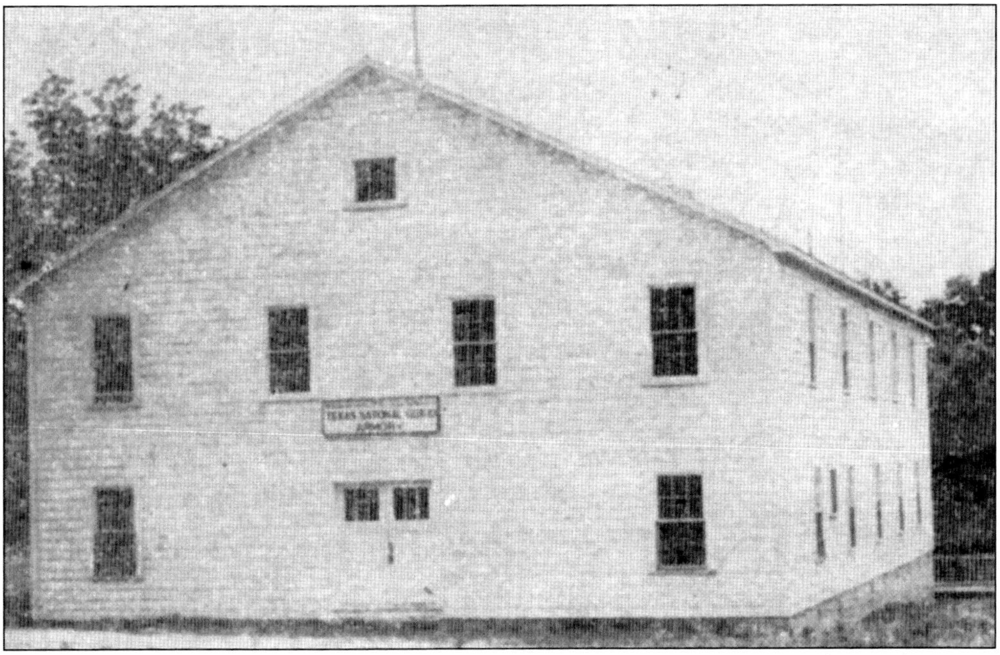

This photograph of Atlanta's National Guard Armory building was taken around 1940. (Courtesy of Cass County Genealogical Society.)

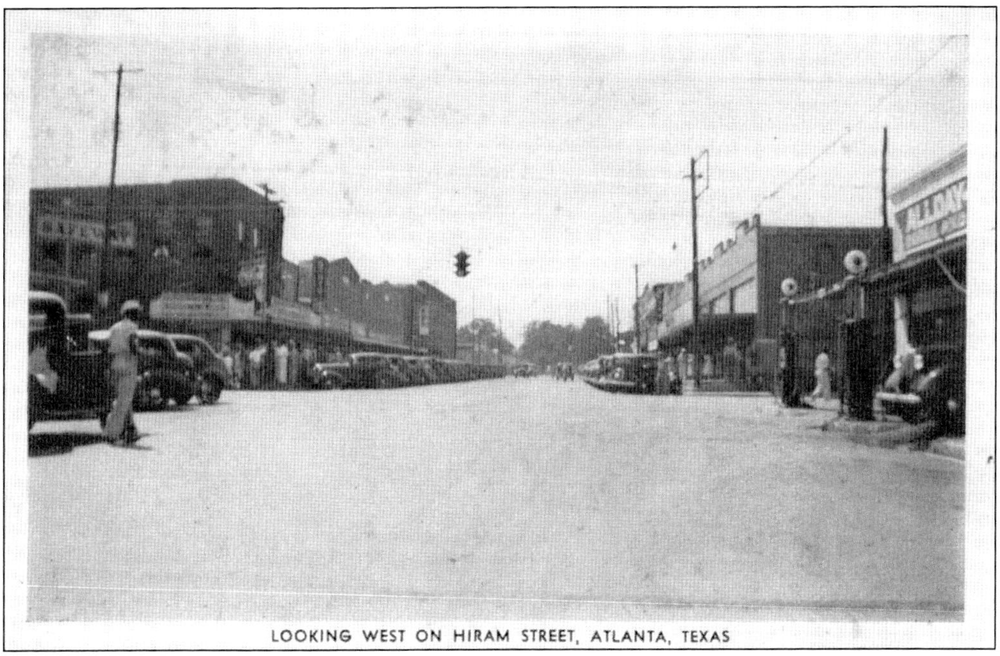

This postcard image of Hiram Street looking west shows how busy downtown was in the 1930s. People are crowded on the sidewalk to the left, and cars lined the street. When compared to the same view from around 1900 on page 12, the horses are gone, and Hiram Street has been paved for the automobile traffic that now dominate. (Courtesy of Russ Harrison.)

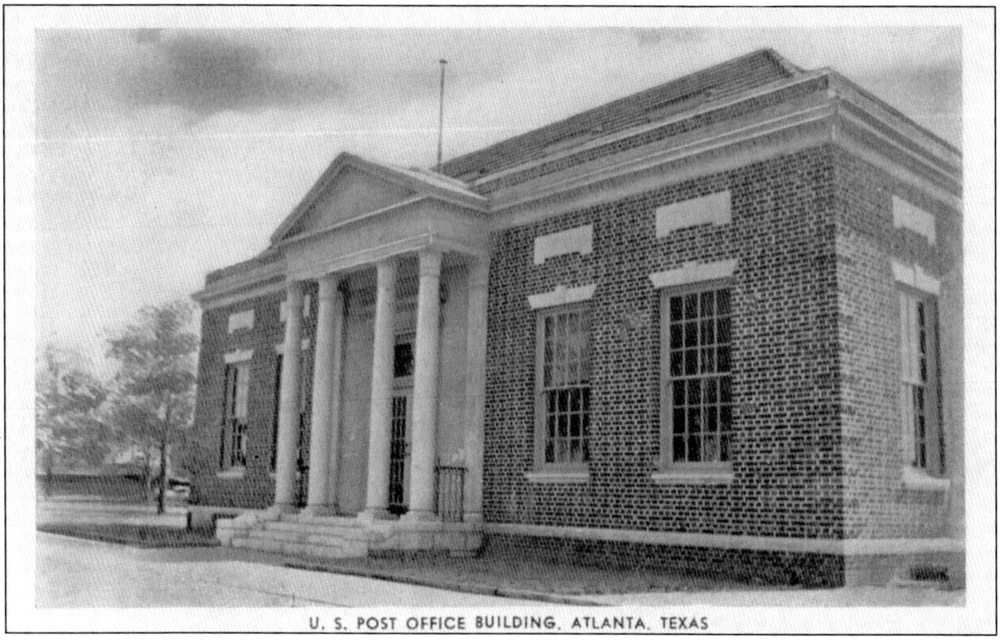

The above photograph of the US Post Office in Atlanta was taken around 1940. The postcard below has writing on the back and is postmarked September 25, 1941. (Courtesy of Heather Ridpath Pilcher.)

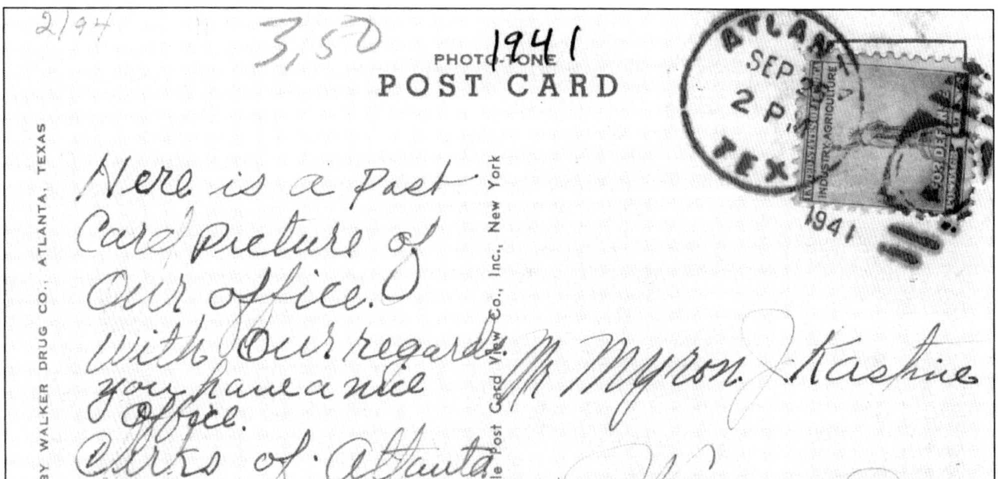

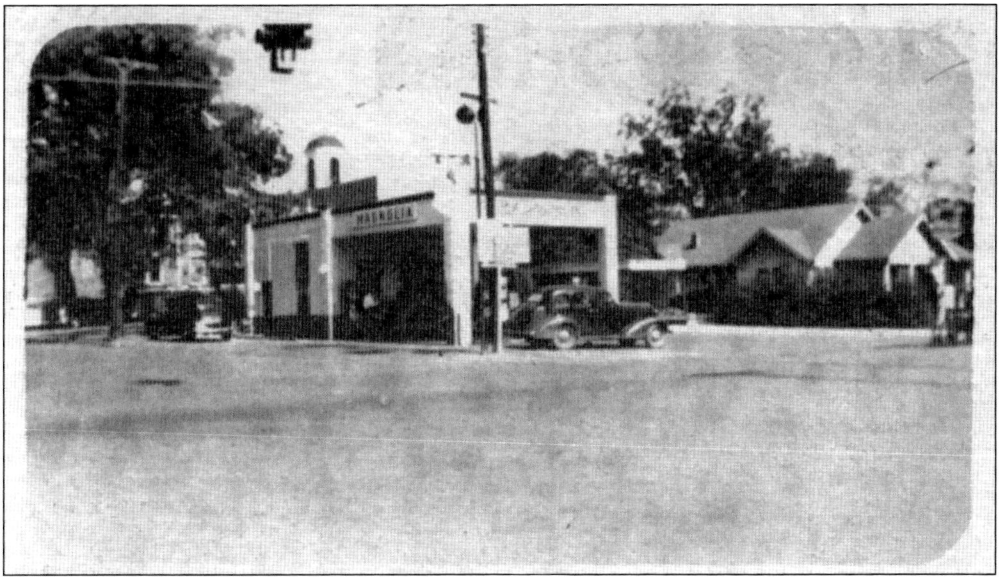

This is a 1940s view of H.E. “Hoddy” Oden’s service station. In the 1970s, the Gulf station and Safeway across the street kept him company, and the First Methodist Church flanked him on the right. (Courtesy of Cass County Genealogical Society.)

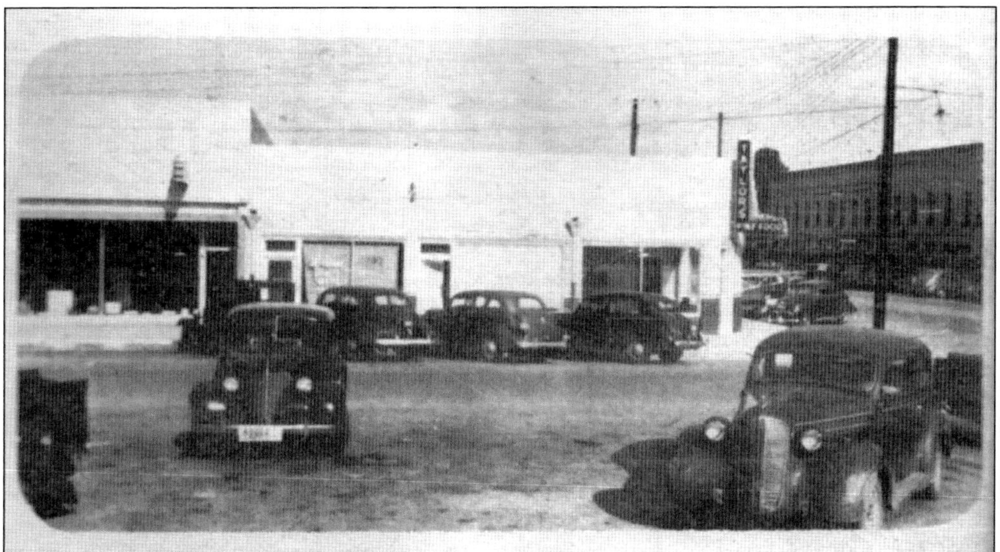

ANOTHER ATLANTA business from bygone days - - Taylor’s Fine Foods.

Taylor’s Fine Foods was located downtown. This picture was taken around 1945. (Courtesy of Cass County Genealogical Society.)

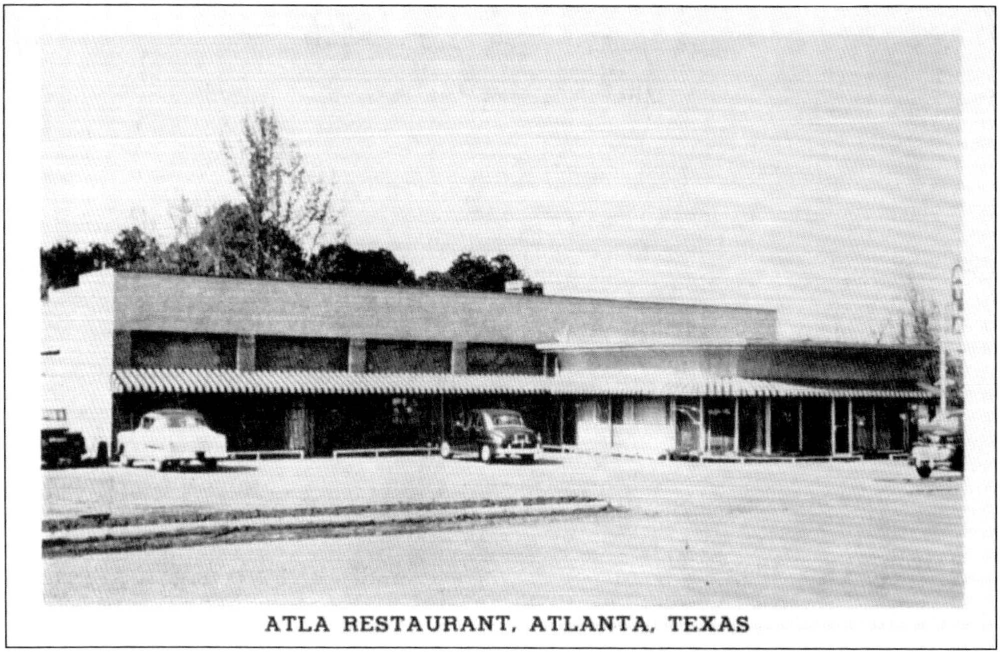

This postcard shows the Alta Restaurant is from the 1950s. The building is still located on West Main Street. Several restaurants and businesses have occupied the structure since it was built. (Courtesy of Heather Ridpath Pilcher.)

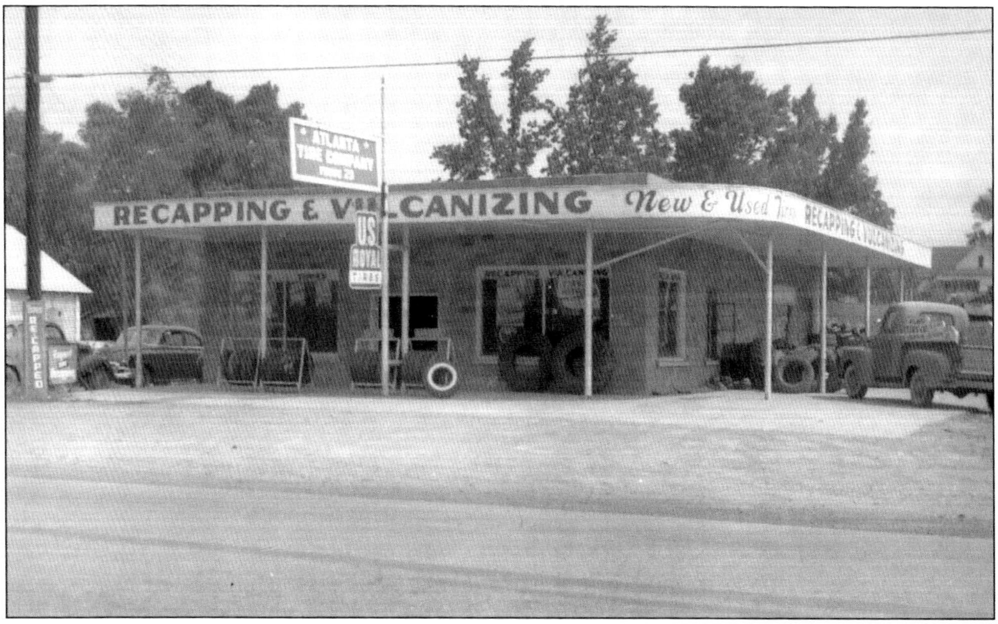

The Atlanta Tire Shop was in business for many decades. The business, owned by Oliver E. and Pearl Brown, was located on East Main Street. The building still operates as a tire company but has a different owner. This picture was taken around 1955. The Browns were also founding members of the Atlanta Church of God. (Courtesy of Pearl Brown.)

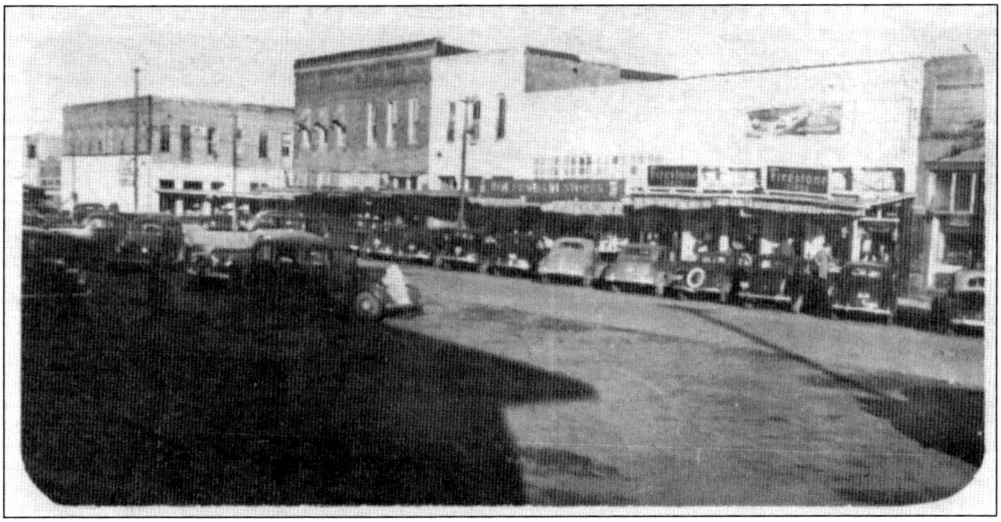

Pictured is a c. 1950 view of South East Street looking north towards the intersection of East Hiram Street. Ben Franklin's and Firestone can be seen in the picture. (Courtesy of Cass County Genealogical Society.)

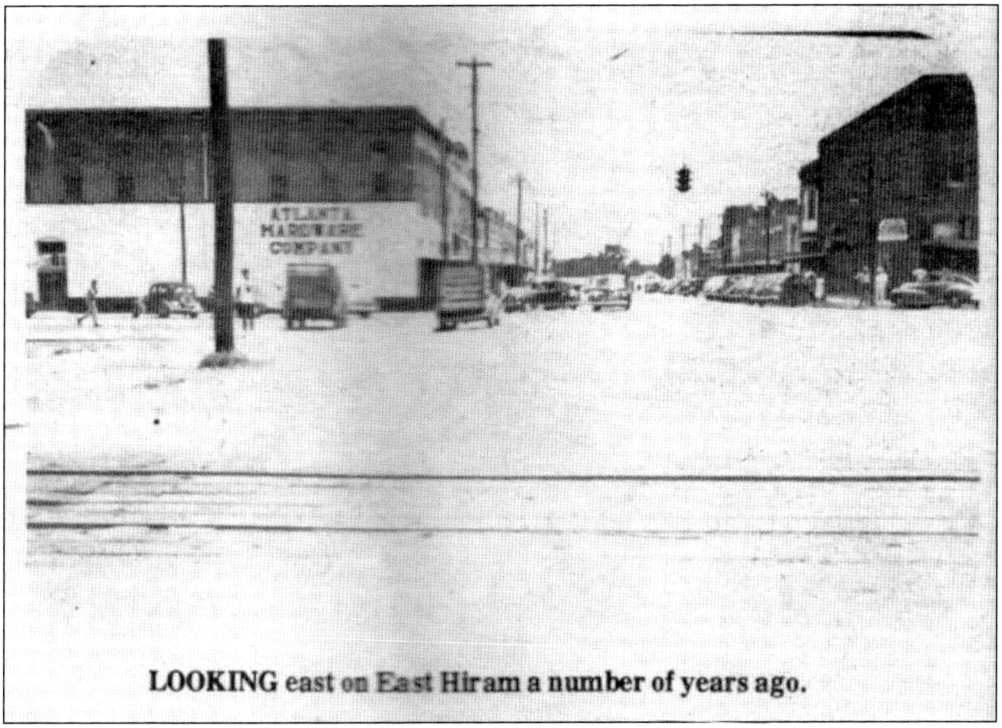

This photograph from the 1950s shows a view of East Hiram Street looking east from the railroad tracks. The Atlanta Hardware Company is clearly visible. (Courtesy of Cass County Genealogical Society.)

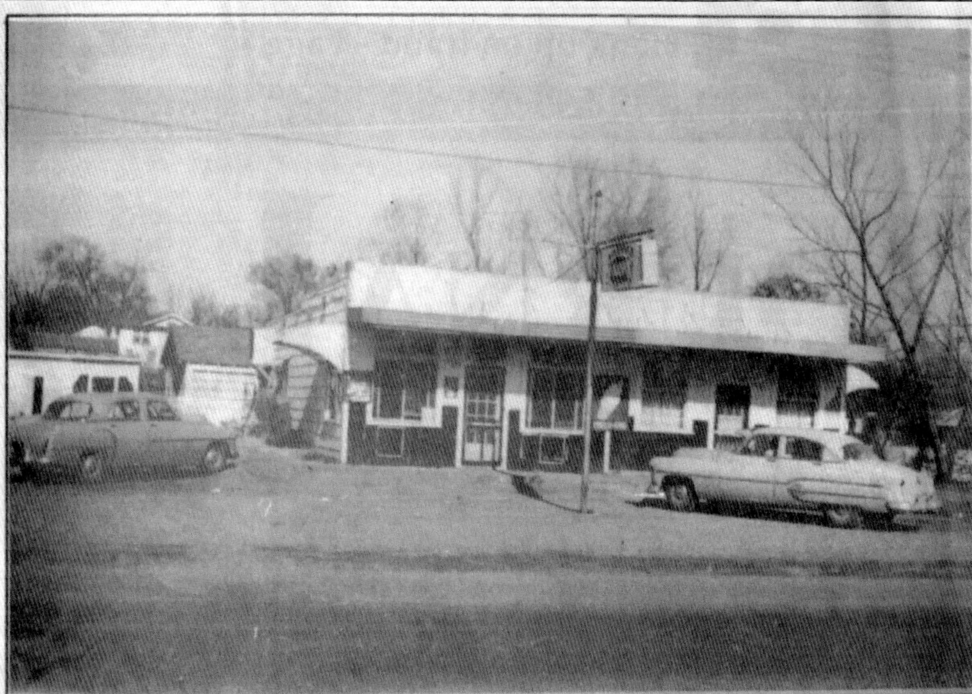

Brown's Drive-In in its heyday.

Tom Brown began selling food in town in 1884. After World War II, Brown's Drive-In was built and quickly became a popular place to go after football games. The favorite team meal was a barbecue platter with fries and a salad. This picture taken around 1950, and the building was located on East Main Street. (Courtesy of Cass County Genealogical Society.)

CITIZENS JOURNAL, ATLANTA, TEXAS, MARCH 29, 1979-PAGE 67

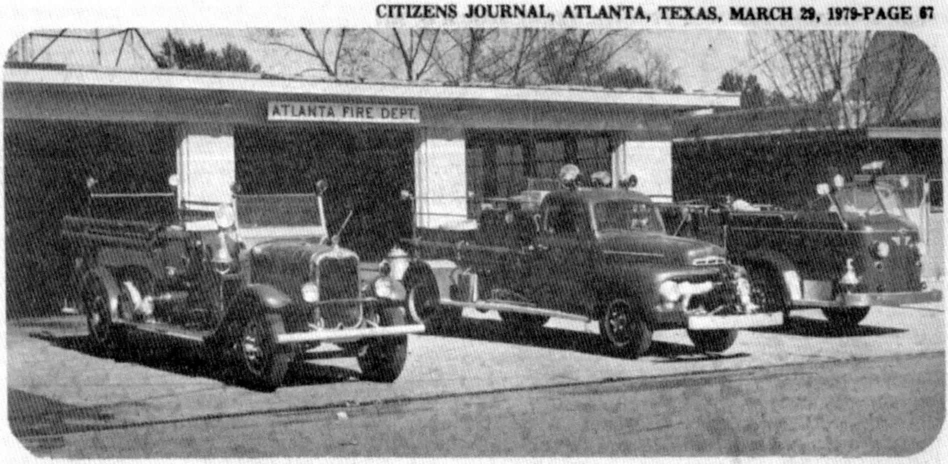

Atlanta's Fire Department In 1950's

This is a view from the 1950s of Atlanta's fire department, which was located on East Main Street. (Courtesy of Cass County Genealogical Society.)

Two

WORKING IN ATLANTA

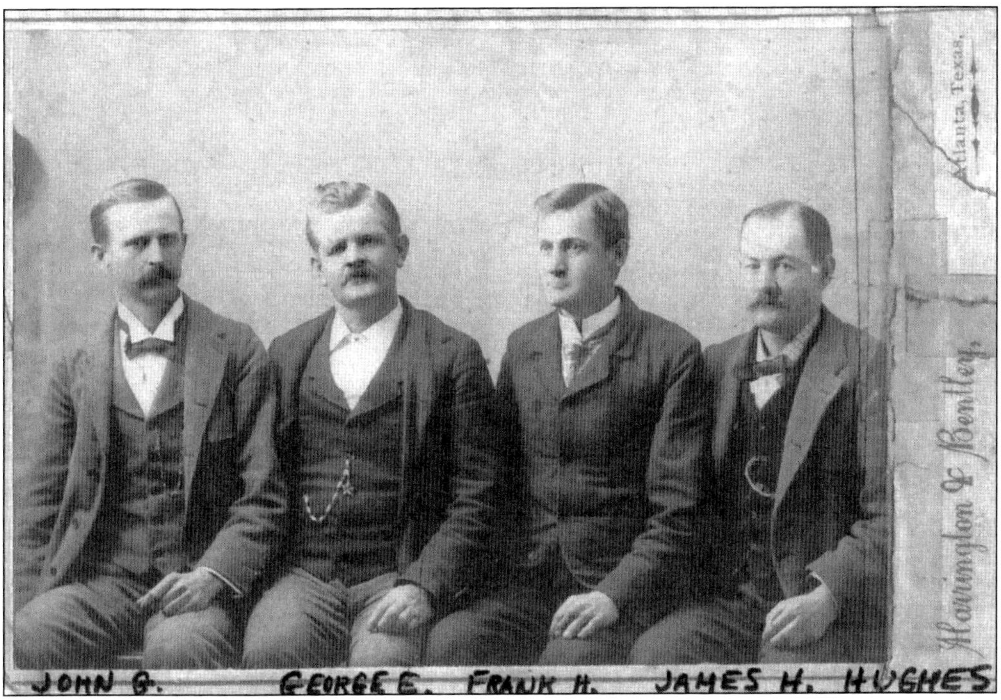

Shown here are the Hughes brothers, who were early merchants in Atlanta. From left to right are John, George, Frank, and James. George and James owned a general store, a hotel, and a livery stable. The livery stable was located on the present site of the Atlanta Public Library. John owned a grocery store, and Frank operated a grocery and general merchandise store. The Hughes brothers came to Atlanta from Tennessee in the early 1880s. (Courtesy of Cass County Genealogical Society.)

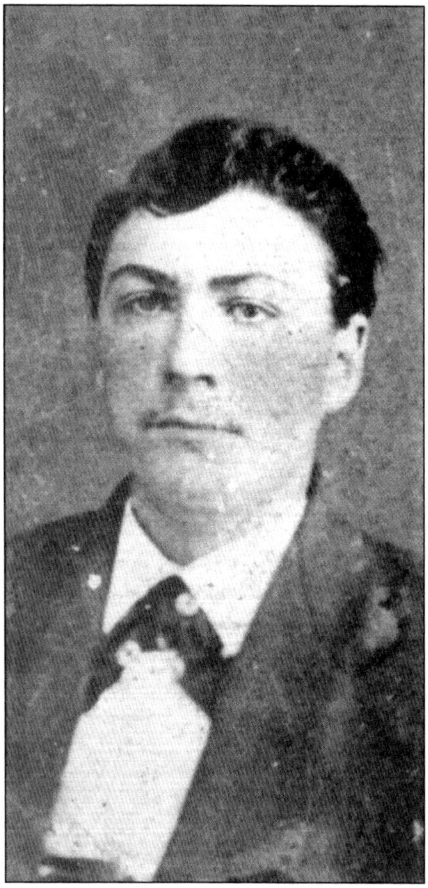

William A. Stuckey was one of Atlanta's early pioneers and a brick mason. The son of I. Stuckey, he built many of the first buildings in town. (Courtesy of Pearl Brown.)

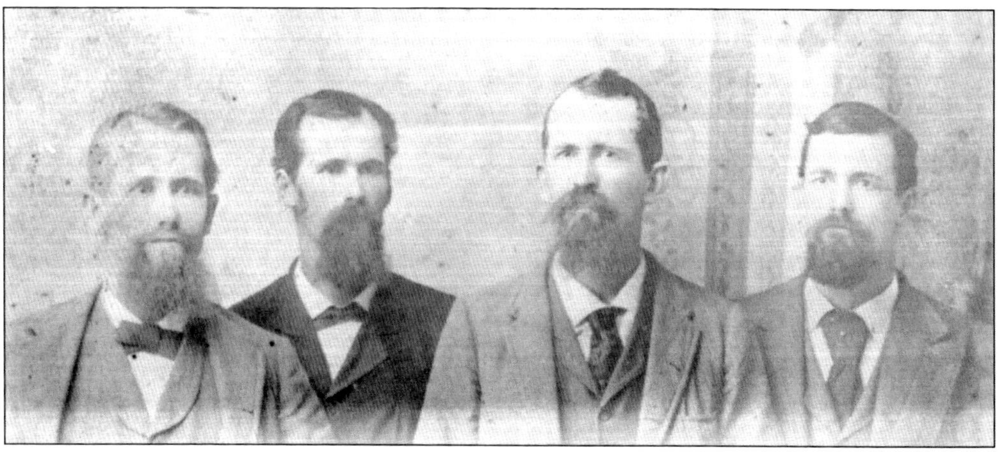

The Johnson brothers were early merchants in Atlanta. They arrived in town in the 1880s, and all four went into business. Pictured from left to right are J.D.; O.L., who jointly ran a general merchandise store near the location of Walker's Drug Store; William, who owned a livery stable; and Cary, who was a hardware merchant. (Courtesy of Pearl Brown.)

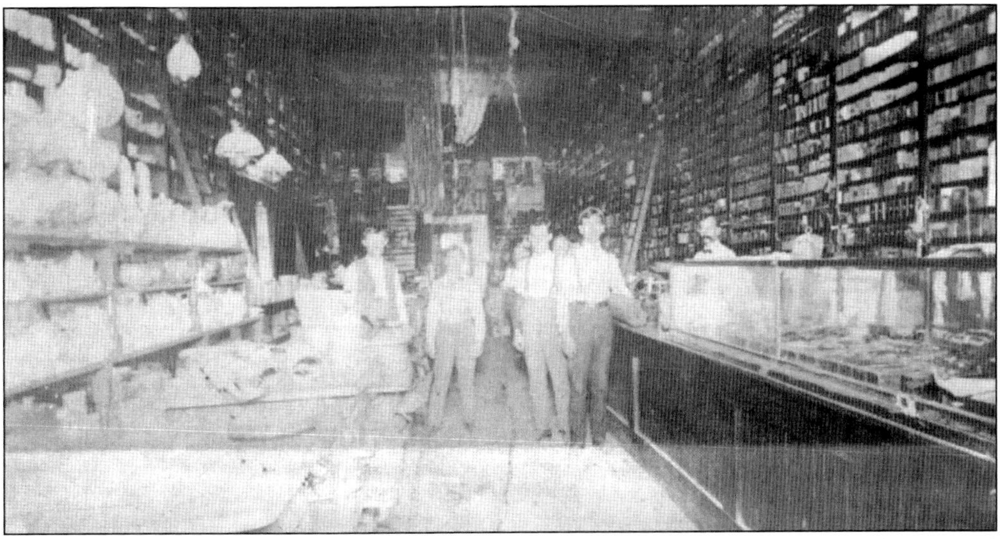

A.C. Smith ran one of the early businesses in Atlanta. This photograph shows his general merchandise store as it looked in the late 1800s. (Courtesy of Pearl Brown.)

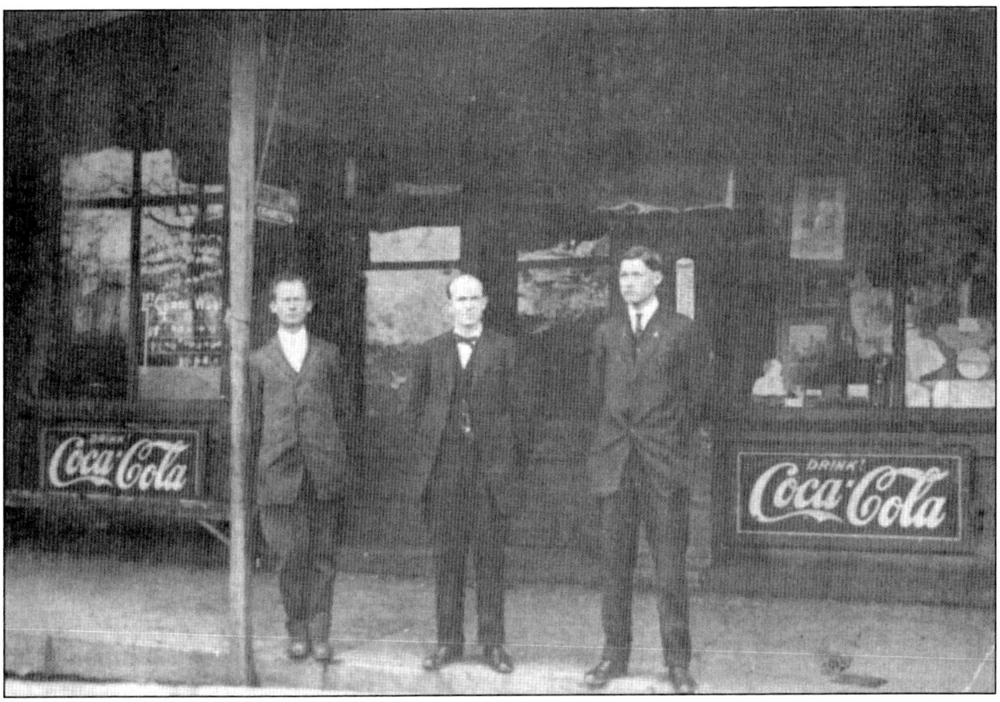

This early Walker's Drug Store was located on East Street facing the depot. The men are, from left to right, W.P. Walker, owner of the store and father of Wayne Walker, who later owned Walker's Drug; G.G. Pynes, who owned a jewelry store inside the drug store; and Jim Alexander, an employee who later opened his own store in Atlanta. (Courtesy of Pearl Brown.)

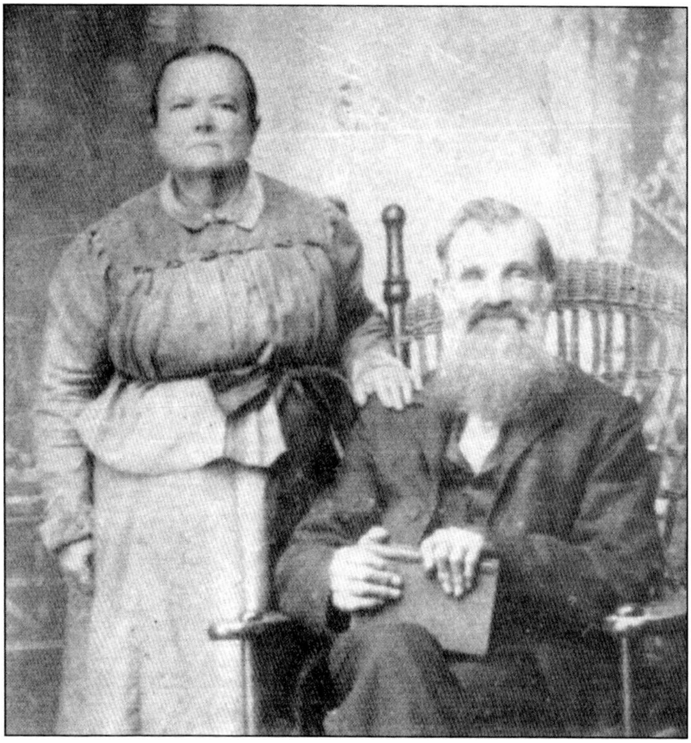

Isaac Wright, an early Atlanta mail carrier, came from Georgia to the East Texas area in 1869 with his wife, Betty Griffin, who he married in 1867. They lived in the Antioch community where Wright was the first mail carrier. He would come to Atlanta twice a week to receive anti-mail (anything too big for an envelope). His salary was two dollars a week. This photograph was taken around 1900. (Courtesy of Pearl Brown.)

This photograph from 1903 shows women preparing peaches for shipping. (Courtesy of Cass County Genealogical Society.)

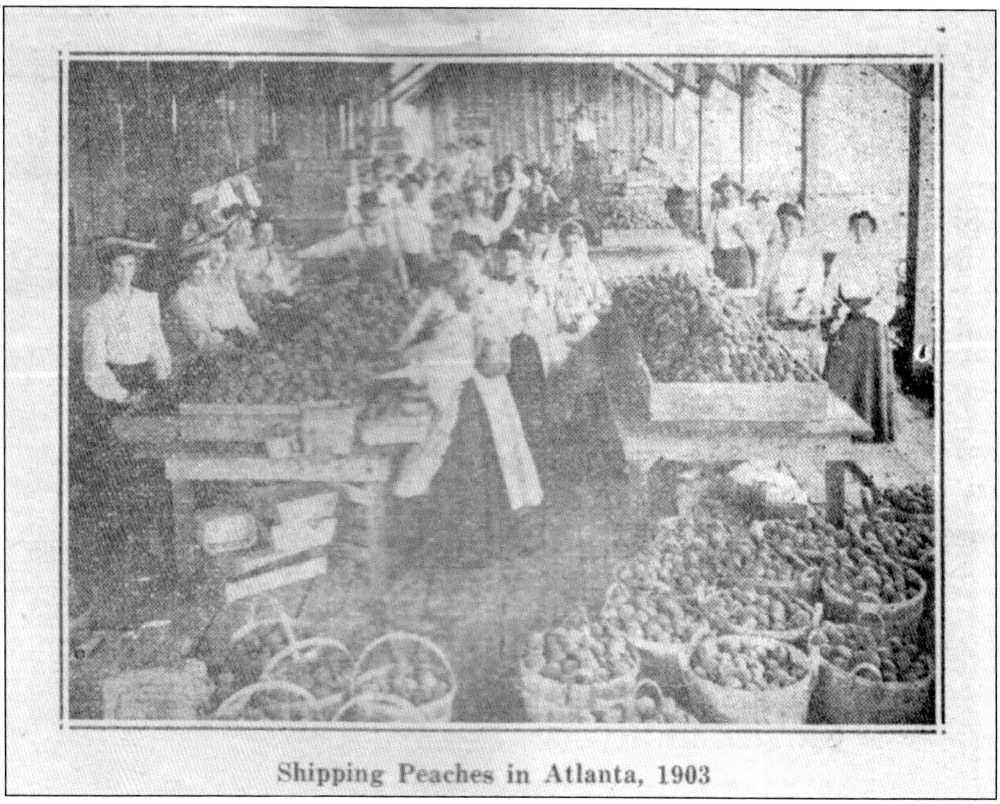

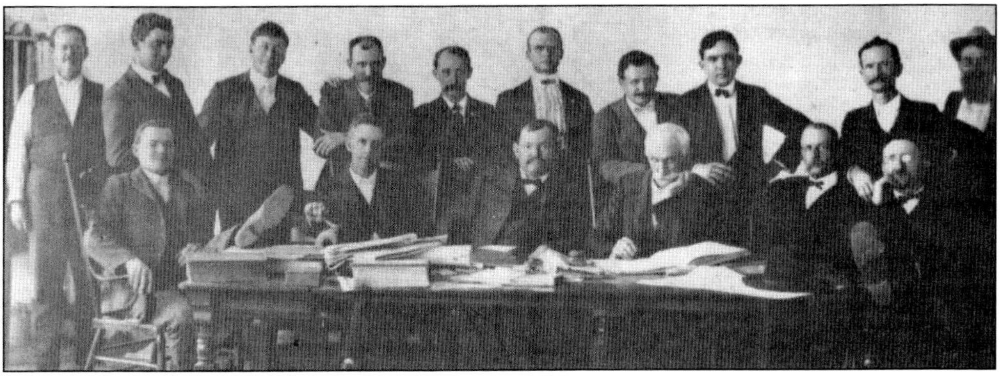

Doctors and dentists attended a meeting of the Cass County Medical Association held in Atlanta around 1906. Sitting and standing around the table are, from left to right, (first row) Doctors Sherman, Starkey, Jeter, and McClung, unidentified, and Doctor Gowan; (second row) meeting guest John McWilliams, unidentified, Doctors Long, Connerly, Neal, Glass, Lee, Ledbetter, and Crossley, and journal editor John M. Fletcher. (Courtesy of Pearl Brown.)

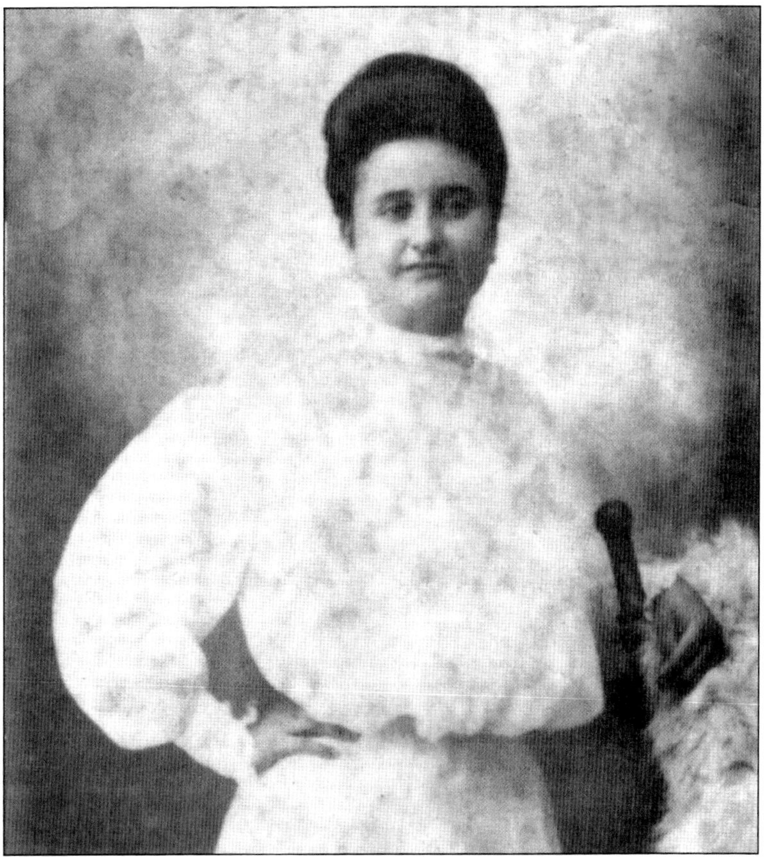

Effie Lee Holt, a former typesetter for the *Citizens Journal*, is shown here around 1909. She worked at the newspaper in 1907–1908 during the years the *Journal* was under the ownership of John M. Fletcher. (Courtesy of Pearl Brown.)

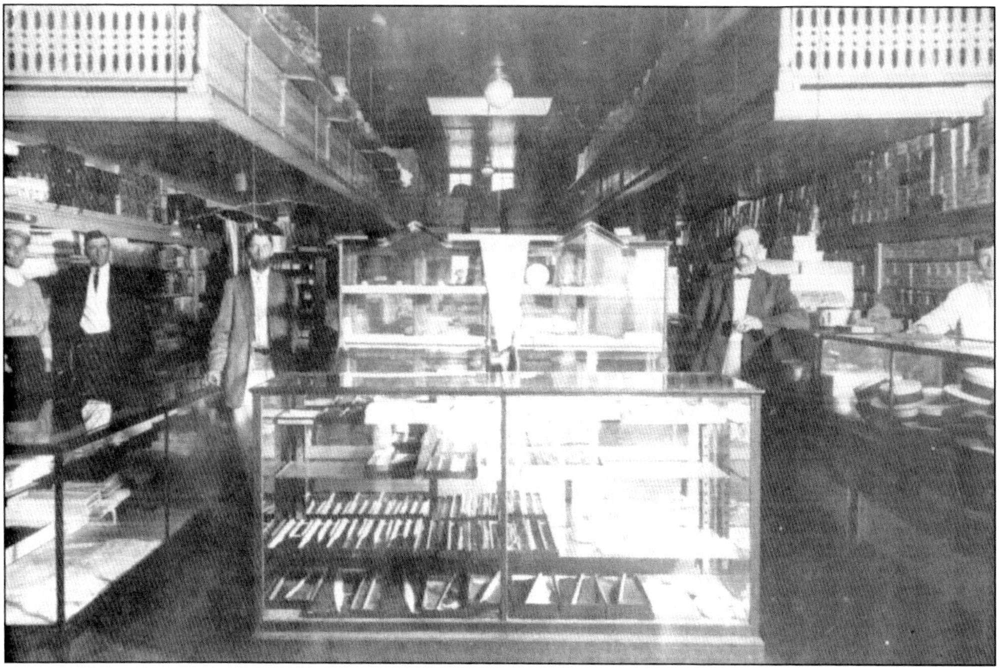

This photograph showing an inside view of Allday's Department Store located on Hiram Street was taken around 1910. (Courtesy of Cass County Genealogical Society.)

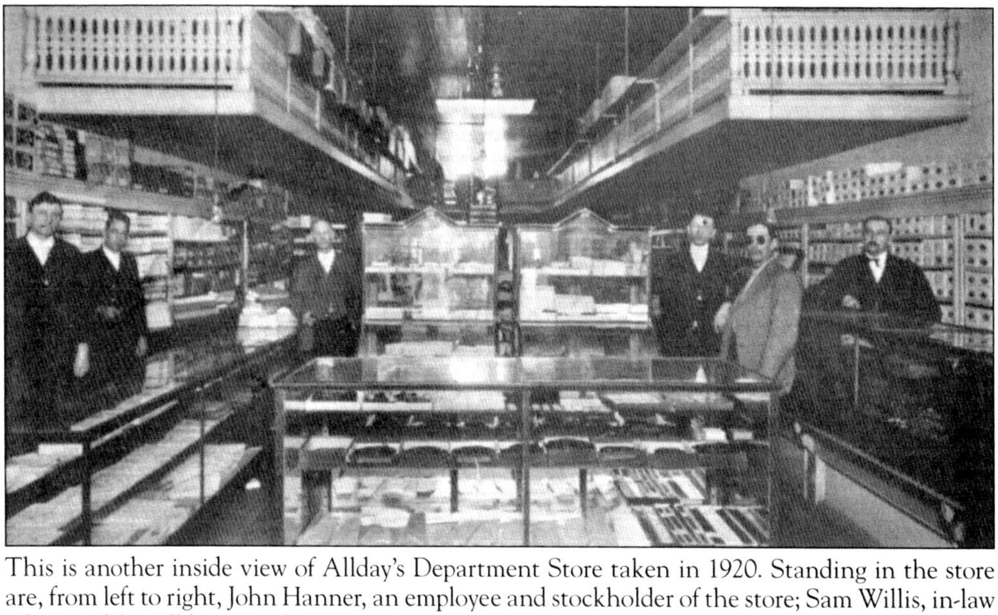

This is another inside view of Allday's Department Store taken in 1920. Standing in the store are, from left to right, John Hanner, an employee and stockholder of the store; Sam Willis, in-law relative of the Alldays; Frank Allday, owner; Nath Hanner, employee and stockholder of the store; an unidentified salesman; and Ben Singletary, a store employee. (Courtesy of Pearl Brown.)

This is a piece of Hughes House stationery from around 1911 with names and dates written on it. George and James Hughes, two of the four Hughes brothers, were the proprietors of the businesses advertised on the stationery. (Courtesy of Cass County Genealogical Society.)

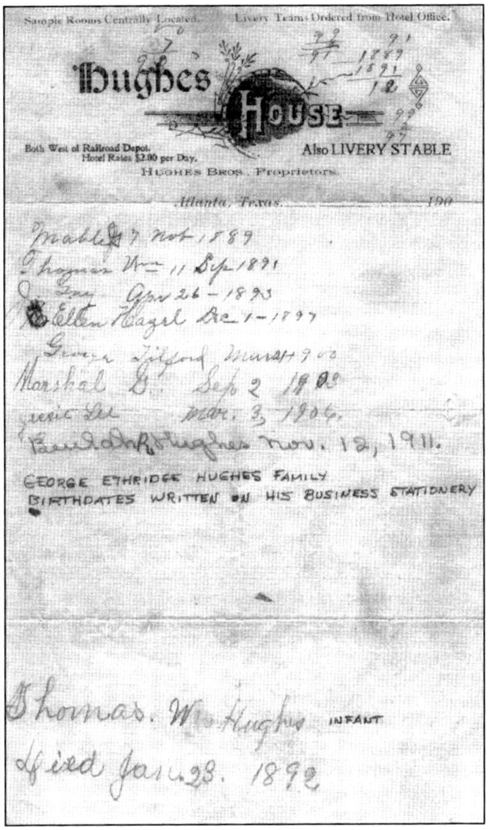
Sample Rooms Centrally Located. Livery Teams Ordered from Hotel Office.

Hughes House

Both West of Railroad Depot. Hotel Rates $2.00 per Day.

Also LIVERY STABLE

Hughes Bros., Proprietors.

Atlanta, Texas, 190

GEORGE ETHRIDGE HUGHES FAMILY BIRTHDATES WRITTEN ON HIS BUSINESS STATIONERY

Thomas W. Hughes INFANT

Died Jan 28. 1892

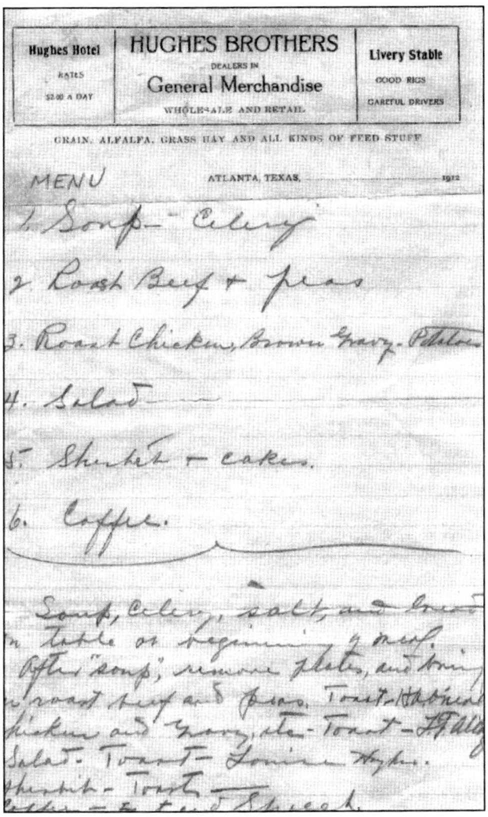
Hughes Hotel RATES $2.00 A DAY	HUGHES BROTHERS DEALERS IN General Merchandise WHOLESALE AND RETAIL	Livery Stable GOOD RIGS CAREFUL DRIVERS

GRAIN, ALFALFA, GRASS HAY AND ALL KINDS OF FEED STUFF

MENU

ATLANTA, TEXAS, 1912

1. Soup – Celery
2. Roast Beef + peas
3. Roast Chicken, Brown Gravy - Potatoes
4. Salad
5. Sherbet + cakes.
6. Coffee.

This is a piece of Hughes Brothers stationery from 1912. The top left reads, "Hughes Hotel RATES $2.00 A DAY," and at the top right, "Livery Stable GOOD RIGS CAREFUL DRIVERS." An order of events for a program was handwritten on the stationery with a food order and names included at the bottom: "Soup, celery, salt, and bread on the table at beginning of meal. After 'soup,' remove plates and bring in roast beef and peas. Toast–H.A. O'Neal. Chicken and gravy, etc.–Toast–L.T. [last name illegible] Salad–Toast–Louise Hughes. [illegible]–Toast–Coffee–Toast and Speech." (Courtesy of Cass County Genealogical Society.)

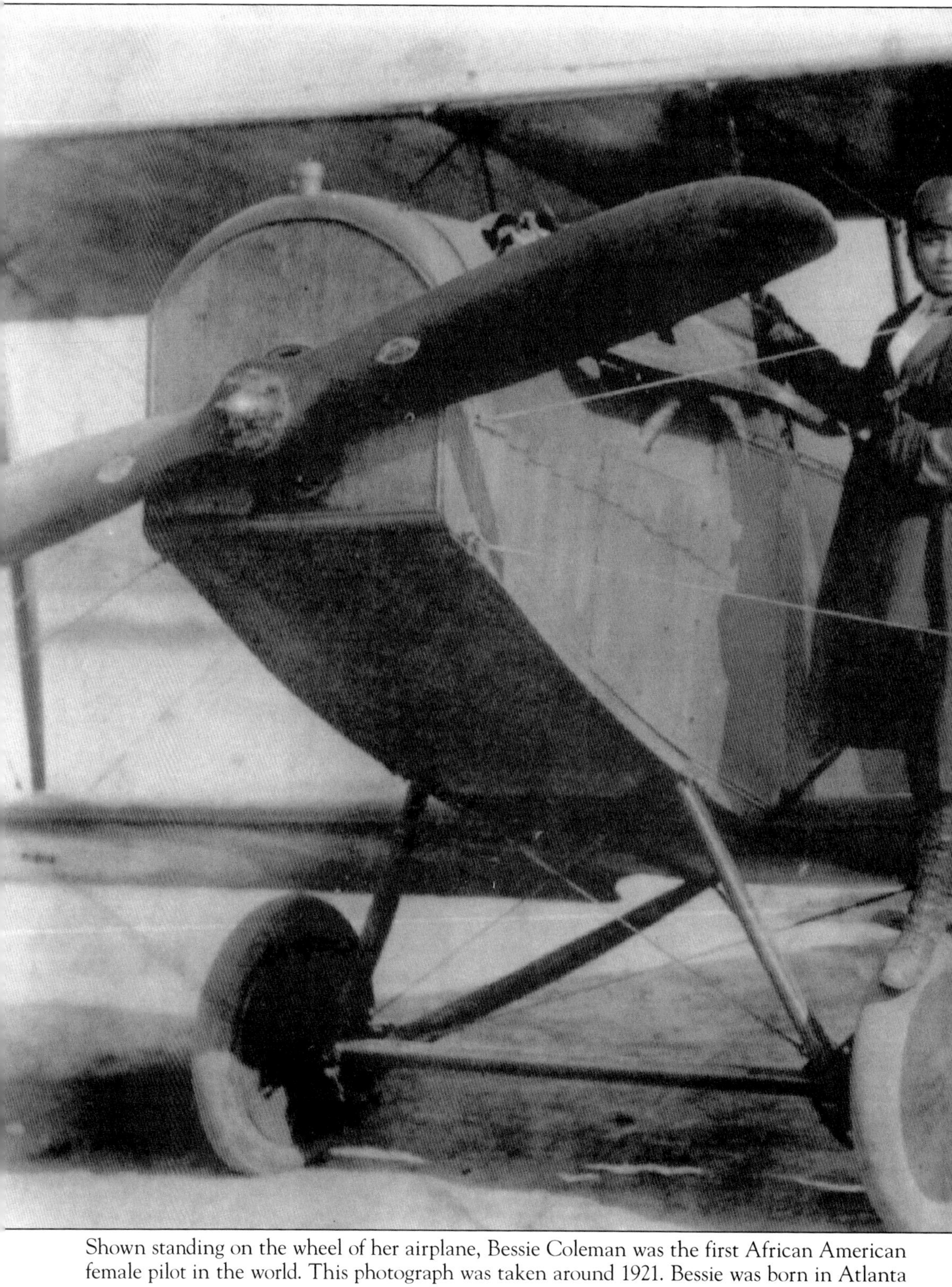

Shown standing on the wheel of her airplane, Bessie Coleman was the first African American female pilot in the world. This photograph was taken around 1921. Bessie was born in Atlanta

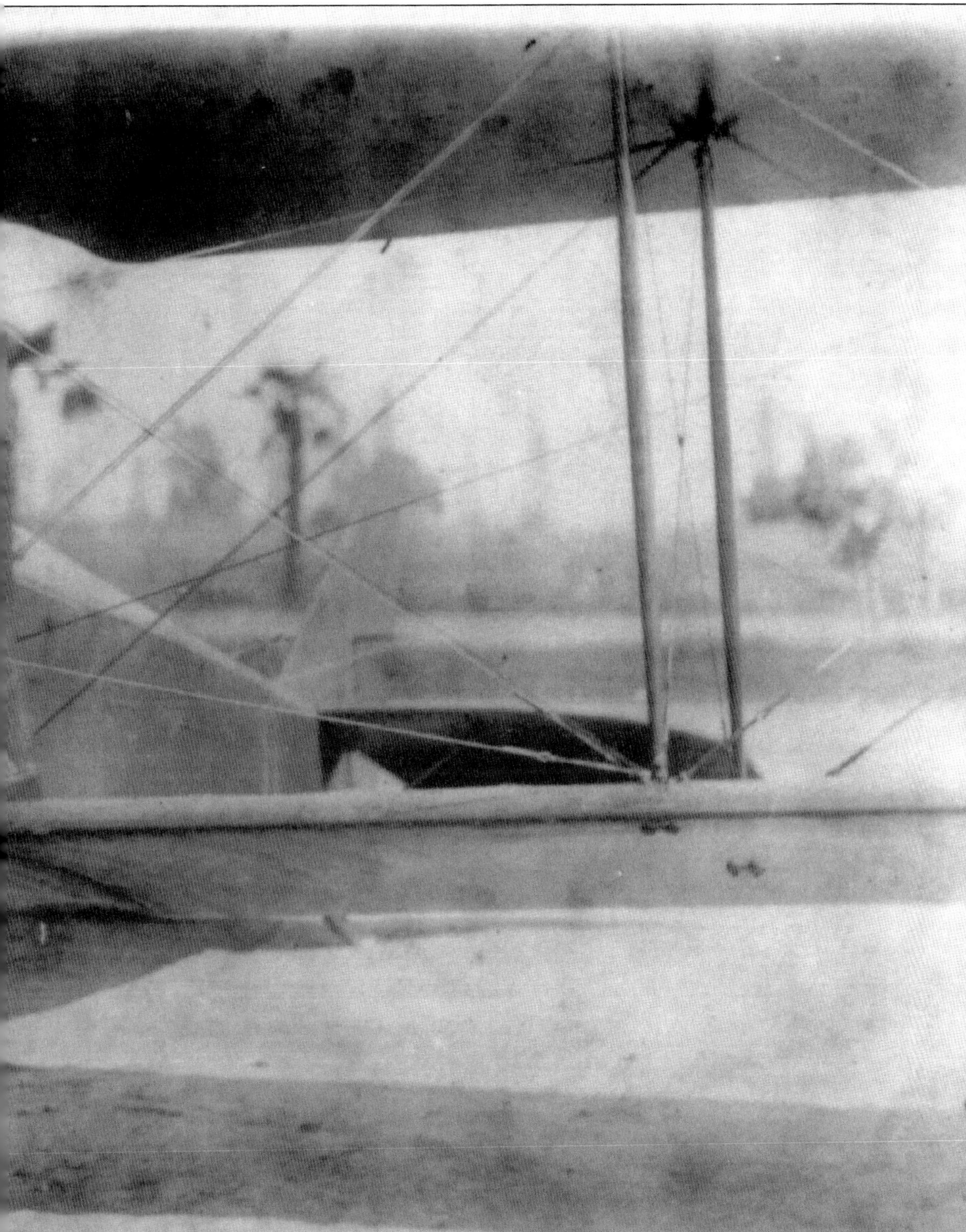

in 1892 and died in 1926. (Courtesy of Cass County Genealogical Society.)

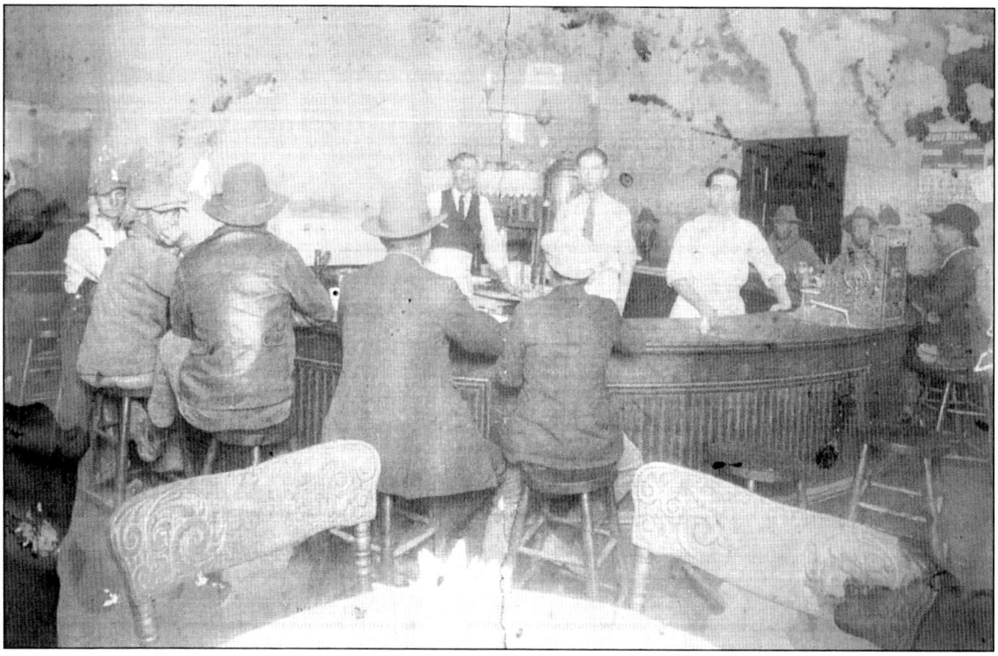

This is an inside view of Tom Brown's restaurant in 1918. The two men seated at the counter on the far left and facing the camera are Bully Clements (left) and Ray Bedgood. The people standing behind the counter are, from left to right, brothers Tom, Hershel, and J.T. Brown. (Courtesy of Cass County Genealogical Society.)

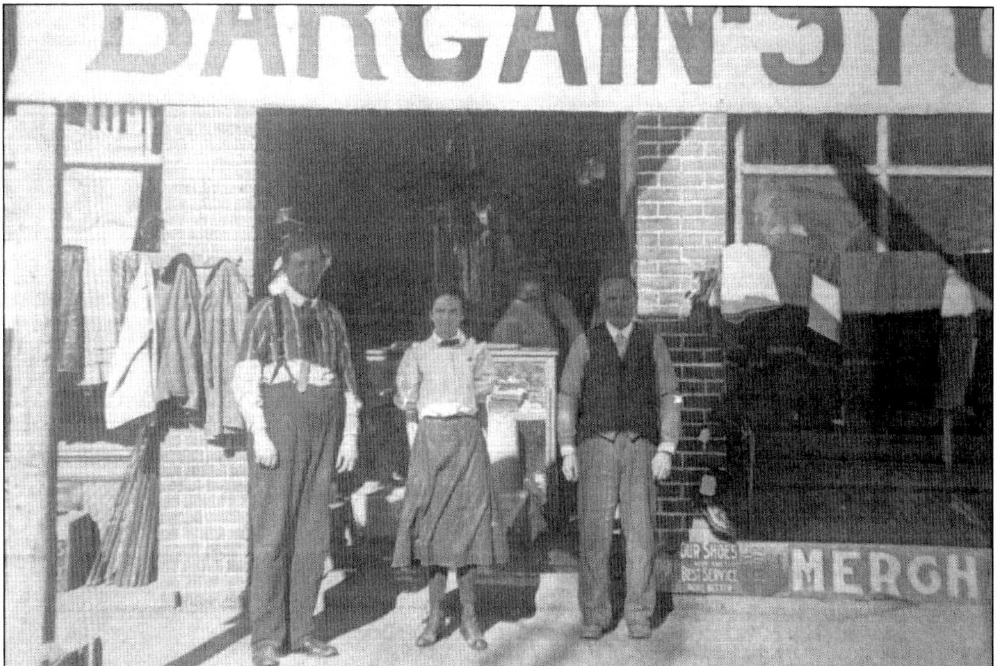

Frank Hughes, one of the four Hughes brothers, is standing in front of his general merchandise store around 1920 with two employees. Hughes is believed to be the man standing on the left. (Courtesy of Cass County Genealogical Society.)

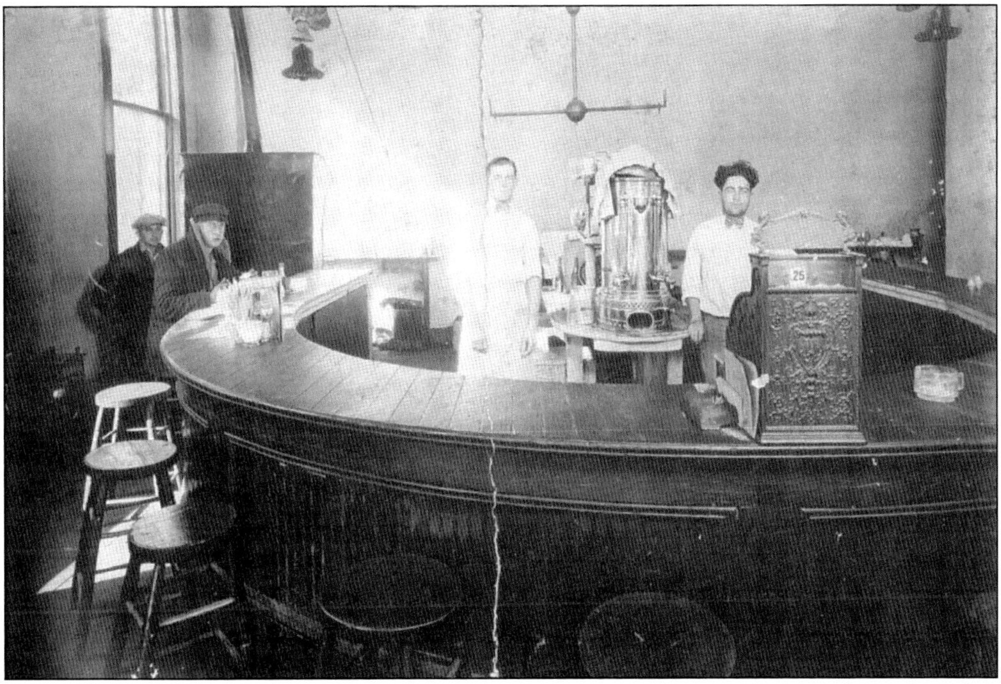

This is another view of the inside of Tom Brown's restaurant in 1924. Pictured are, from left to right, Ray Bedgood, Jess Moore, Hershel Brown, and J.T. Brown. (Courtesy of Cass County Genealogical Society.)

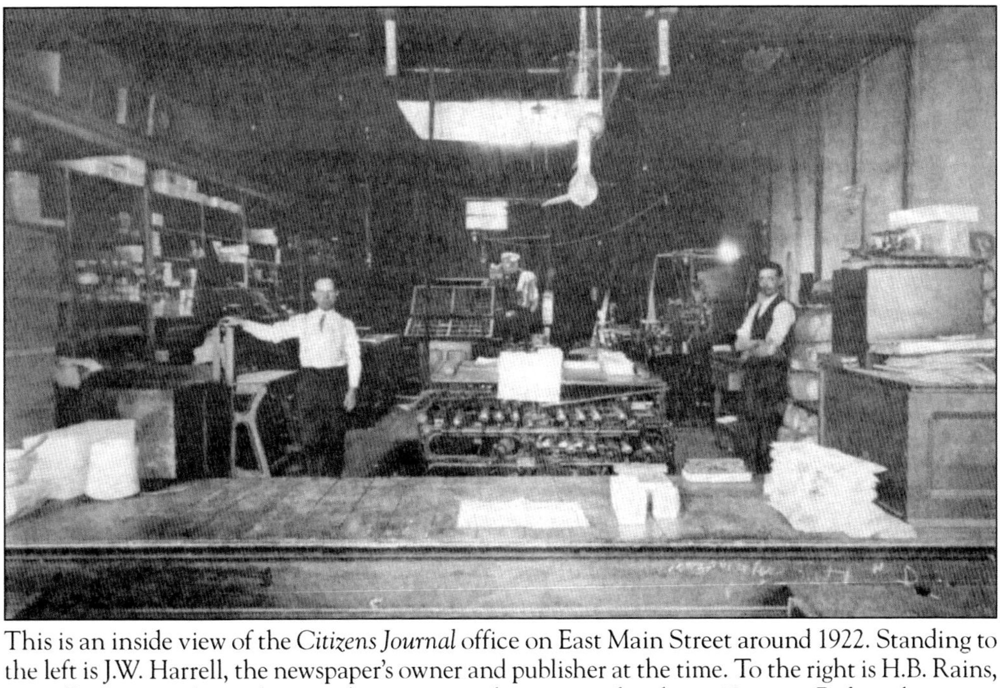

This is an inside view of the *Citizens Journal* office on East Main Street around 1922. Standing to the left is J.W. Harrell, the newspaper's owner and publisher at the time. To the right is H.B. Rains, Harrell's first employee; he was the printer and pressman for about 40 years. Before electricity, a gasoline motor ran the presses; its pipes can be seen on the ceiling. (Courtesy of Cass County Genealogical Society.)

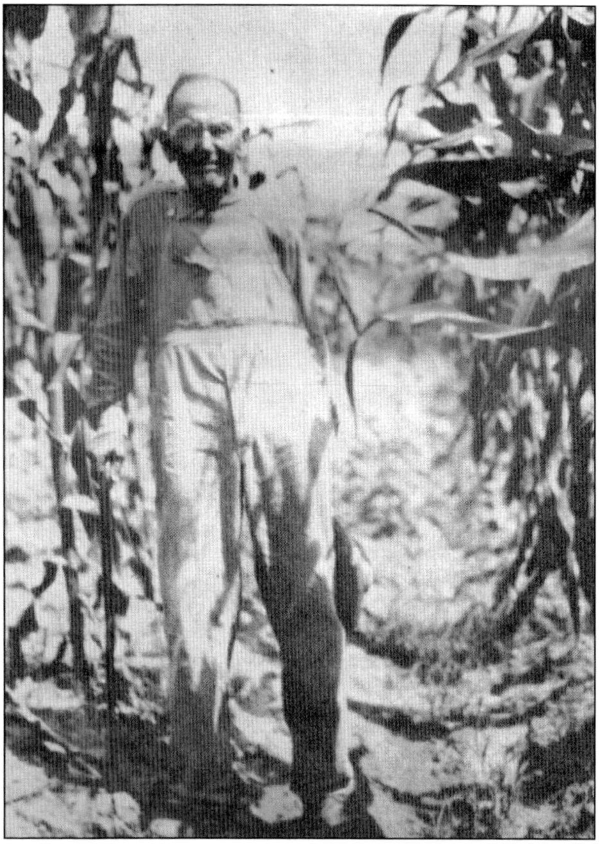

Wash Harper was considered one of the top farmers in the Atlanta area. He is shown in a photograph from *Farm and Ranch* in September 1928. (Courtesy of Pearl Brown.)

Workers are busy in this photograph of the Atlanta city secretary's office taken around 1920. Pictured are Don Cameron (left) and William F. Cameron. (Courtesy of Cass County Genealogical Society.)

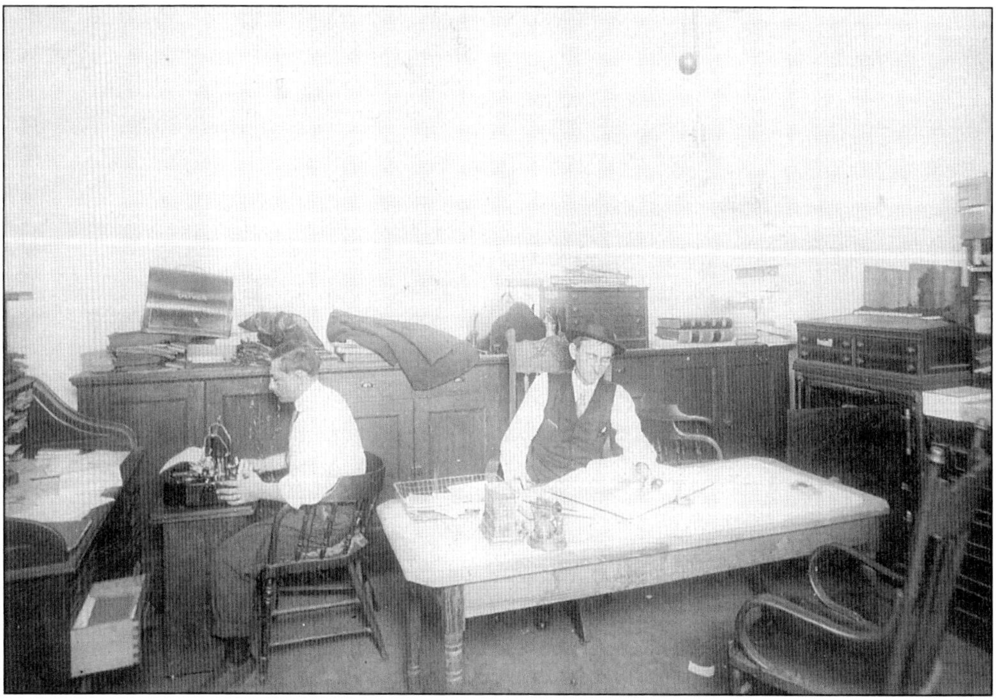

R.W. Grogan and his wife settled in the Atlanta area in 1886, and four years later he purchased a sawmill. The Grogan business became a dominant force in the history and economy of Atlanta. (Courtesy of Cass County Genealogical Society.)

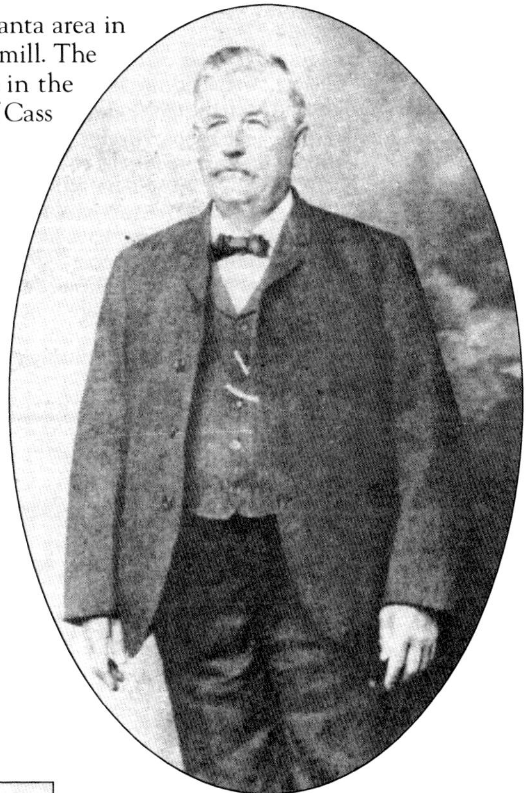

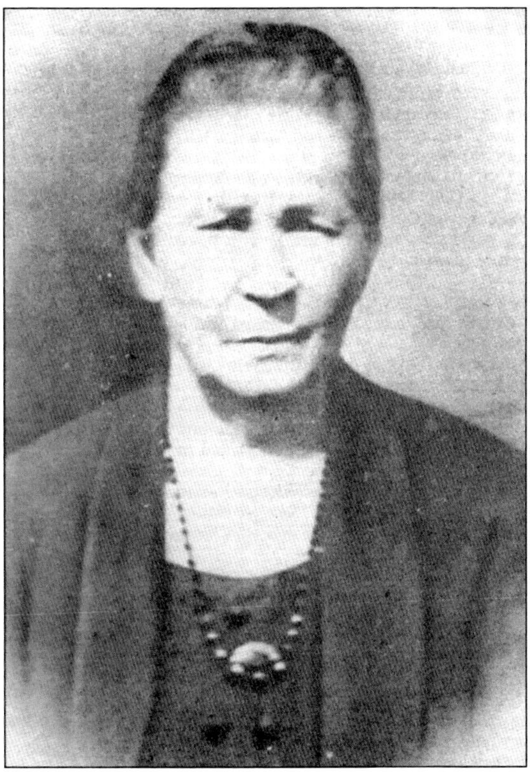

This portrait is of R.W. Grogan's wife around age 50. (Courtesy of Cass County Genealogical Society.)

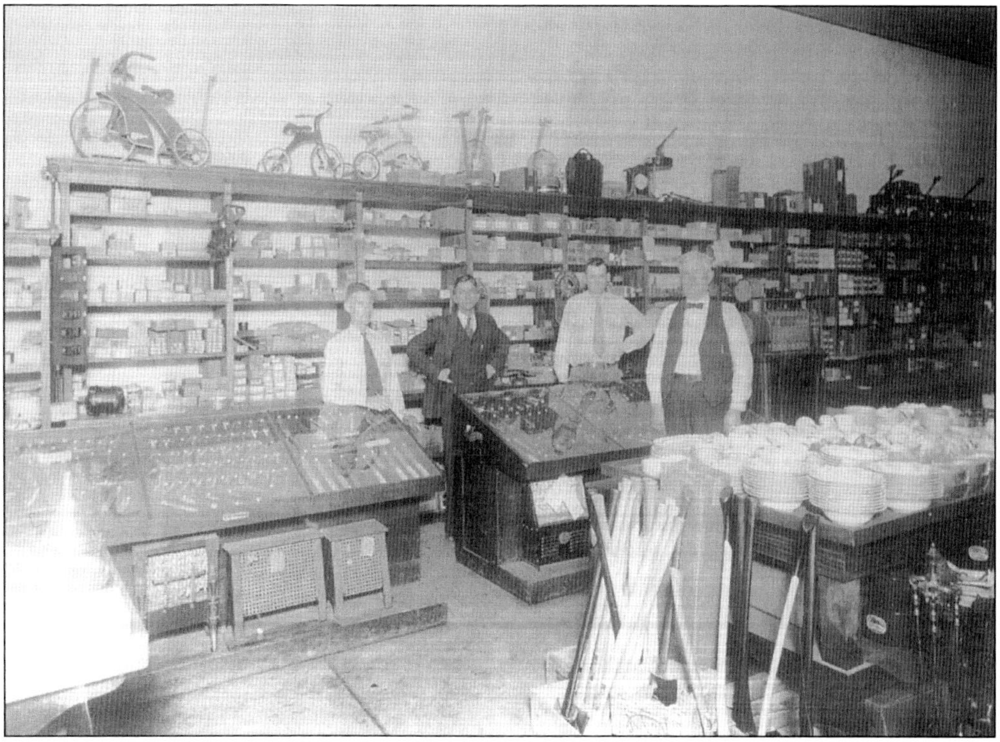

Workers are standing at the counter inside the R.H. Price Store around 1930. (Courtesy of Cass County Genealogical Society.)

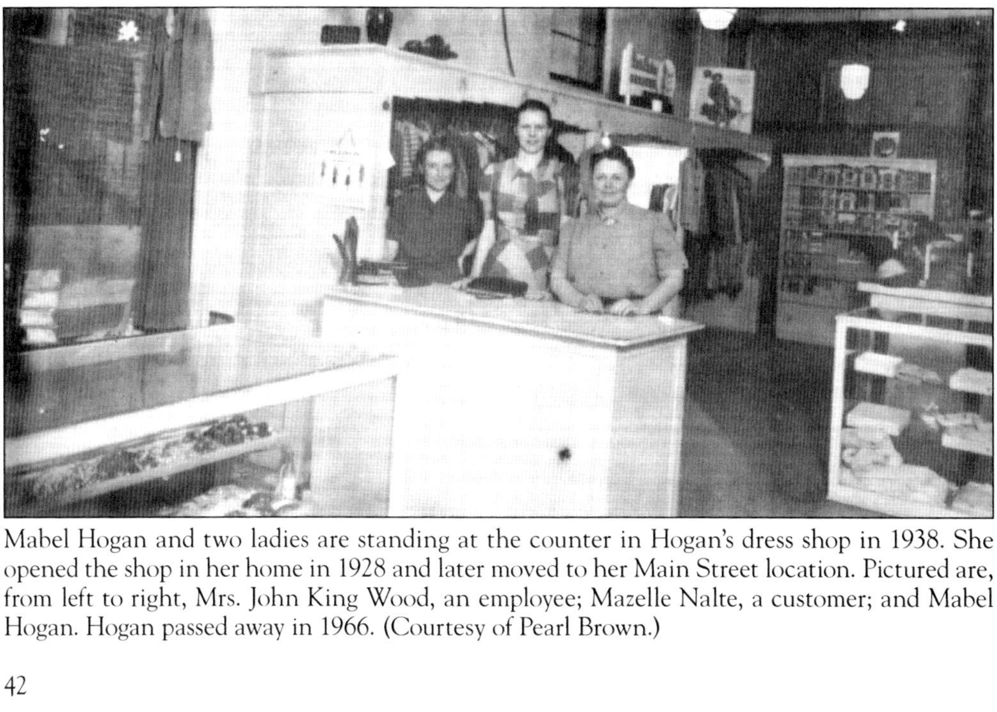

Mabel Hogan and two ladies are standing at the counter in Hogan's dress shop in 1938. She opened the shop in her home in 1928 and later moved to her Main Street location. Pictured are, from left to right, Mrs. John King Wood, an employee; Mazelle Nalte, a customer; and Mabel Hogan. Hogan passed away in 1966. (Courtesy of Pearl Brown.)

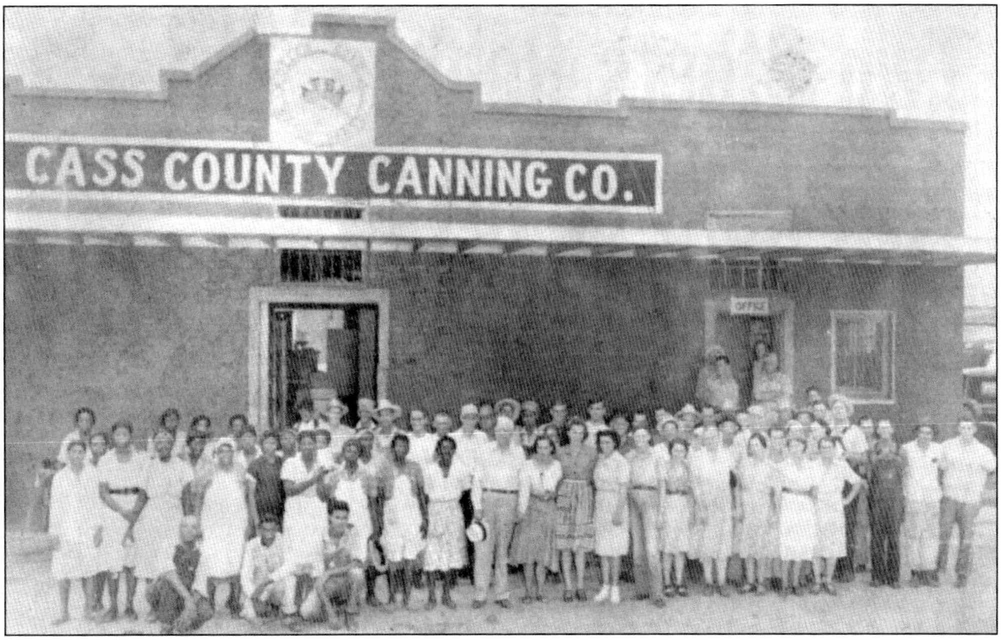

One of the largest businesses during its time, the Cass County Canning Company came to Atlanta in 1938 and stayed until it was sold out in the mid-1950s. Shown here are some of the employees in 1946. Pictured in the center of the first row is E.R. Adams, who was a longtime veteran of the canning business and owner of the Atlanta firm. (Courtesy of Pearl Brown.)

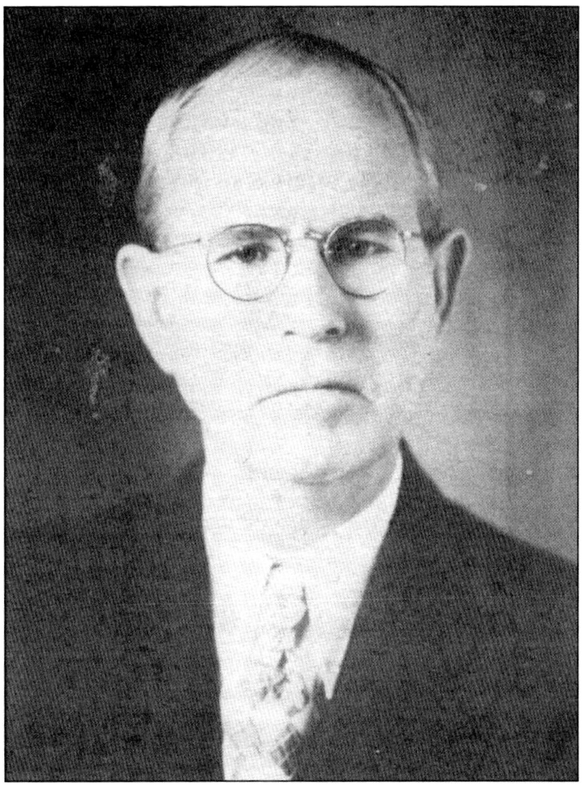

J.W. Harrell was the publisher of the *Citizens Journal* from 1914 to 1940. (Courtesy of Cass County Genealogical Society.)

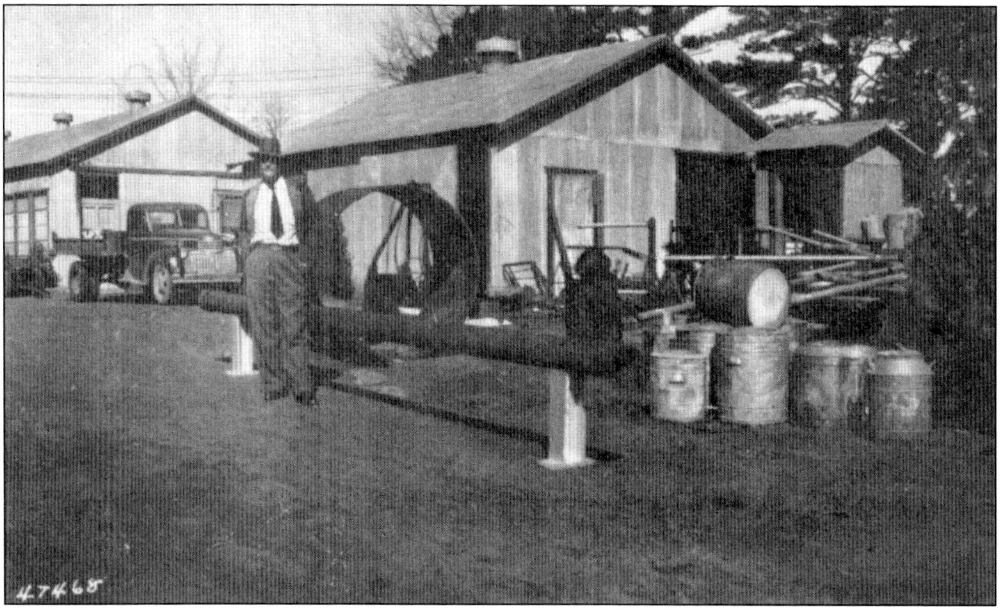

The old blacksmith and paint shops at the Texas Highway Department's District 19 headquarters in Atlanta are pictured around 1940. (Courtesy of Pearl Brown.)

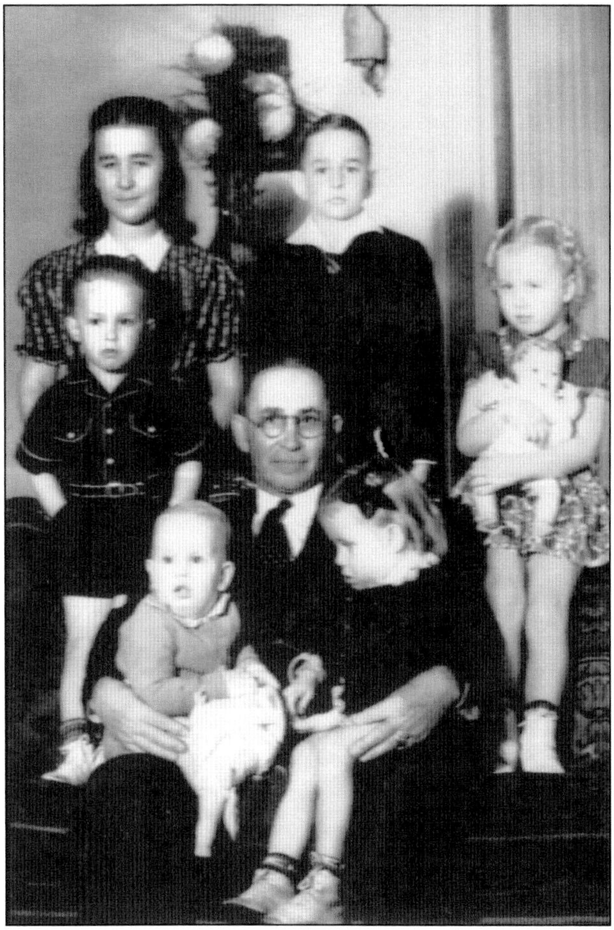

T.R. Richey is posing for a portrait with his grandchildren in the 1940s. Seated on Mr. Richey's lap are David M. Richey (left) and Shirley S. Smith. The boy standing to the left of Richey is Heartsill L. Richey, and standing behind Richey are Diane Richey (left), Norman L. Smith (center), and Robin Richey. (Courtesy of Cass County Genealogical Society.)

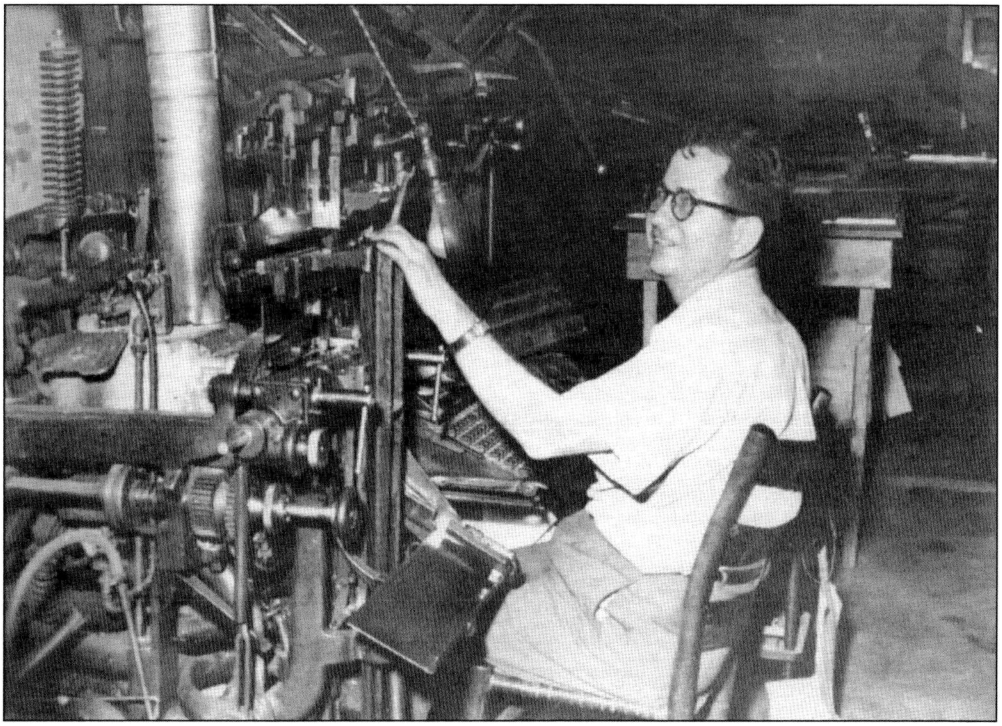

D.P. Harrell is pictured while working on the linotype machine at the *Citizens Journal* in the 1940s. The linotype machine turned molten lead into metal type letters, which were formed into paragraphs one line at a time. The linotype was used at the *Journal* until about 1968. Harrell was the publisher from 1940 to 1963. (Courtesy of Cass County Genealogical Society.)

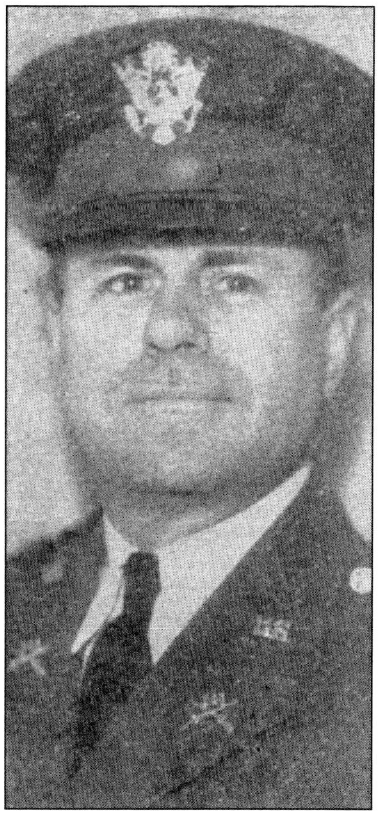

This military photograph is of Lt. W.E. Rabb, possibly the nephew of coach William E. Rabb. (Courtesy of Cass County Genealogical Society.)

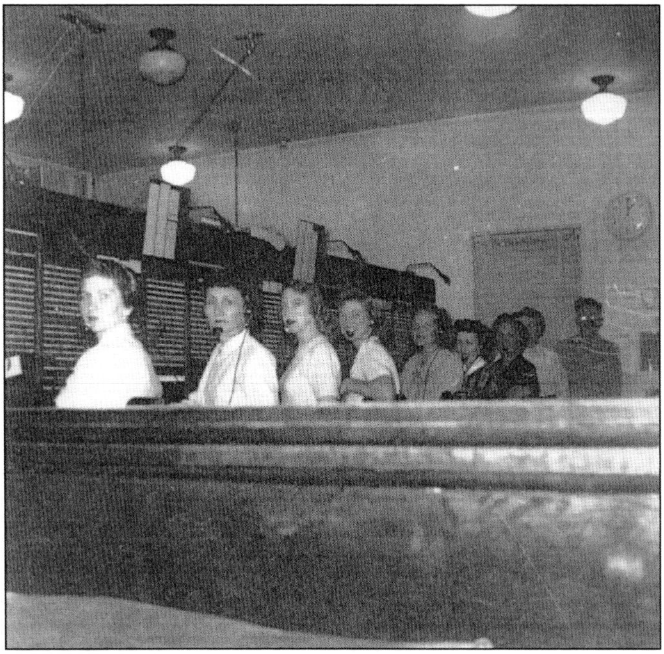

This is a view of the telephone company in Atlanta, which was located on Miller Street in the 1950s. The workers pictured are, from left to right, Irene Bradley, Mary E. Clements, Gloria Wiggins, June Law, Emma G. Green, Betty Randolph, Mozell Thomas, Babe Evans, and Joe "Pop" Evans. (Courtesy of Irene Bradley.)

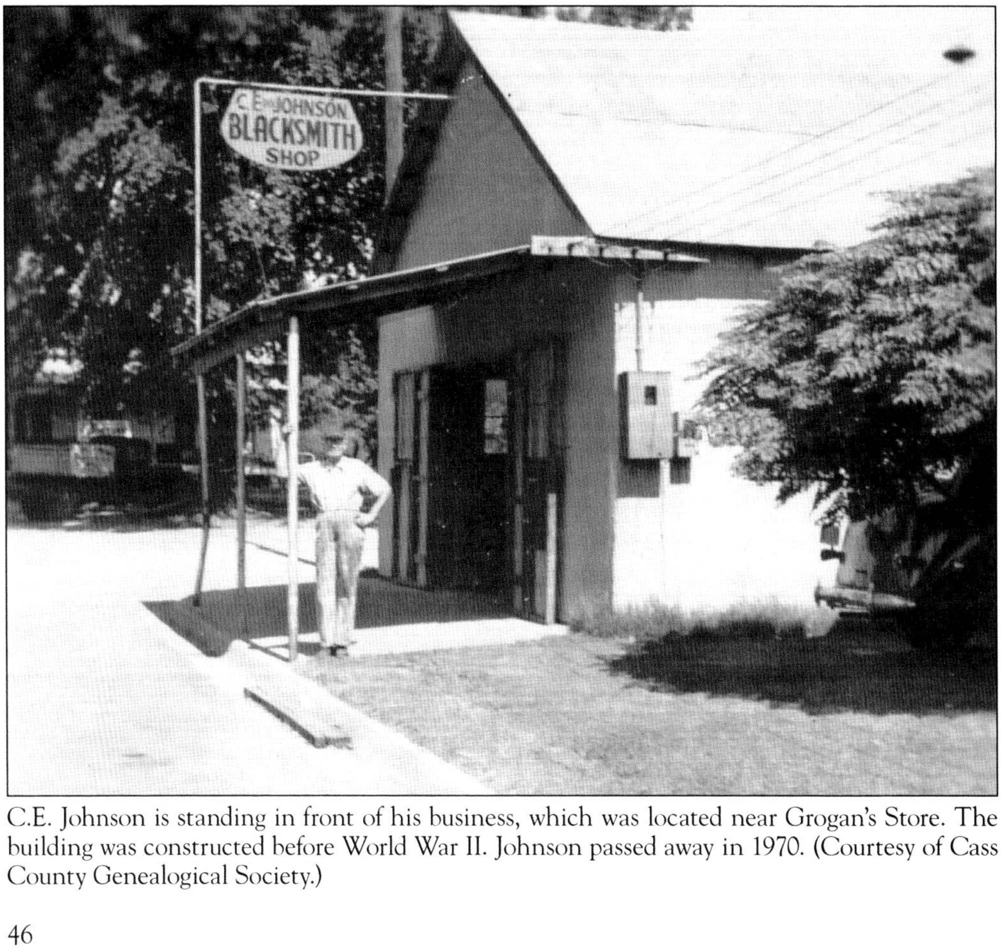

C.E. Johnson is standing in front of his business, which was located near Grogan's Store. The building was constructed before World War II. Johnson passed away in 1970. (Courtesy of Cass County Genealogical Society.)

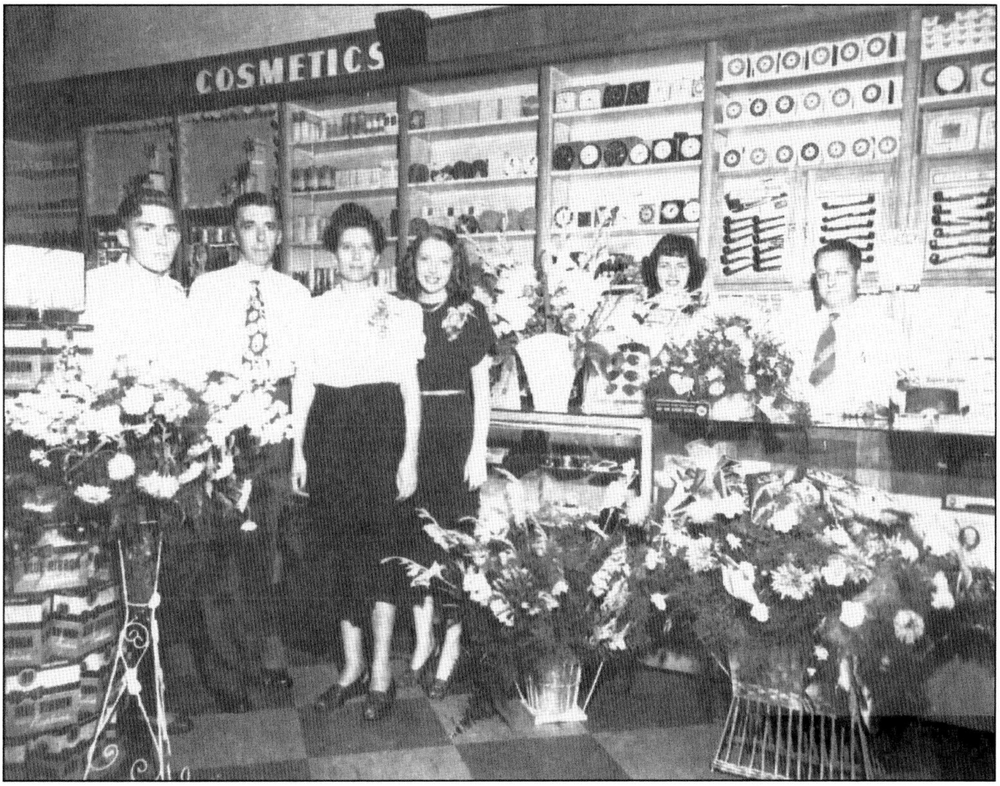

Customers and employees are standing at the counter of Tri-State Drugs during its grand opening in 1948. People standing at the counter are, from left to right, unidentified, George Reed (or Reid), unidentified, Jimmie McDuff, unidentified, and pharmacist and manager Raymond Braddock. (Courtesy of Cass County Genealogical Society.)

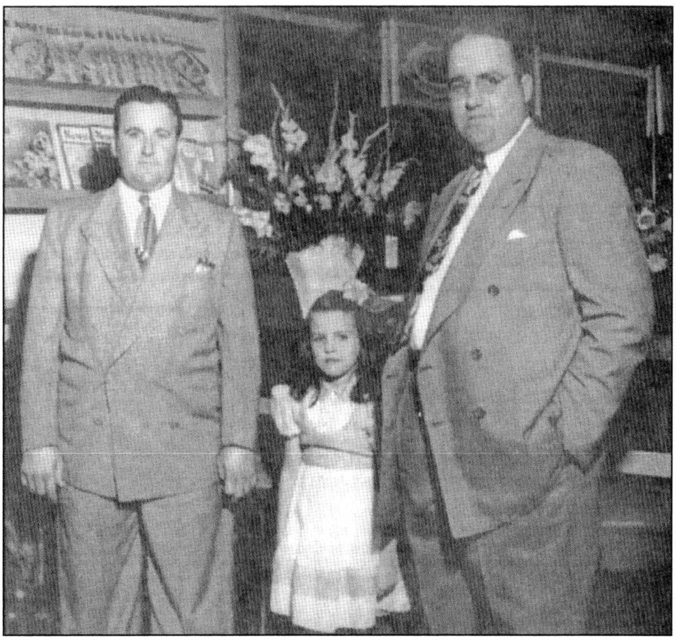

The Brooks brothers opened Tri-State Drugs, a franchise of Walgreen's Drug Store, in 1948. Pictured in the store are, from left to right, Dr. Jesse Brooks, Kathleen Brooks Verschoyle, and her father, Dr. James Brooks. (Courtesy of Cass County Genealogical Society.)

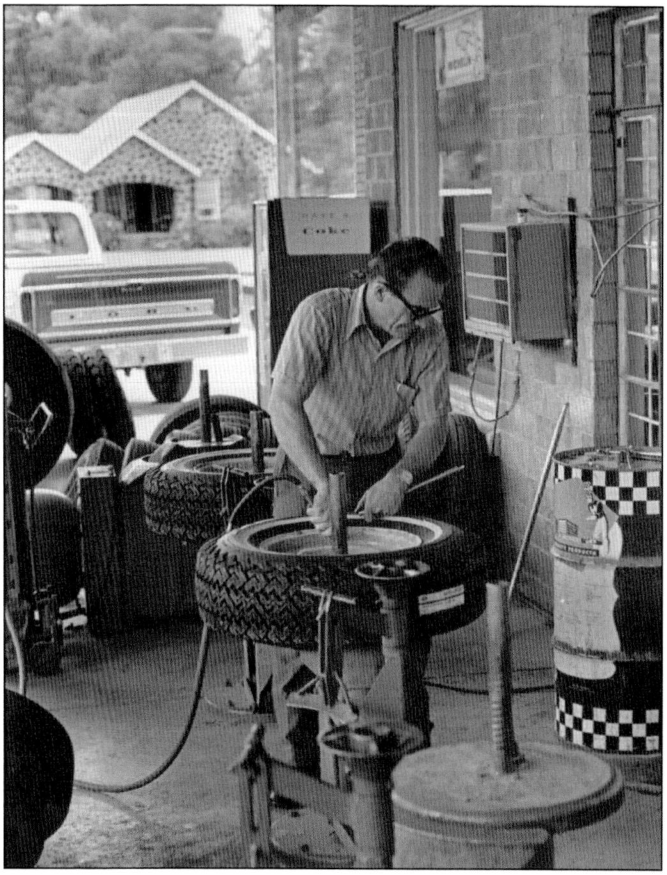

Oliver E. Brown is repairing a tire at Atlanta Tire Shop around 1970. The house that belonged to R.R. Lyle can be seen across the street. (Courtesy of Pearl Brown.)

Rodney Brown, son of Oliver E. and Pearl Brown, is shown working at Atlanta Tire Shop around 1970. (Courtesy of Pearl Brown.)

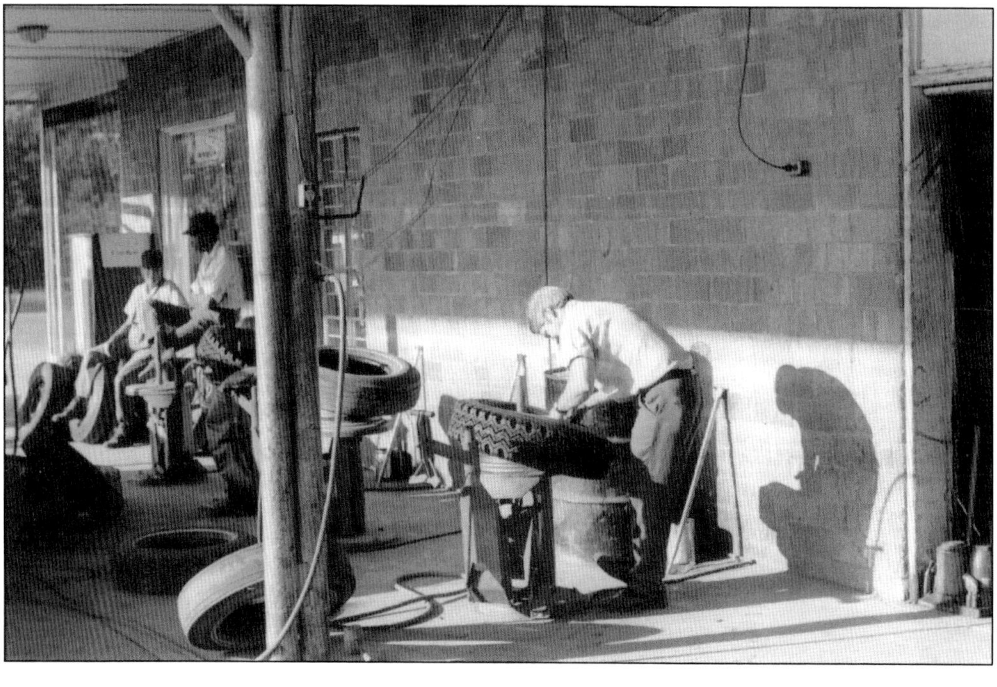

Three

FAMILY WORSHIP

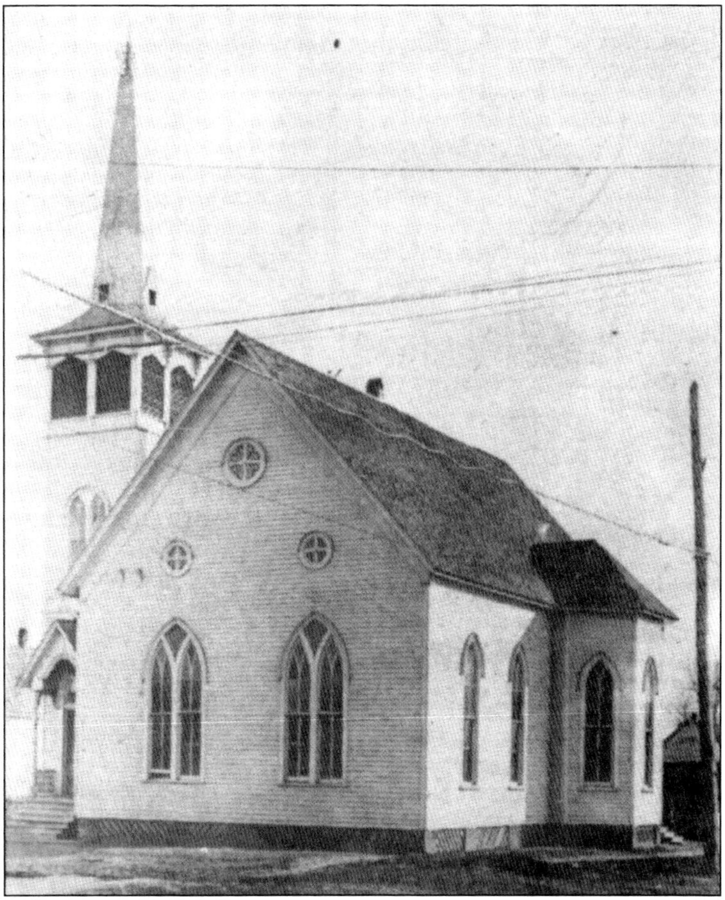

The First Methodist Church of Atlanta has had four buildings at its former location on Louise Street. Shown is the second church building, which was erected in 1890. The first building was erected in 1875 and later was sold to an African American congregation, at which time the First Methodist Church of Atlanta moved to its lot on North Louise Street. (Courtesy of Pearl Brown.)

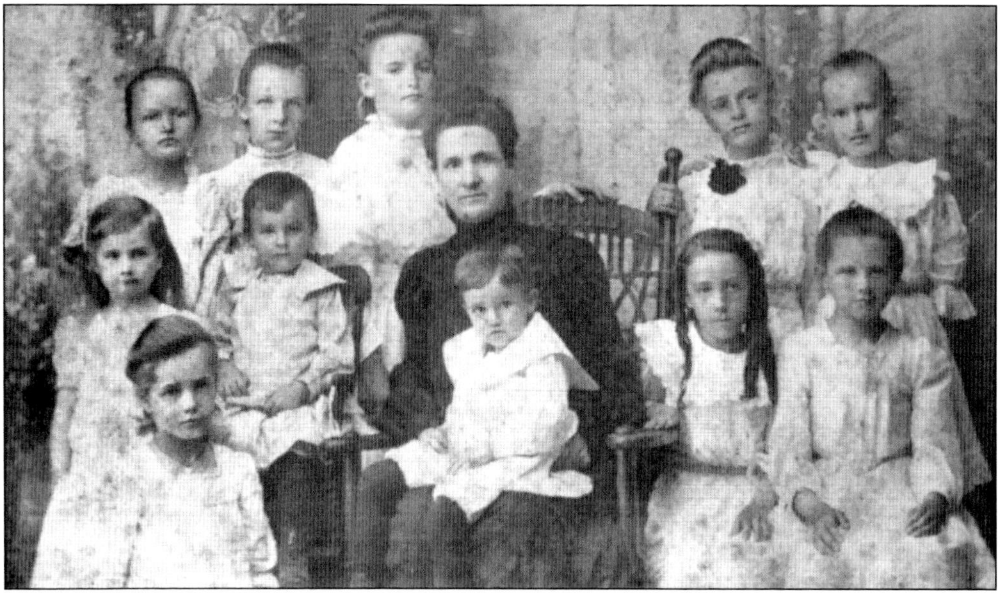

The beginning of the Gleaners Sunday school class at the Methodist church in Atlanta is shown around 1910. The woman wearing black and seated in the center is Onie Willis, a teacher. The children include, from left to right, (seated, front left) Mattie McClung; (first row) Mary McClung (Caldwell), a Birmingham child, Carey Johnson (seated on Willis's lap), Beulah Bransford, and Eunice McCasland; (second row) Gladys Johnson (Walker), Clara Birmingham, Janie O'Neal (Johnson), Onie Pepper (Lummus), and Gertis Johnson (Morgan). (Courtesy of Pearl Brown.)

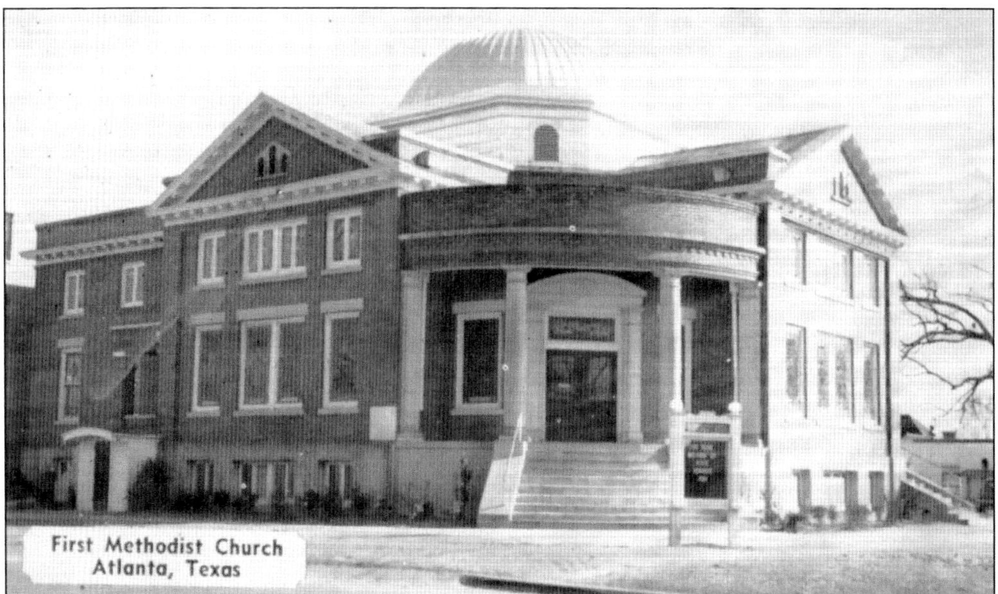

This is a postcard of the First Methodist Church from around 1950. Built in 1917, this was the third church building the Methodists built on this site. (Courtesy of Heather Ridpath Pilcher.)

The Annie Greene-Willis Memorial Building was presented to the First Methodist Church in 1938 by Meda Greene, Annie's mother. (Courtesy of Cass County Genealogical Society.)

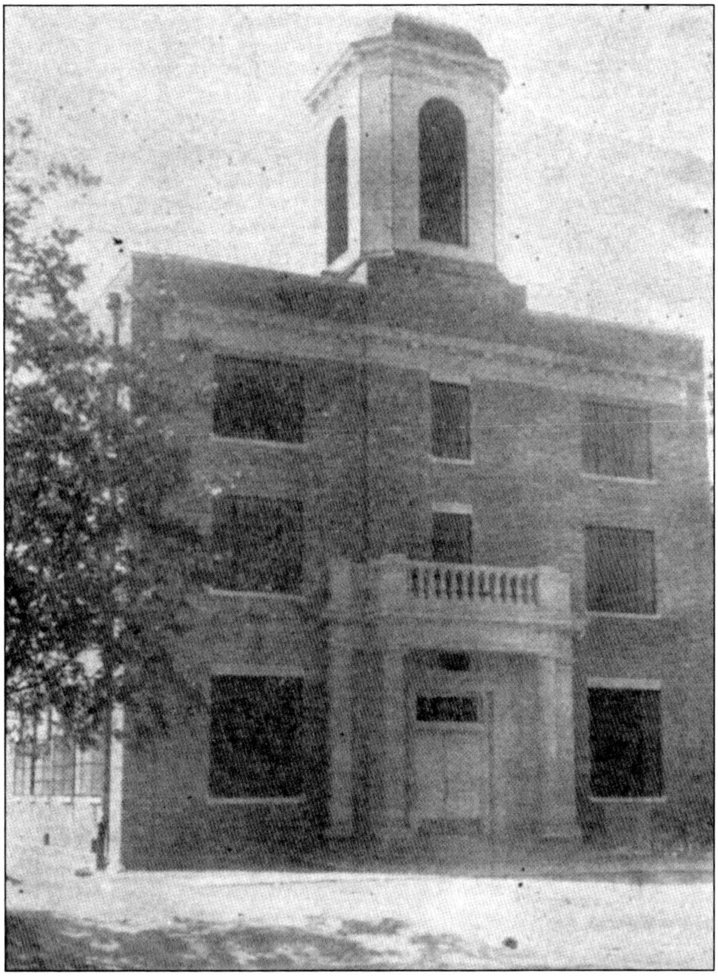

This wider view of the First Methodist Church shows the Annie Greene-Willis Memorial Building behind the main church building. This photograph was taken around 1950. The congregation recently moved to a new location on Lindsey Lane. The Nazarene congregation now occupies the site. (Courtesy of Pearl Brown.)

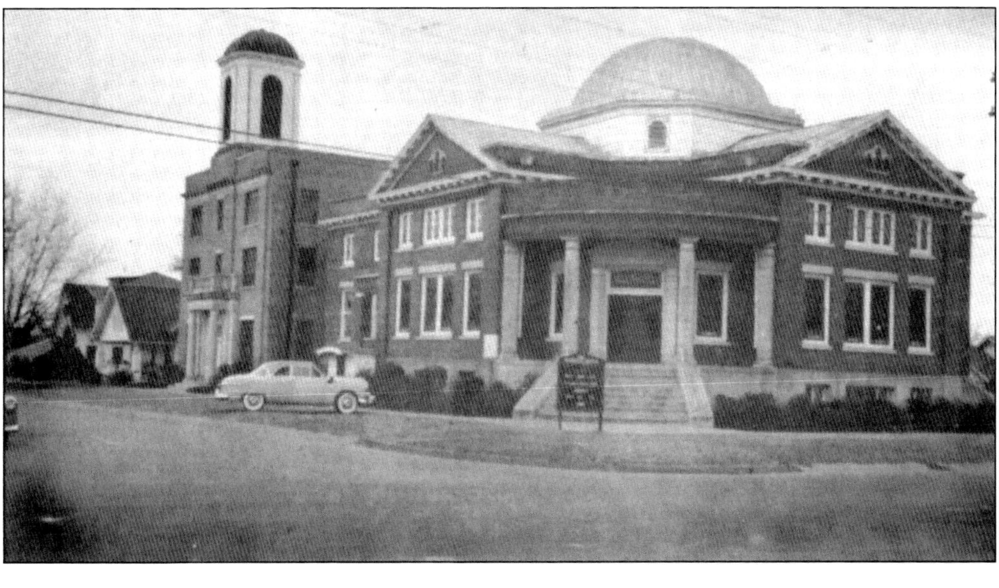

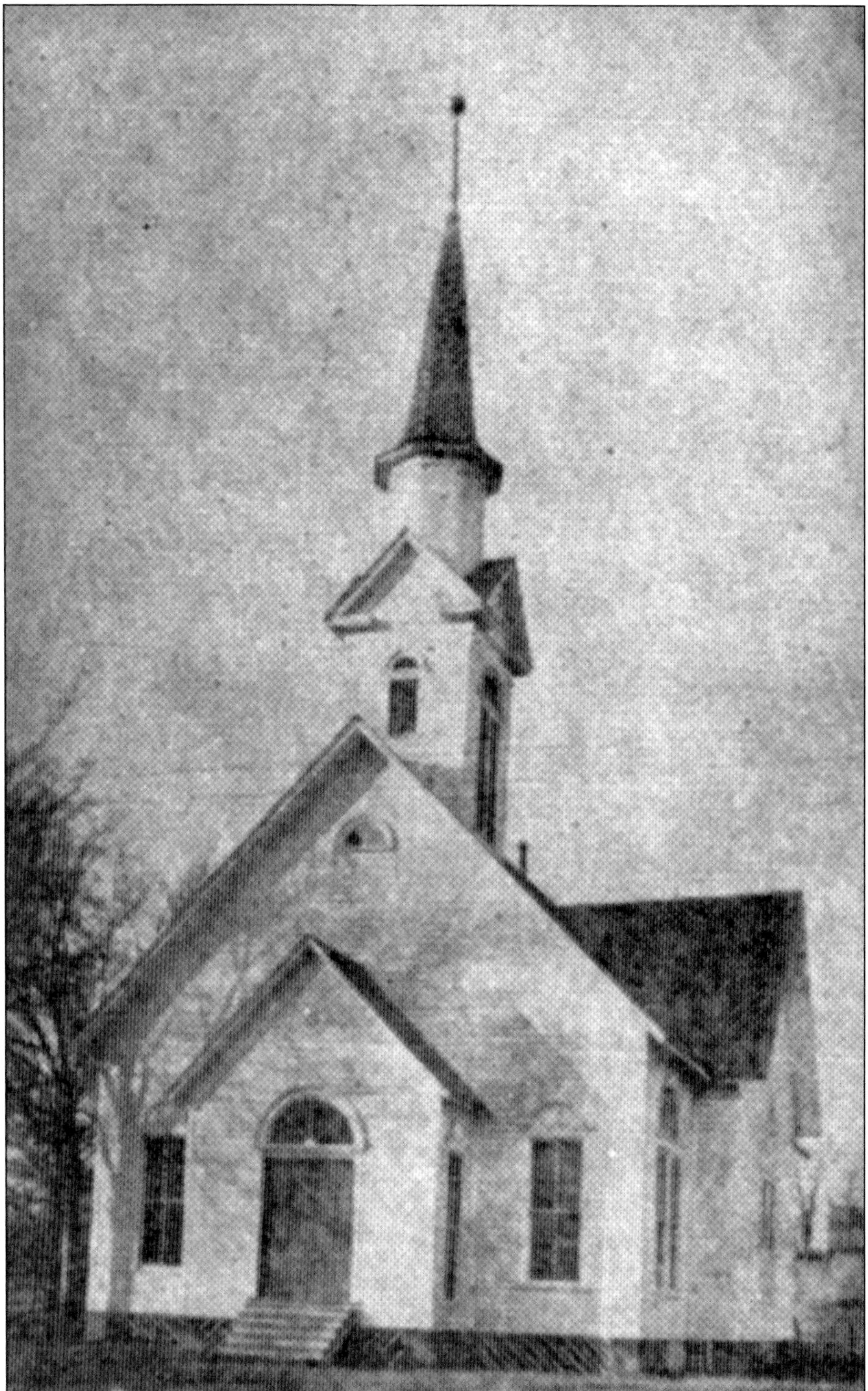

The First Baptist Church of Atlanta was established in 1874. This first structure was erected in 1896. (Courtesy of Pearl Brown.)

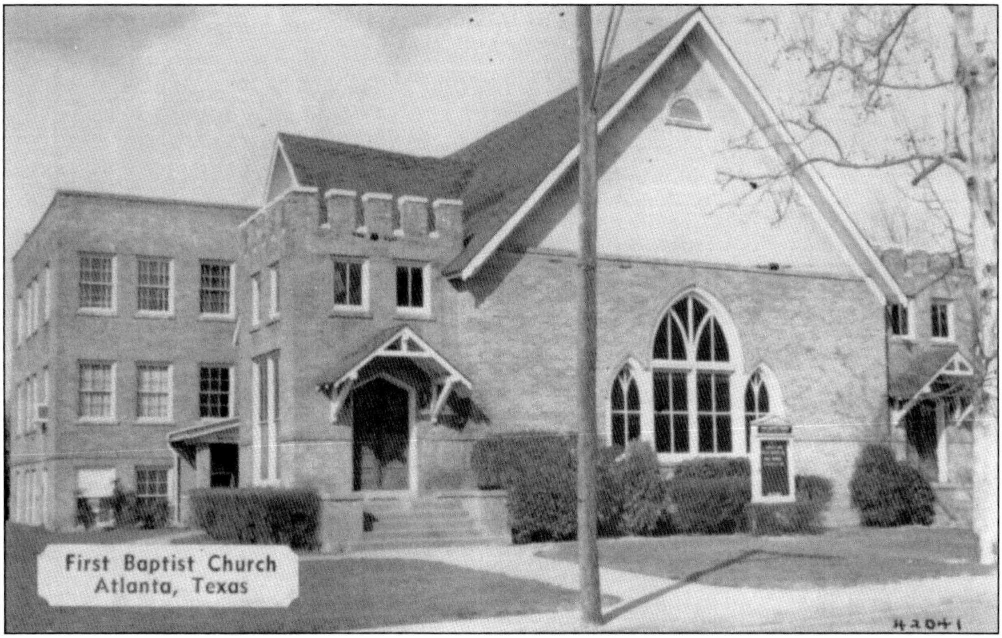

This postcard image of a newer First Baptist Church building was taken around 1950. (Courtesy of Heather Ridpath Pilcher.)

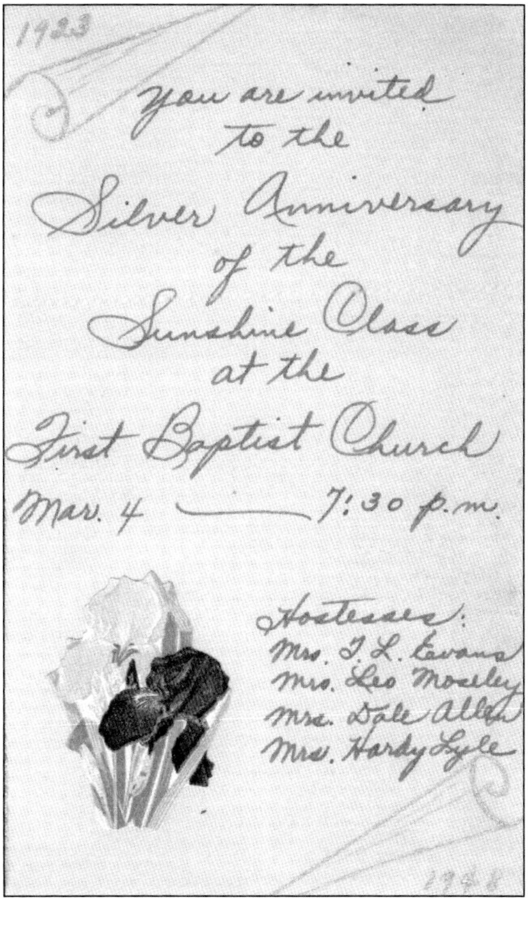

Shown is a First Baptist Church invitation for the silver anniversary of the Sunshine class from 1923. The hostesses were the wives of T.R. Evans, Leo Moseley, Dale Allen, and Hardy Lyle. (Courtesy of Cass County Genealogical Society.)

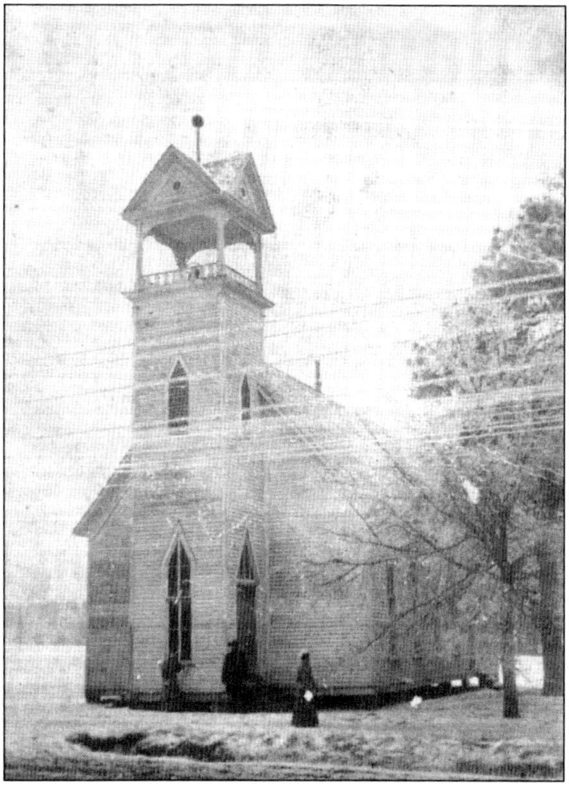

The Cumberland Presbyterian Church was the first church built in the young settlement of Atlanta. According to the centennial edition of the *Citizens Journal* from 1972, the building was erected in 1885 at the present church site and was destroyed by a windstorm in 1946. (Courtesy of Pearl Brown.)

The African American First Baptist Church congregation poses for a photograph on the front steps of the church during a homecoming celebration in 1953. (Courtesy of Pearl Brown.)

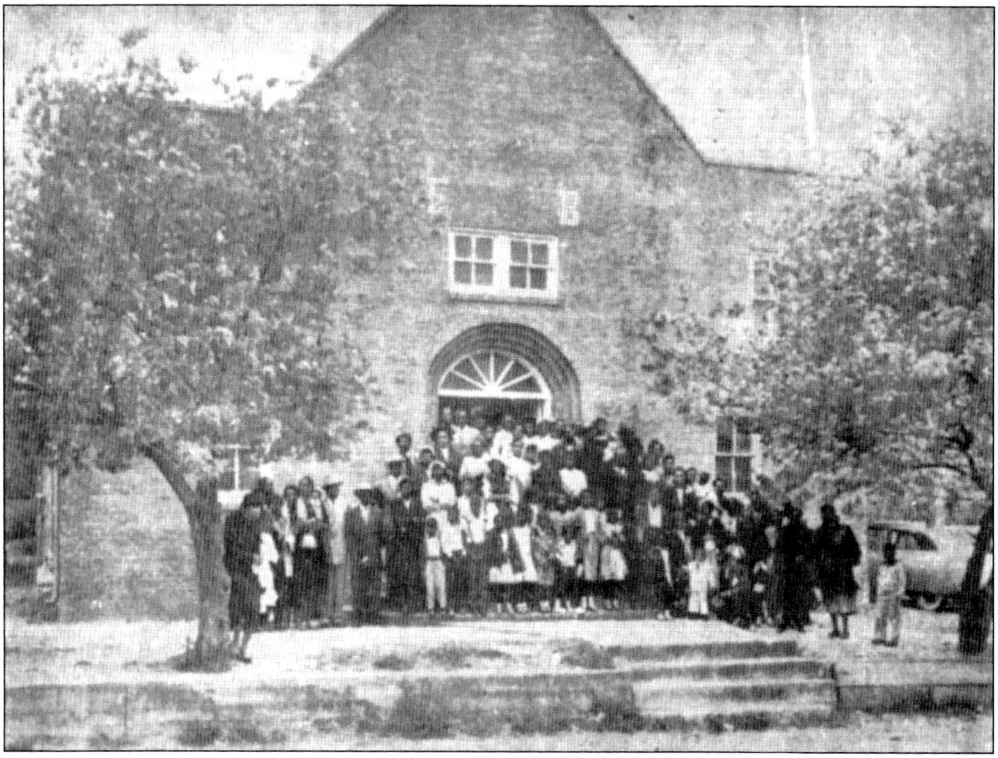

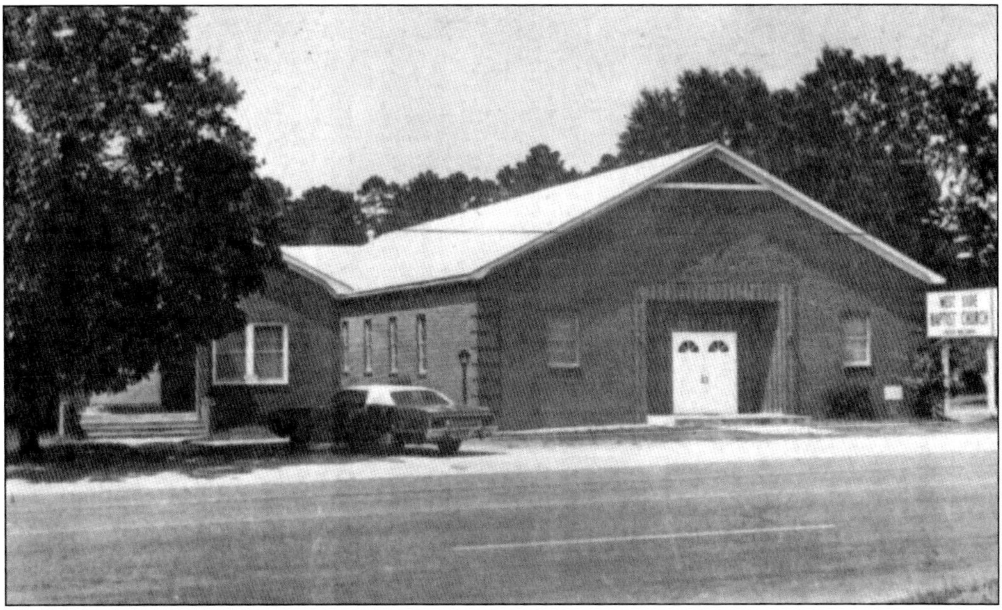

Pictured is West Side Baptist Church on West Main Street. Services began in 1948 and continue in the same building today. (Courtesy of Pearl Brown.)

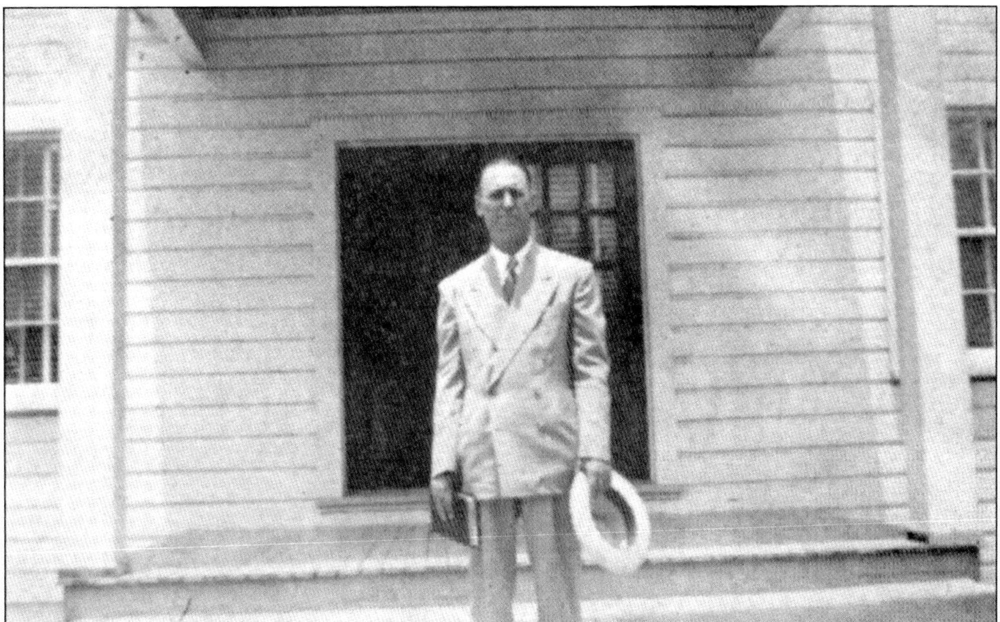

Rev. Ennis Anderson was one of the former pastors of the West Side Baptist Church in Atlanta. (Courtesy of Pearl Brown.)

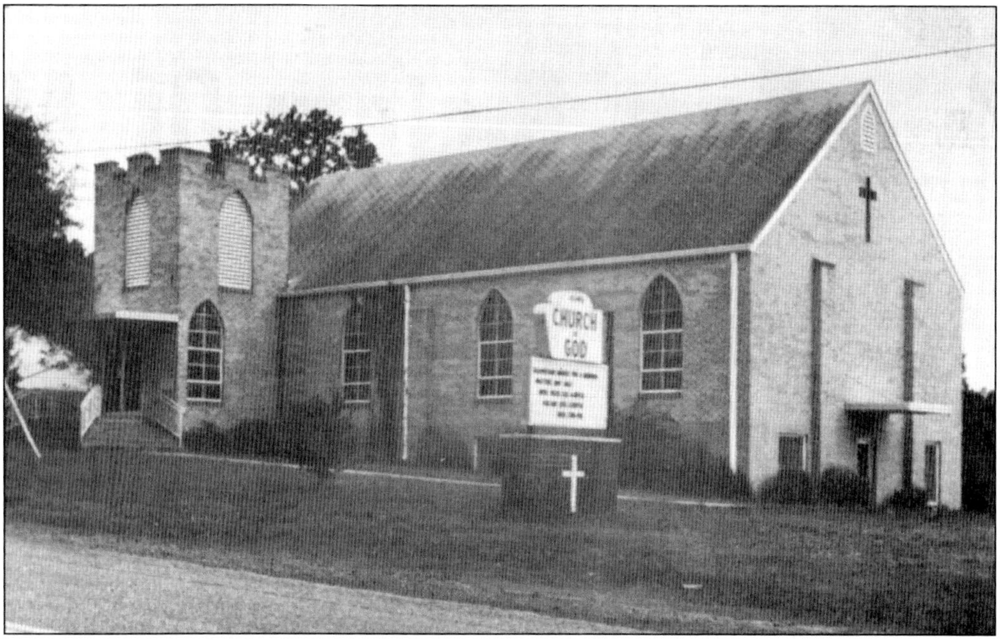

The Atlanta Church of God began services in 1951 in the home of Oliver E. Brown. Land near his house on East Main Street was donated for the church, which was built in 1957. This is a photograph of the church taken around 1970. The church now has a new building located just south of town on South Boggie Street. (Courtesy of Pearl Brown.)

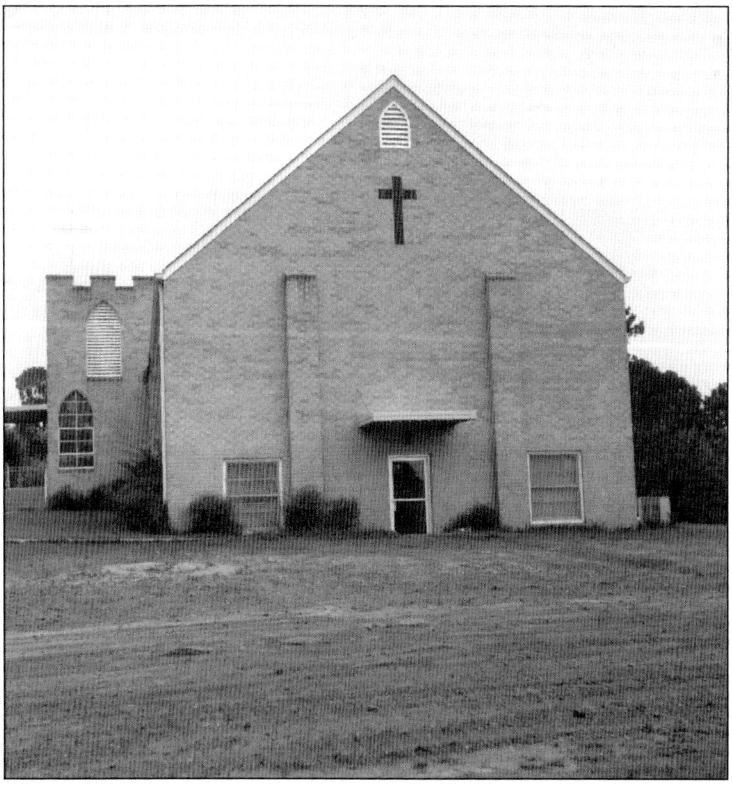

Another view of the Atlanta Church of God shows the parking lot was once unpaved. This photograph was taken in the 1960s. (Courtesy of Pearl Brown.)

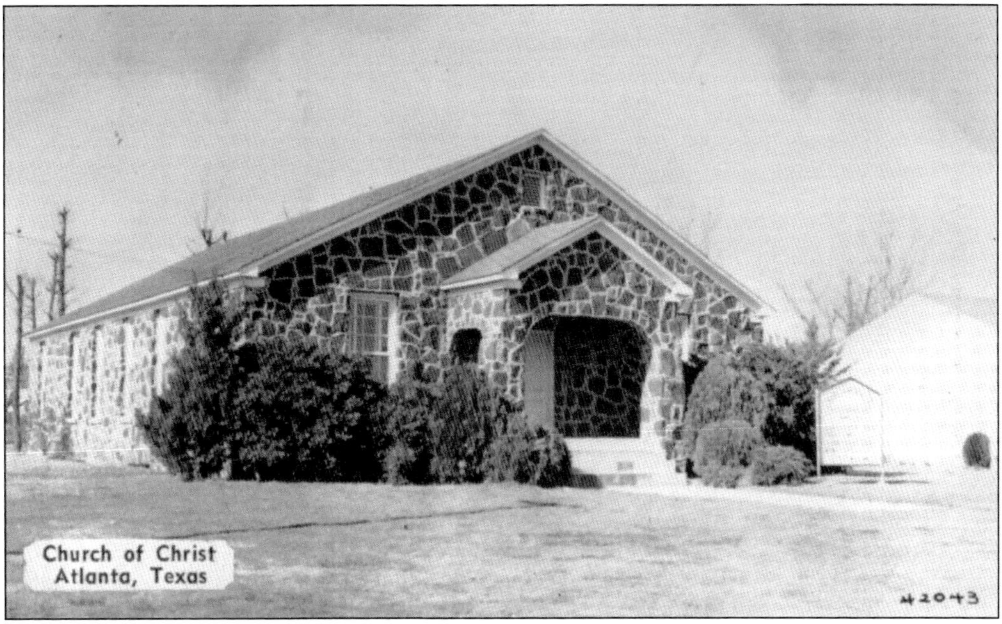

This is a postcard view of the Church of Christ in Atlanta that was taken around 1940. (Courtesy of Heather Ridpath Pilcher.)

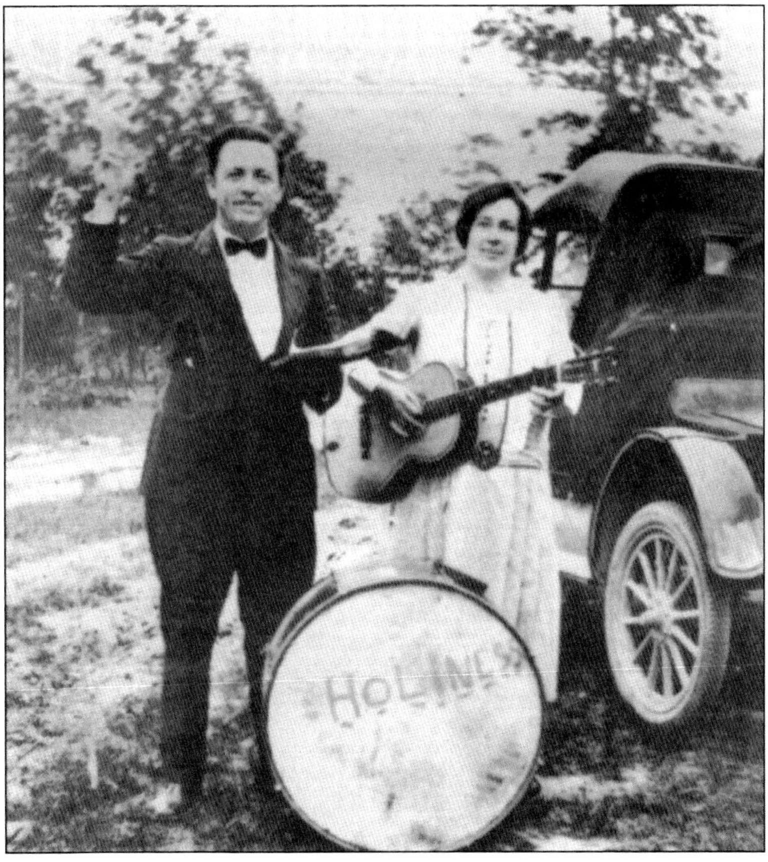

Rev. W.T. Hemphill and his wife held the first revival meeting for what is now the United Pentecostal Church of Atlanta. The photograph dates to July 1927. (Courtesy of Pearl Brown.)

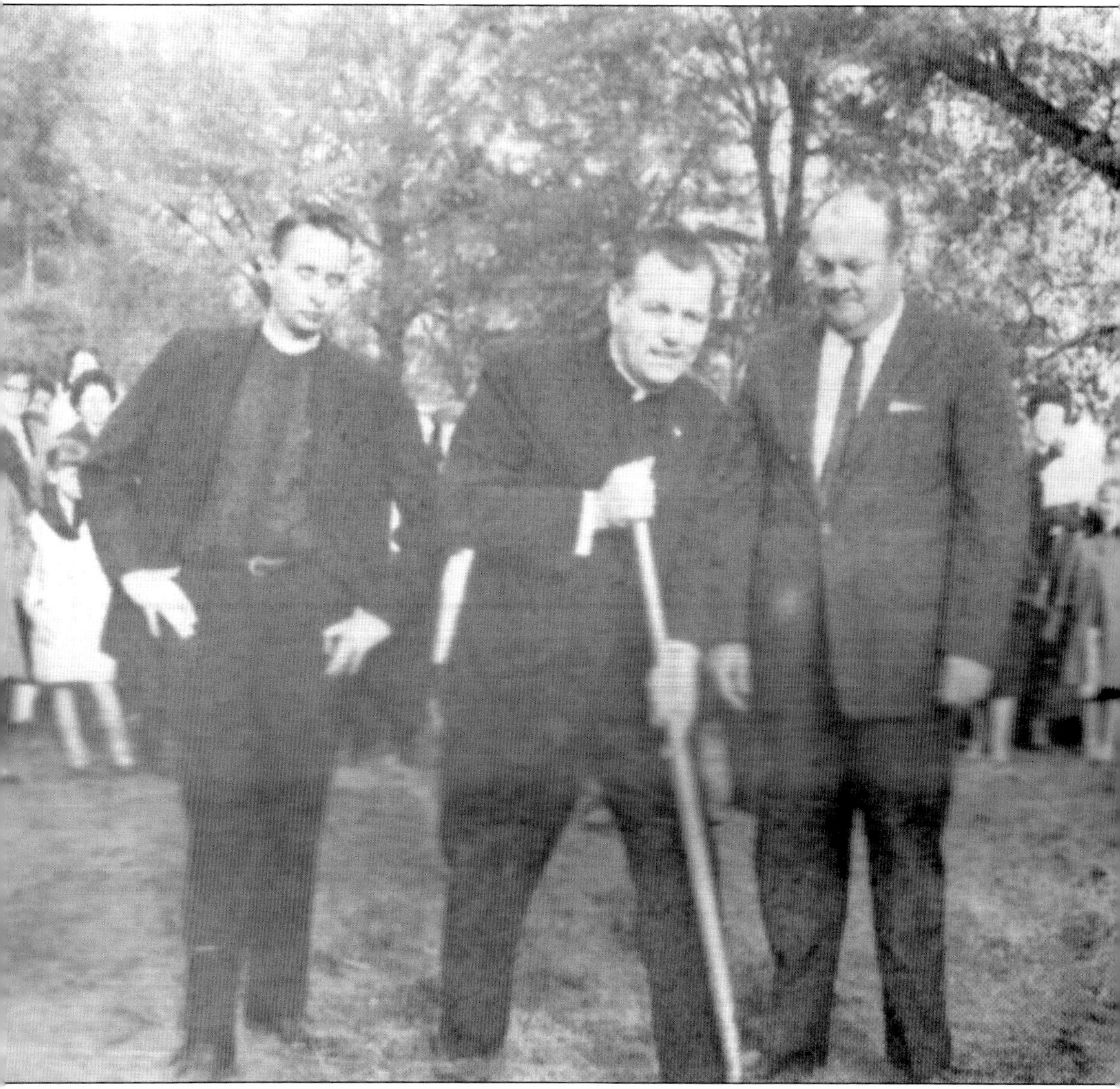

Breaking ground for the construction of St. Catherine's Catholic Church are Fr. James Doell (left) and Fr. John Garry (center), Glenmary priests who were instrumental in beginning the Catholic church in Atlanta. Burr Logwood (right) was member of the Atlanta City Council. The building was completed in 1965. (Courtesy of Pearl Brown.)

Four

The Atlanta Rabbits

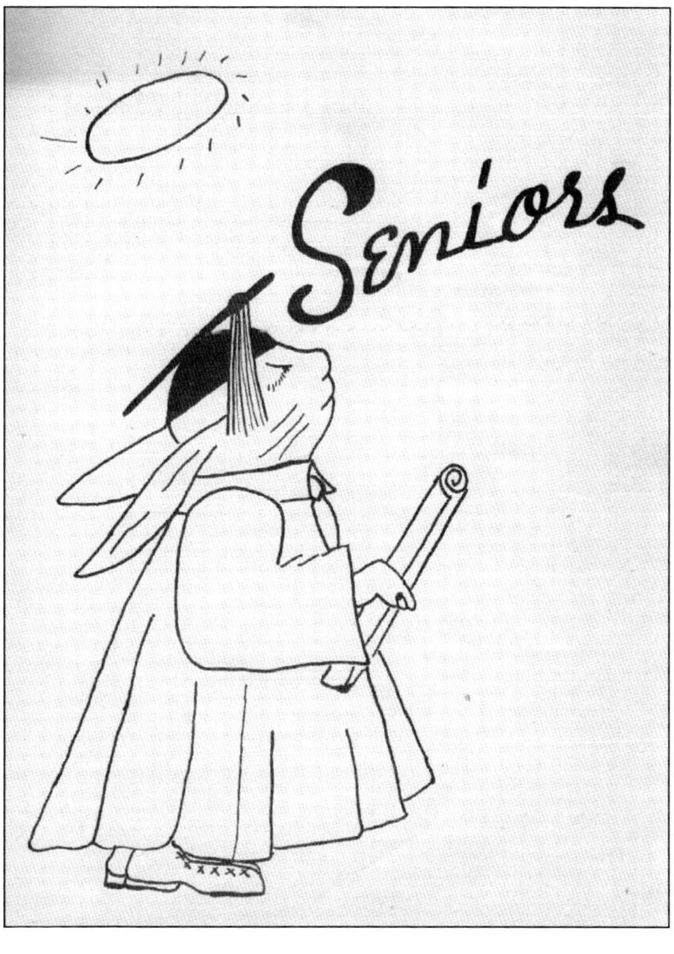

This drawing from a 1946 Atlanta High School yearbook depicts a very studious-looking rabbit wearing a cap and gown while holding its diploma. (Courtesy of Cass County Genealogical Society.)

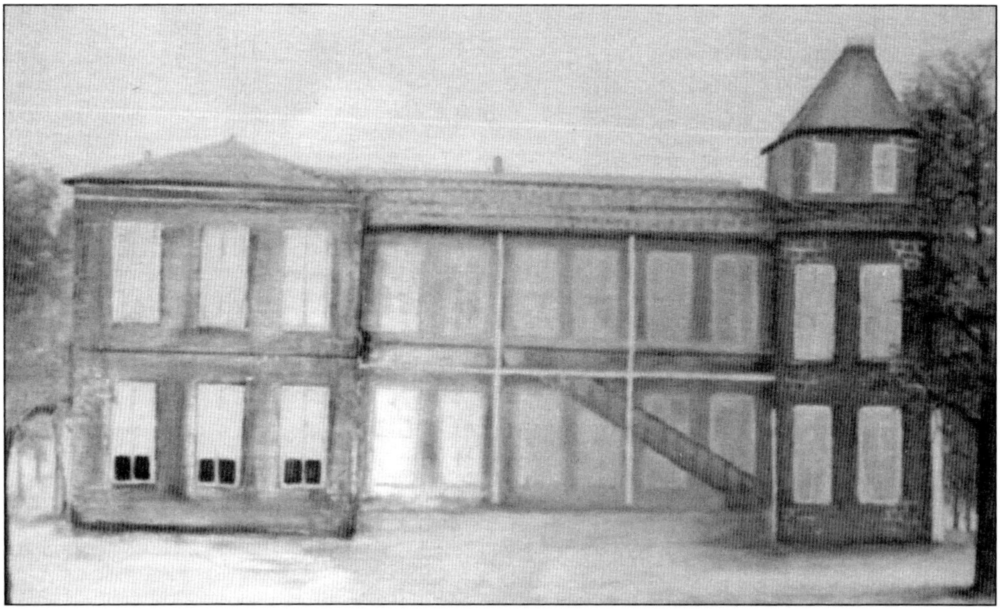

The first Atlanta public school was presumably located near the old Miller Grade School and the site of the high school building that would be constructed in 1922. This first public school building was used from 1905 to 1923. (Courtesy of Cass County Genealogical Society.)

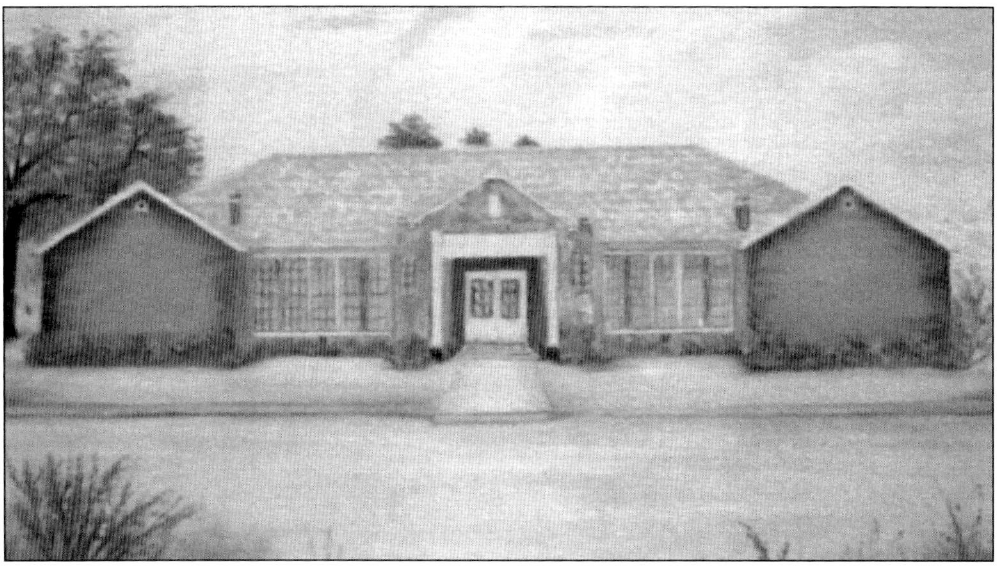

The building that once housed Miller Grade School still stands on West Miller Street. It operated as the elementary school from 1936 until 1974, when it was replaced with a larger, more modern structure at a different site. (Courtesy of Cass County Genealogical Society.)

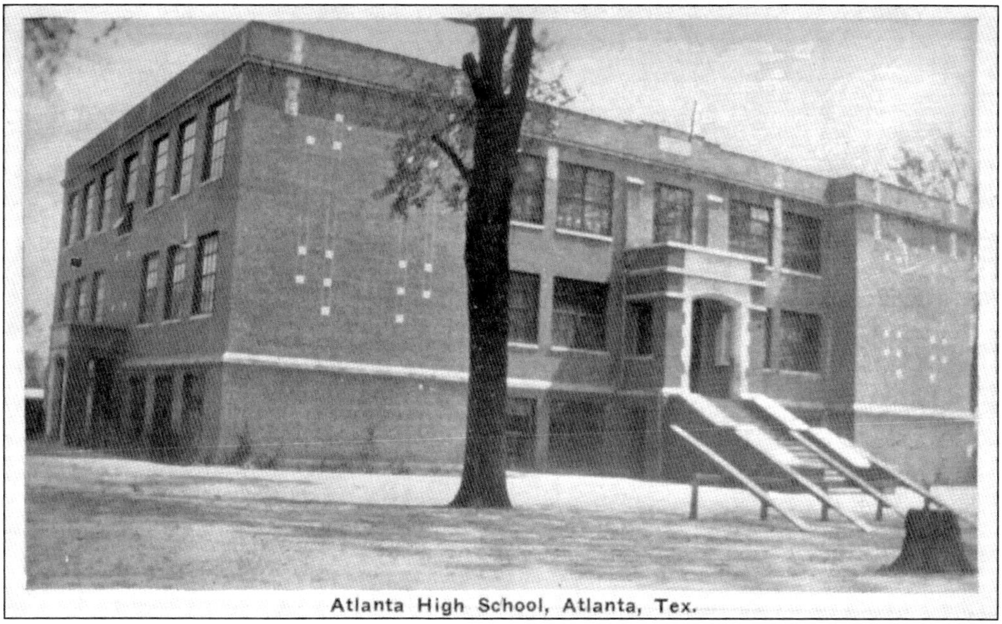

This postcard of Atlanta High School is from around 1940. The building was constructed in 1922 and first occupied by students in January 1923. It was located on the southeast corner of Louise and Allday Streets. (Courtesy of Heather Ridpath Pilcher.)

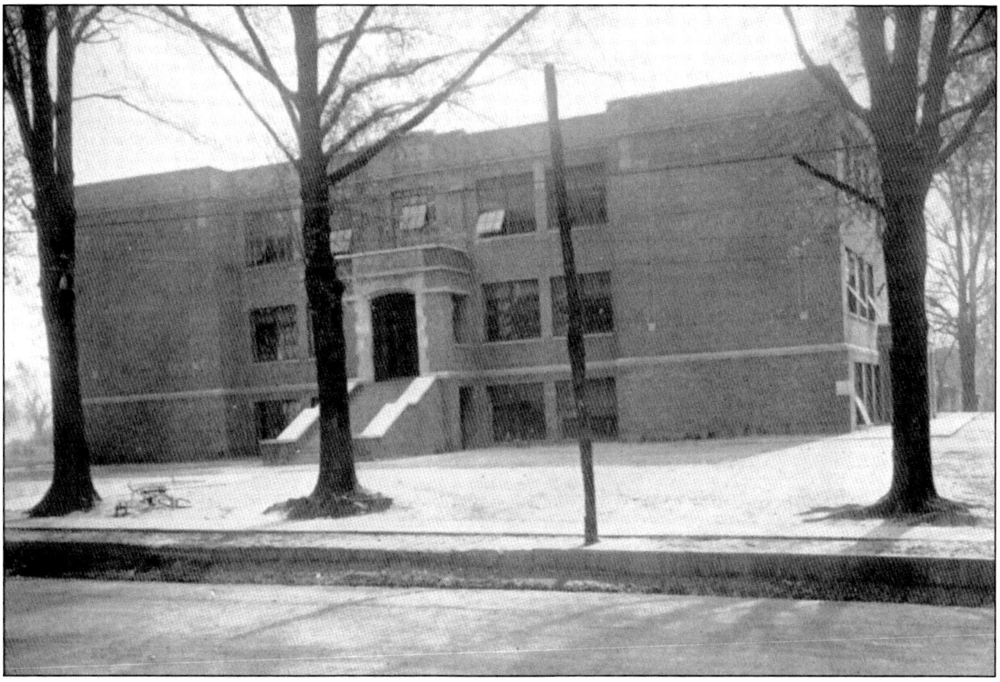

This is another view of Atlanta High School from the 1924 *Archive*, the school's very first yearbook. The building had 10 classrooms, an auditorium, a library, and more. The description in the *Archive* also boasted about its many modern amenities like electricity, gas, water, and sewage infrastructure. The auditorium seated 754 people and featured a roomy stage and a grand piano. (Courtesy of Cass County Genealogical Society.)

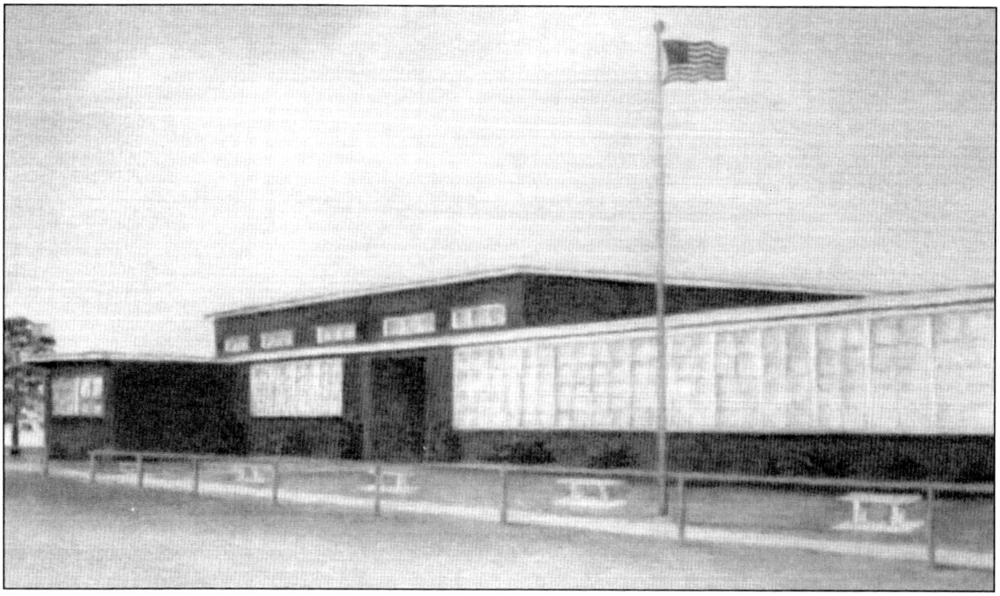

The Booker T. Washington School was the African American school. This drawing shows how the school looked in the 1950s. (Courtesy of Cass County Genealogical Society.)

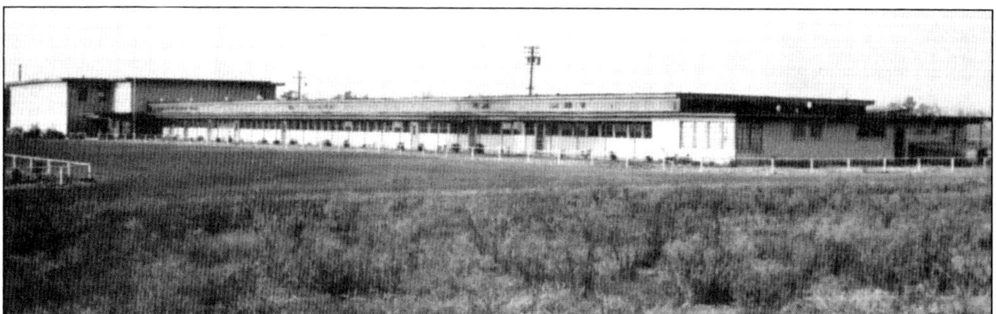

This is a view of the 1951 Atlanta High School building located on High School Lane. The building was constructed in 1950 and remained in use as the high school until 1971 when the current high school was built. This building, currently the Atlanta Middle School, is scheduled for demolition to make way for a new middle school building. (Courtesy of Pearl Brown.)

This group of Atlanta school friends had its picture taken in 1899. Pictured from left to right are (first row) Dell Taylor, Eula Herring, and Lidia Sheppard; (second row) Bulla McLeod, Cora Sheppard, Nannie Herring, and Alice Dauphin. (Courtesy of Pearl Brown.)

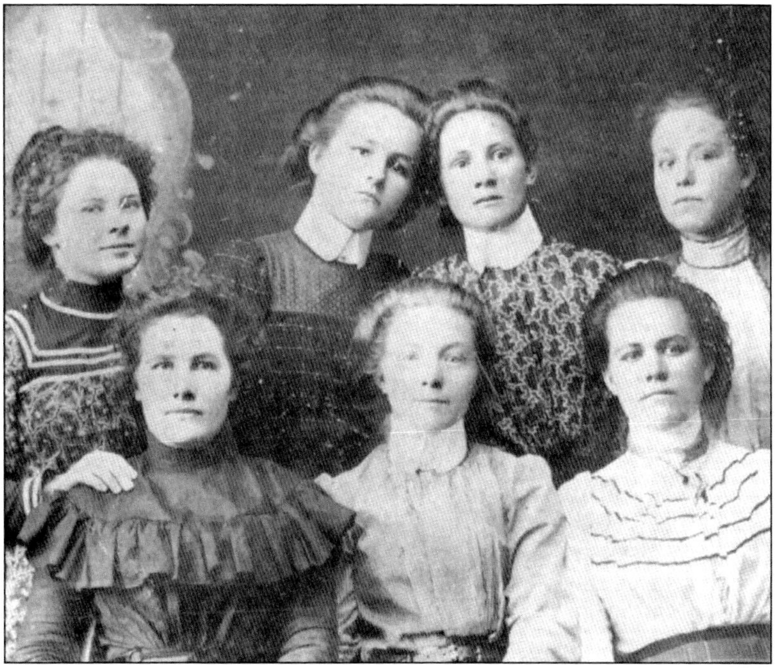

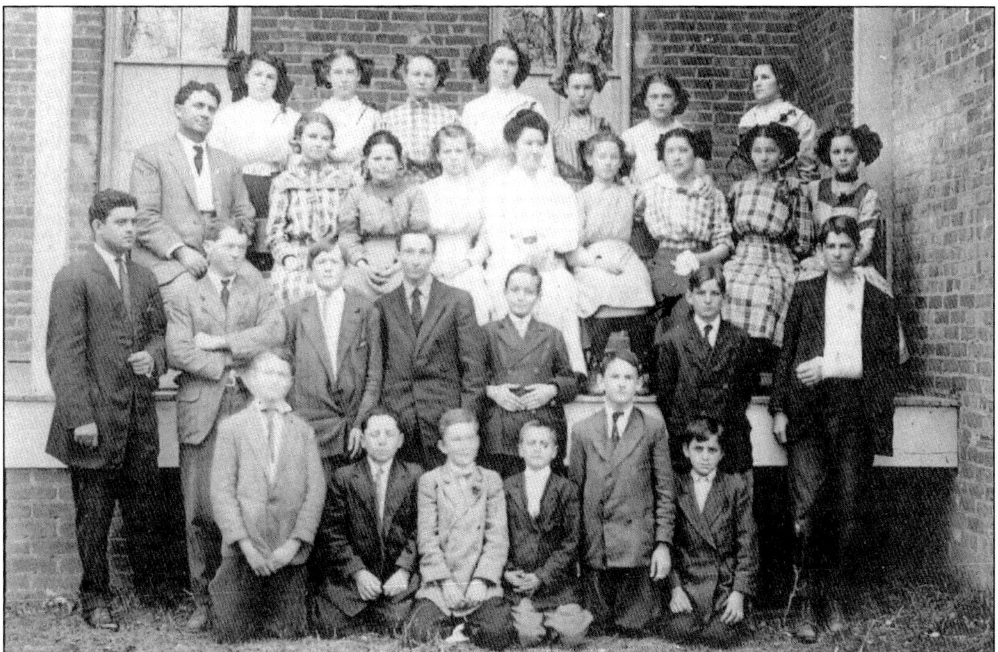

This is an early Atlanta school picture taken in 1910. C.F. Perdue, second from the right in the second row, is the only identified person in the photograph. (Courtesy of Cass County Genealogical Society.)

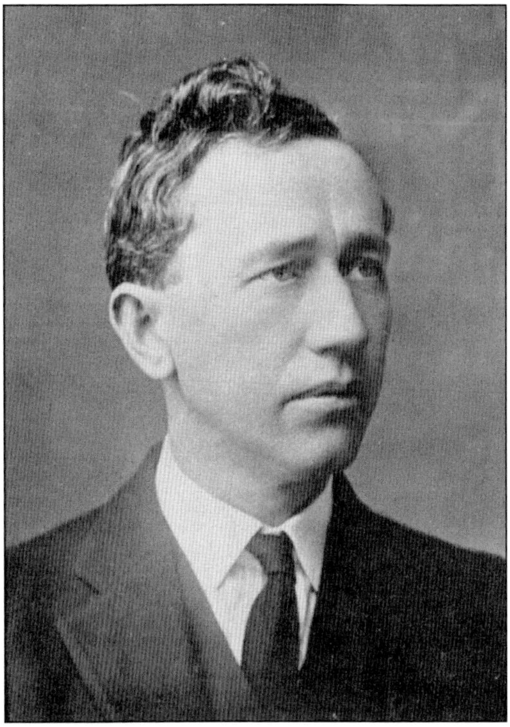

W.H. Galloway was the Atlanta School superintendent in 1924. He was honored in the 1924 *Archive* yearbook for his overall work and specifically for the completion of the new school building. (Courtesy of Cass County Genealogical Society.)

The Atlanta school board of 1924 included, in no particular order, J.W. Hanner, president; Otis Ford Oden, secretary; Hicks Harvey, treasurer; J.E. McCoy, Dr. O.L. Smith, Emmett Florence, and R.J. Daniel. (Courtesy of Cass County Genealogical Society.)

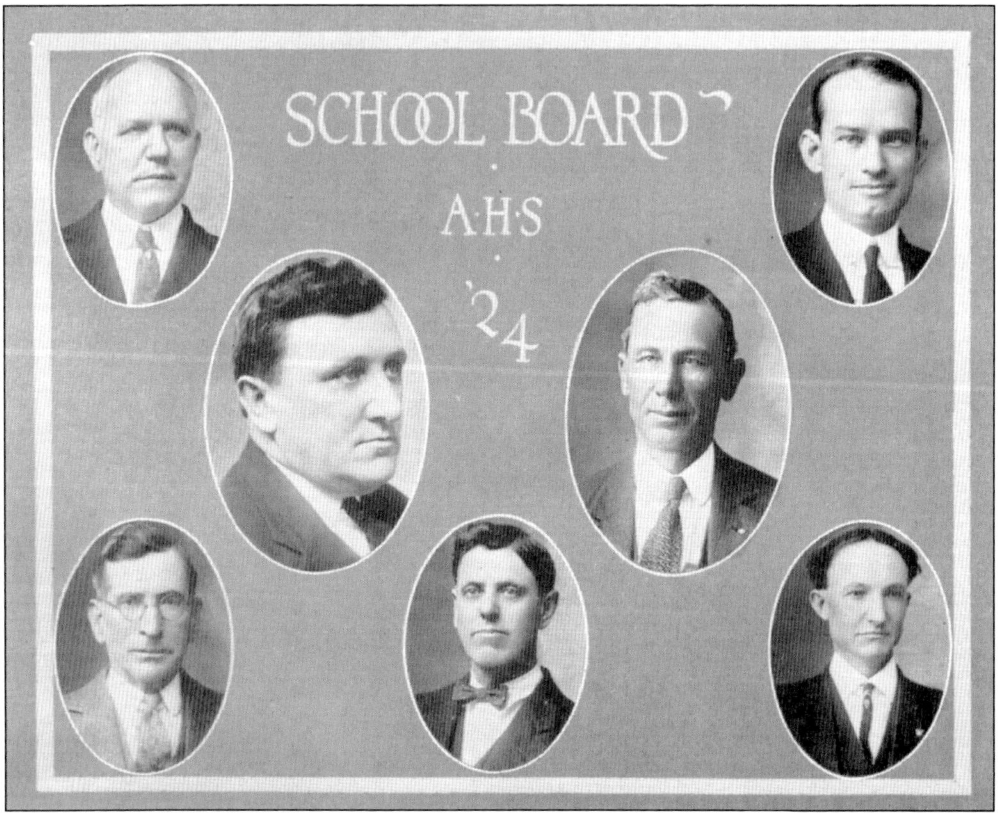

THE-ARCHIVE-1924

LAURA BARNES—"Doodle"
"Her hair is her crowning glory".

RUBY CANON—"Baby"
"Tho she's timid, she holds her own."

KATHLEEN CARNEY—"Sug"
"Her eternal triangle: Papa, Mama, Bill."

ELLA COPE
"She absorbs knowledge like a sponge."

ZETA GAGE
"I just adore dogs."

MERTIE GRAVES
"What do I care for looks when love is so interesting."

D. P. HARRELL "Sleepy"
"If silence were golden, he would be a millionaire."

BESS HATCHER
"Addicted to giggles and chewing gum."

JESSIE LEE HUGHES "Peck"
"Ain't love grand?"

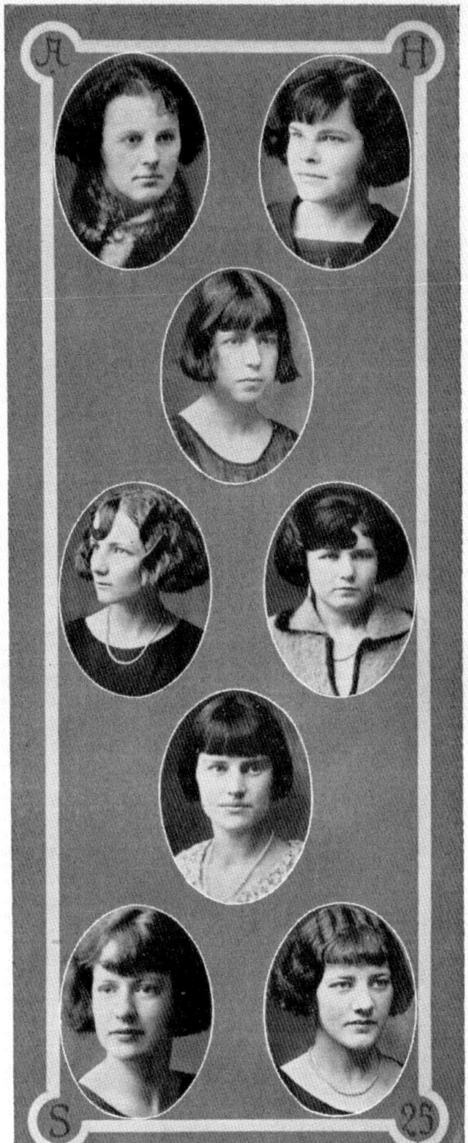

28

A sampling of the junior class from the 1924 *Archive* shows the popular hairstyle for Atlanta girls during that era. (Courtesy of Cass County Genealogical Society.)

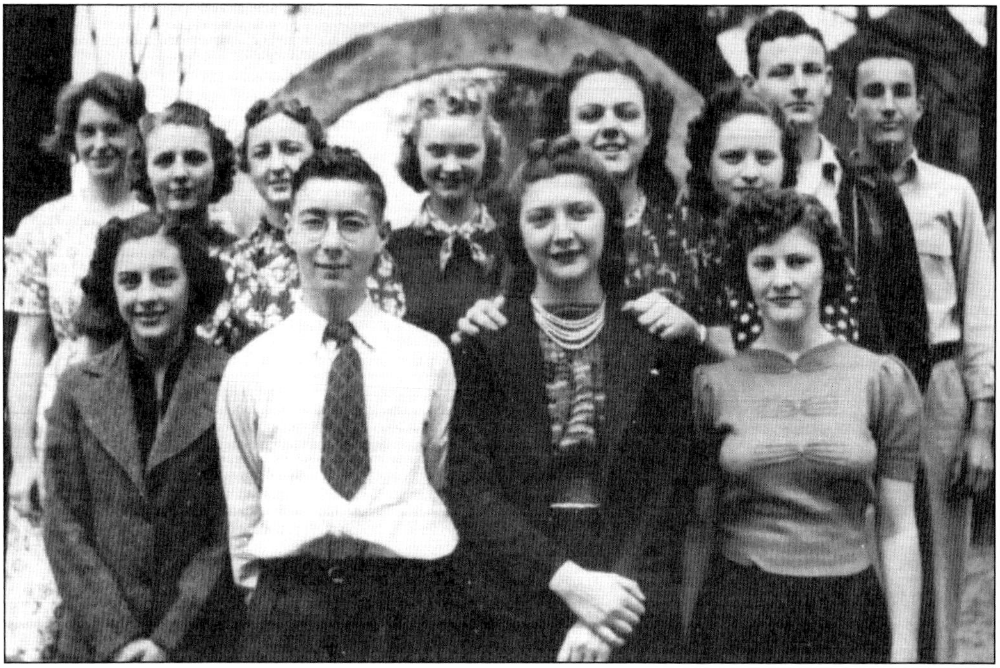

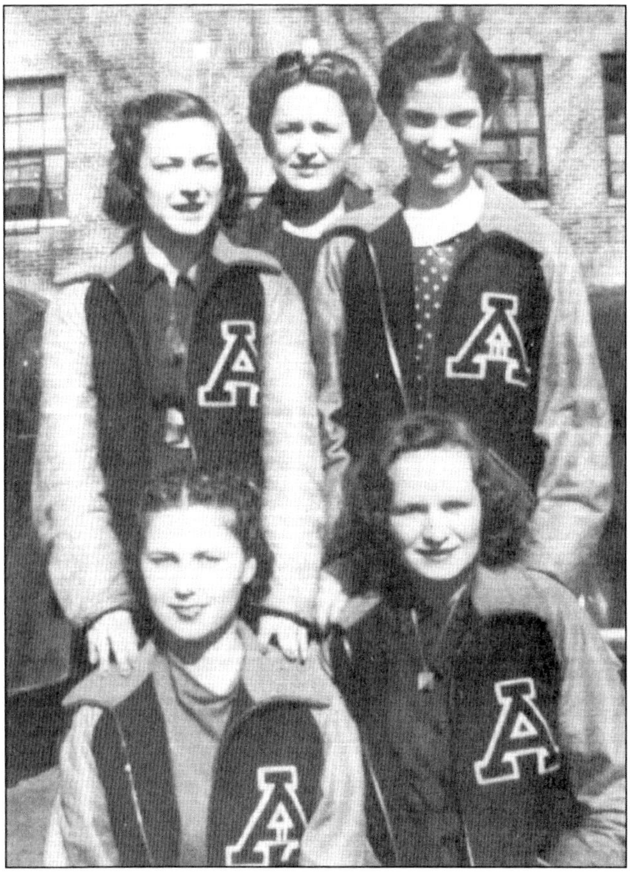

The *Maroon* staff in 1939 were, from left to right, (first row) Betty Jo Rabb, Phil Deam, Anna Mae Jerome, and Carolyn Howe; (second row) Joyce Jett, Nauvaree Grogan, Virginia White (sponsor), Mildred Sneed, Anita Levin, Charline Penn, Kenneth Whisenant, and Joe N. Swanger. (Courtesy of Cass County Genealogical Society.)

A group of Atlanta High School girls poses for a picture wearing letter jackets in 1939. (Courtesy of Cass County Genealogical Society.)

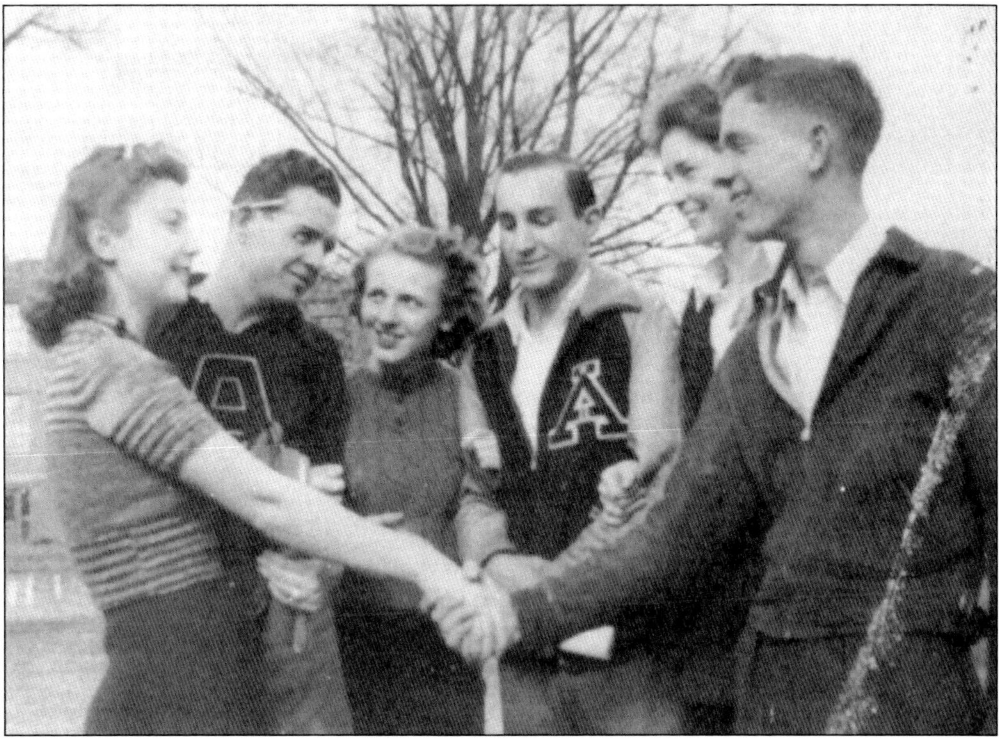

Atlanta High School seniors are posing for this photograph from 1939. (Courtesy of Cass County Genealogical Society.)

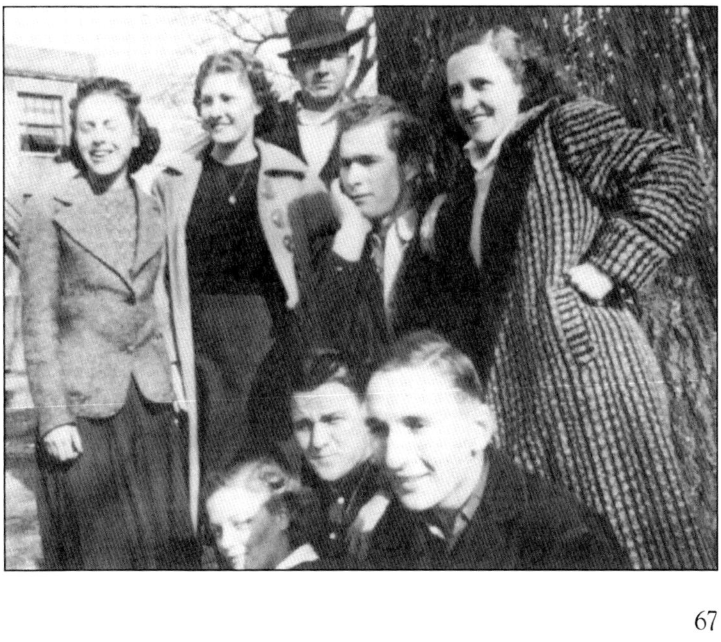

A group of Atlanta High School juniors is standing in front of one the large trees near the school in 1939. Notice the school building in the background. (Courtesy of Cass County Genealogical Society.)

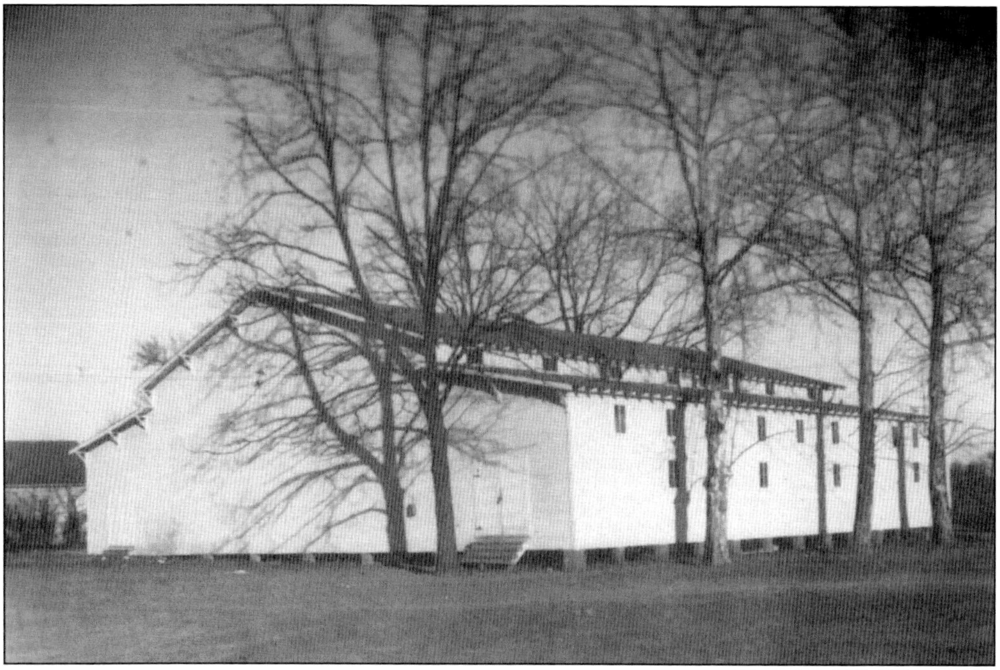

This photograph shows the Atlanta High School athletics building as it looked in 1938. (Courtesy of Cass County Genealogical Society.)

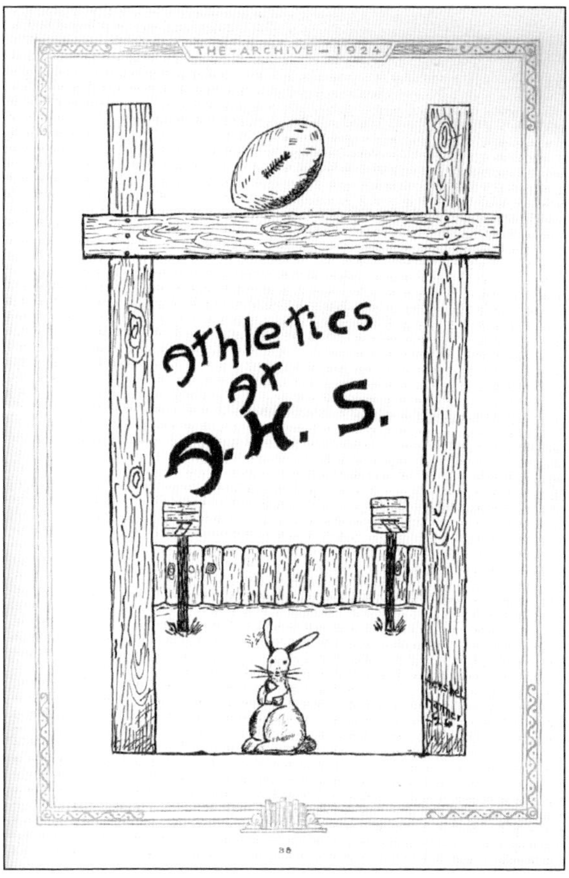

A drawing from the 1924 *Archive* shows the new rabbit mascot. Mr. Rabbit's image has been updated a few times since then. (Courtesy of Cass County Genealogical Society.)

The Atlanta Rabbits were named after coach William E. Rabb, pictured here in 1924. Coach Rabb, Atlanta High's first football coach, introduced football in 1920. Before coaching, he worked as a lawyer. (Courtesy of Cass County Genealogical Society.)

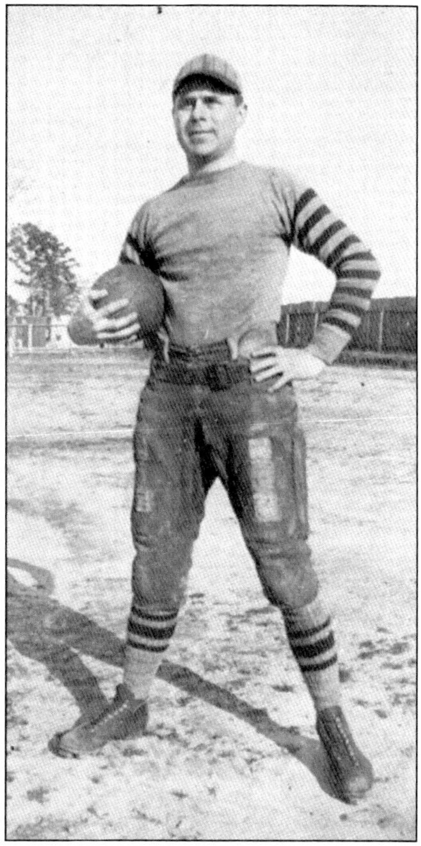

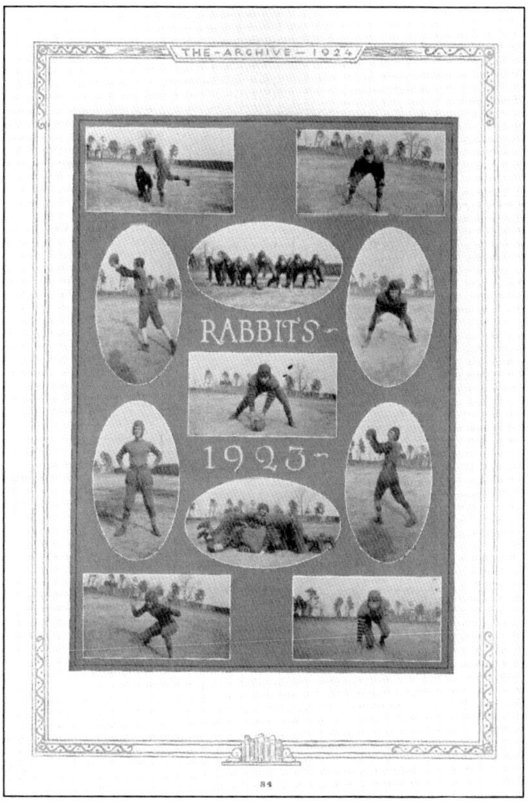

These are action shots of the 1923–1924 Atlanta Rabbits football team from the 1924 *Archive*. (Courtesy of Cass County Genealogical Society.)

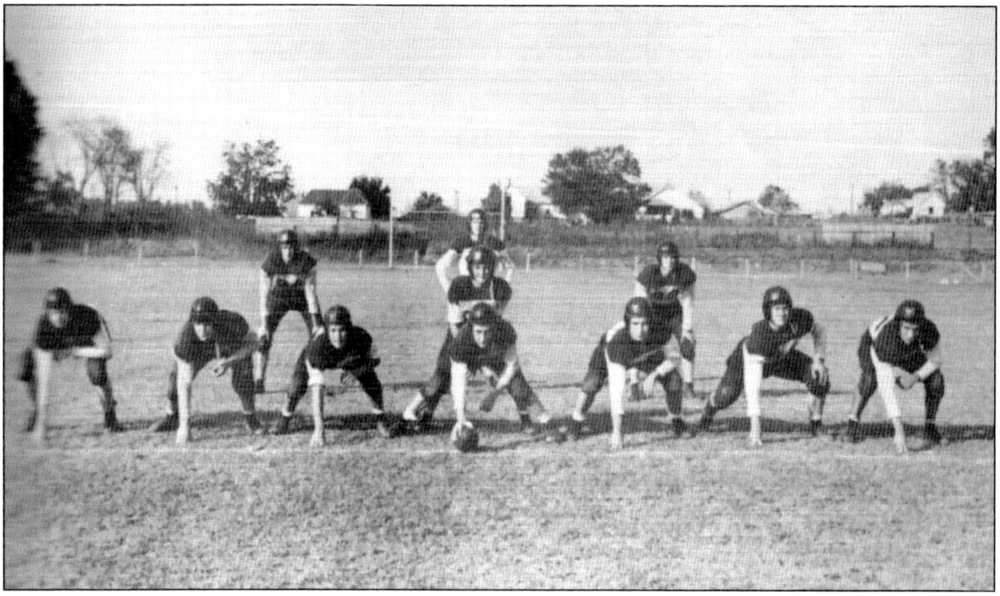

Atlanta football players are practicing on the field in 1946. Pictured are, from left to right, (first row) Billy Nichols, Dan Dean, Arlis Scogin, Don Walker, Eddie Bluestein, James McDaniel, and Donald Blanton; (second row) Vernon McKinney, Harold Murdock, and Bobby Brown; (third row) James Malone. Notice the houses in the background, presumably located on West Taylor Street. (Courtesy of Cass County Genealogical Society.)

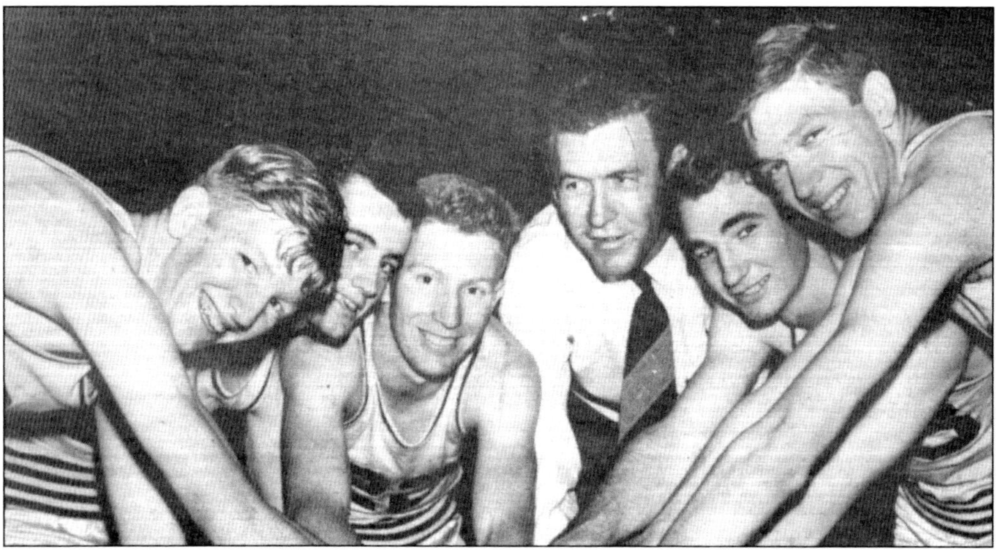

These 1951 starters are ready to go on the court and do battle for good old Atlanta High School. They are, from left to right, Henry Willis, Stanley Cruse Sr., Charles Musgrove, G.L. "Slick" Cannady, James Bass, and Carrell Burleson. Cruse is the only senior; the rest of the players are juniors. (Courtesy of Cass County Genealogical Society.)

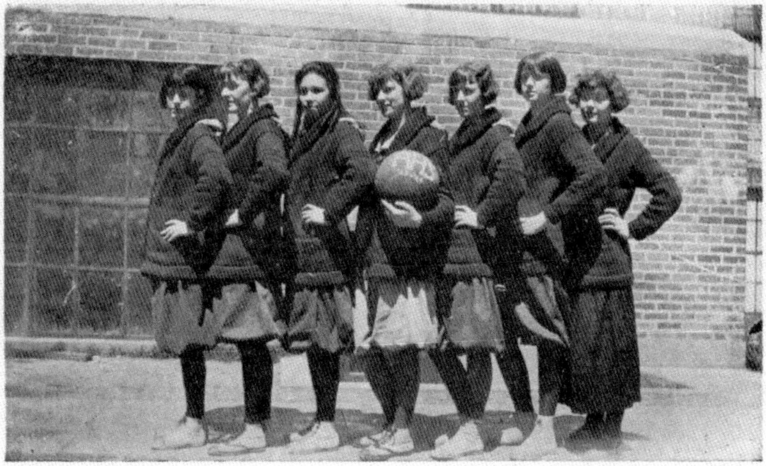

The Season's Schedule with Scores

Atlanta	19	C. O. M.	23
Atlanta	18	Texarkana, Ark.	11
Atlanta	24	C. O. M.	8
Atlanta	18	Texarkana, Tex.	12
Atlanta	18	Marshall Hi.	17
Atlanta	10	Texarkana, Ark.	24
Atlanta	20	Marshall Hi.	23
Atlanta	21	Texarkana, Tex.	23
Totals	148	Totals	141

The 1924 girls' basketball team had a pretty good season, as these score totals indicate. (Courtesy of Cass County Genealogical Society.)

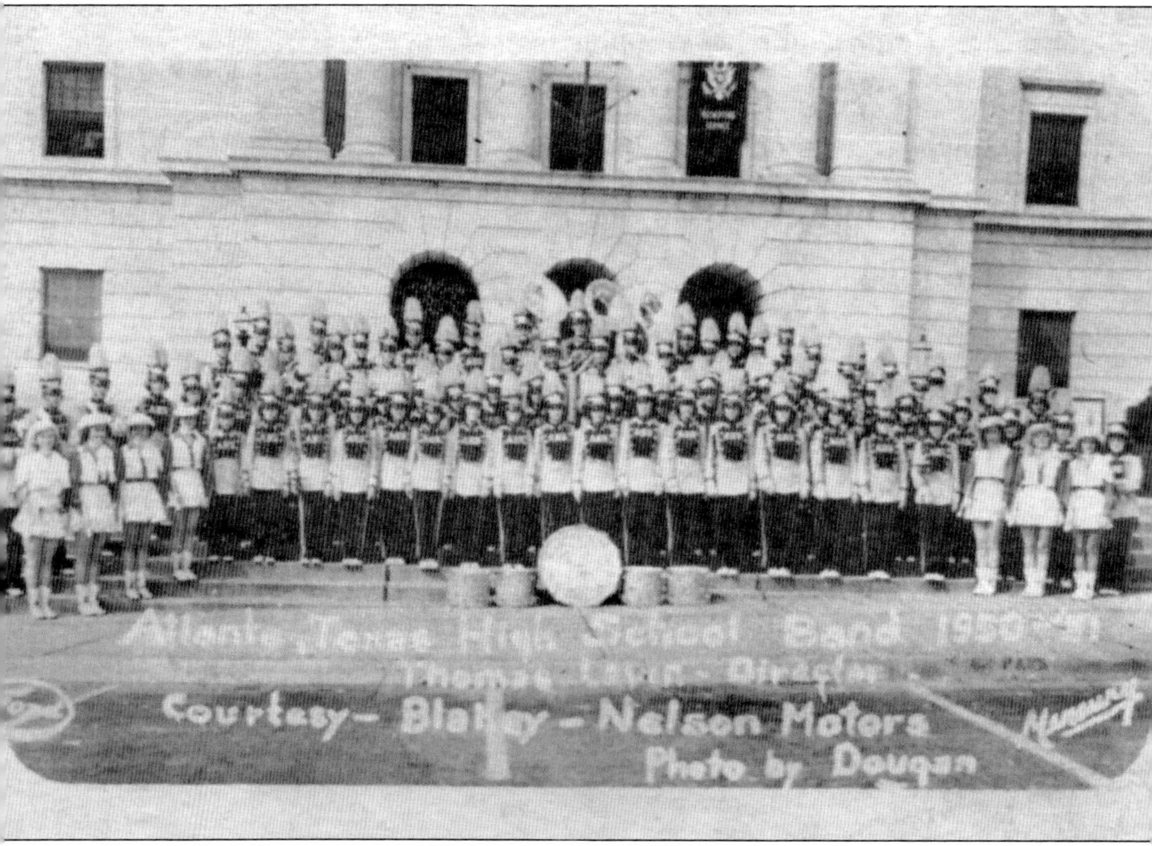

The 1950–1951 Atlanta High School band got to take a trip and made the newspaper. (Courtesy of Cass County Genealogical Society.)

Betty Jo Rabb was crowned the football queen in 1939. (Courtesy of Cass County Genealogical Society.)

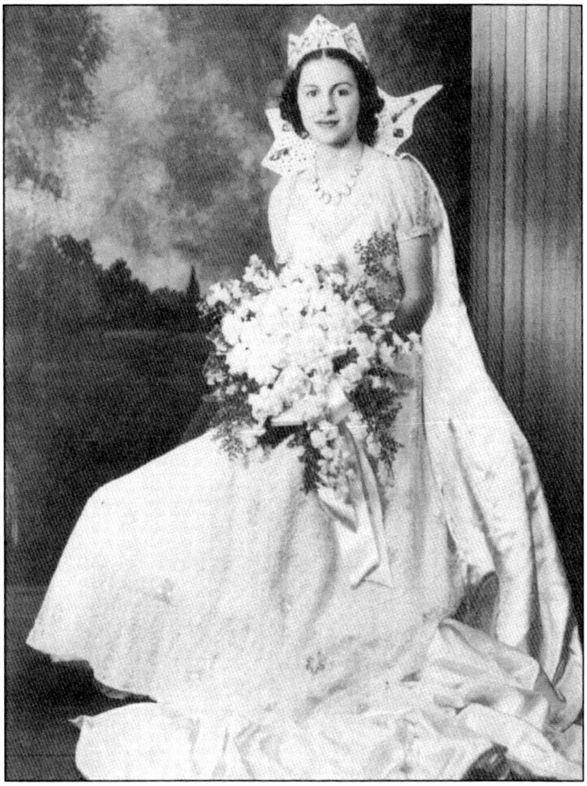

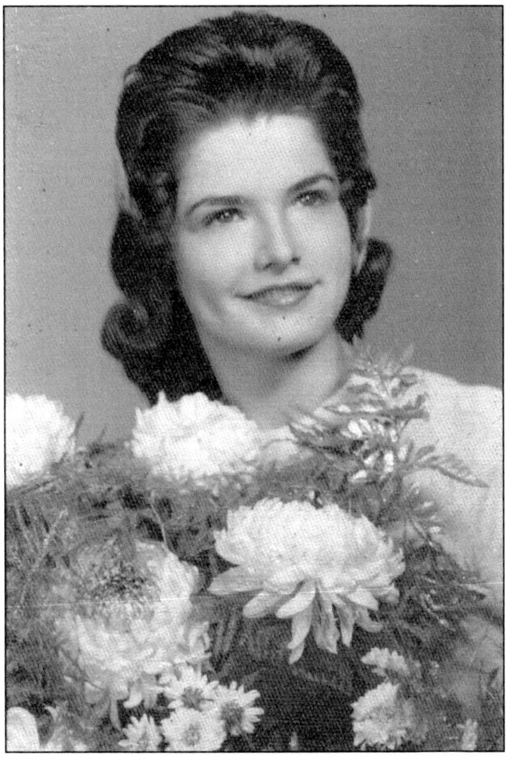

Sondra Dean Smith, daughter of Oliver E. and Pearl Brown, was the football sweetheart in 1963. (Courtesy of Pearl Brown.)

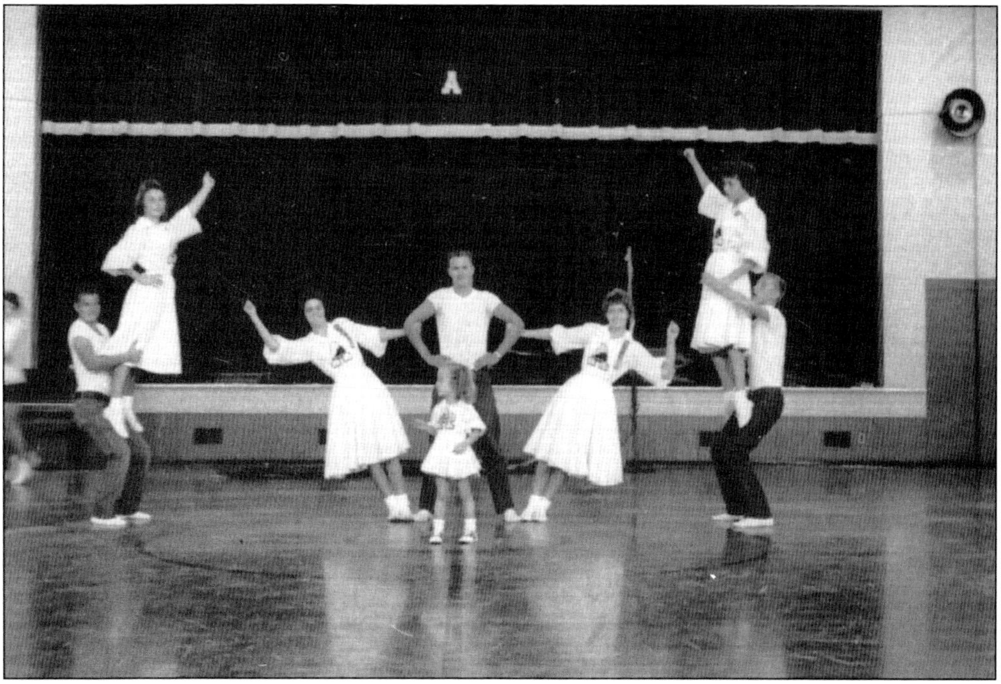
The Atlanta High School cheerleaders practice in the gymnasium about 1961. Rodney Brown, son of Oliver E. and Pearl Brown, is the first boy on the left. (Courtesy of Pearl Brown.)

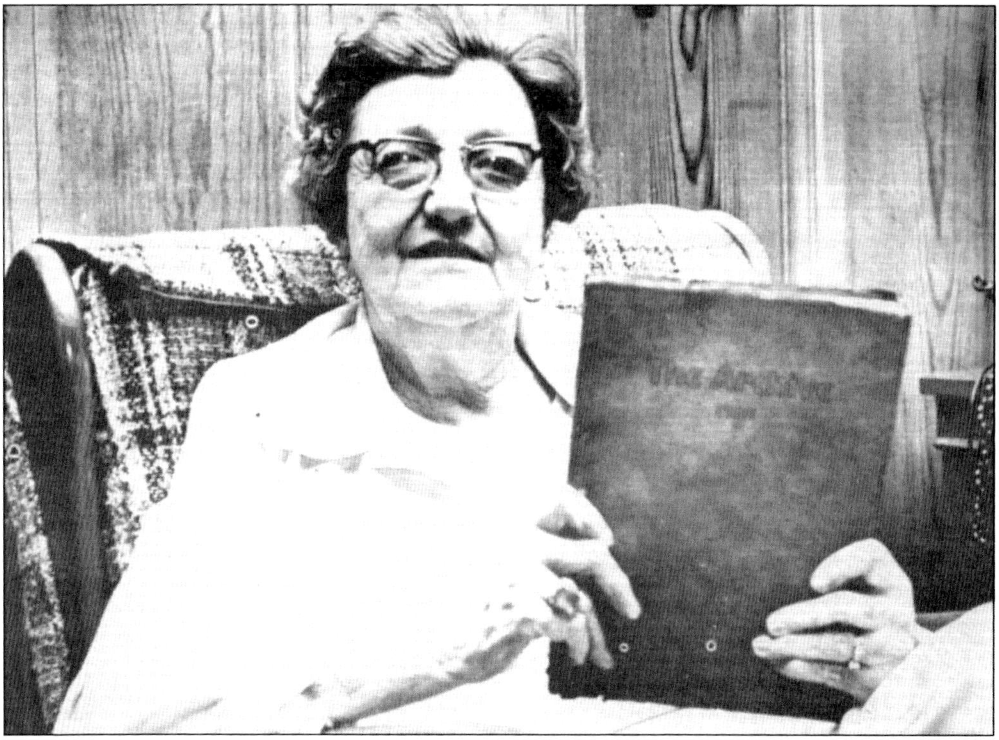
Mildred Mays McClung, the athletic editor for the 1924 *Archive*, is shown here holding up a copy of Atlanta High School's first yearbook. (Courtesy of Cass County Genealogical Society.)

Five

Recreation and Leisure

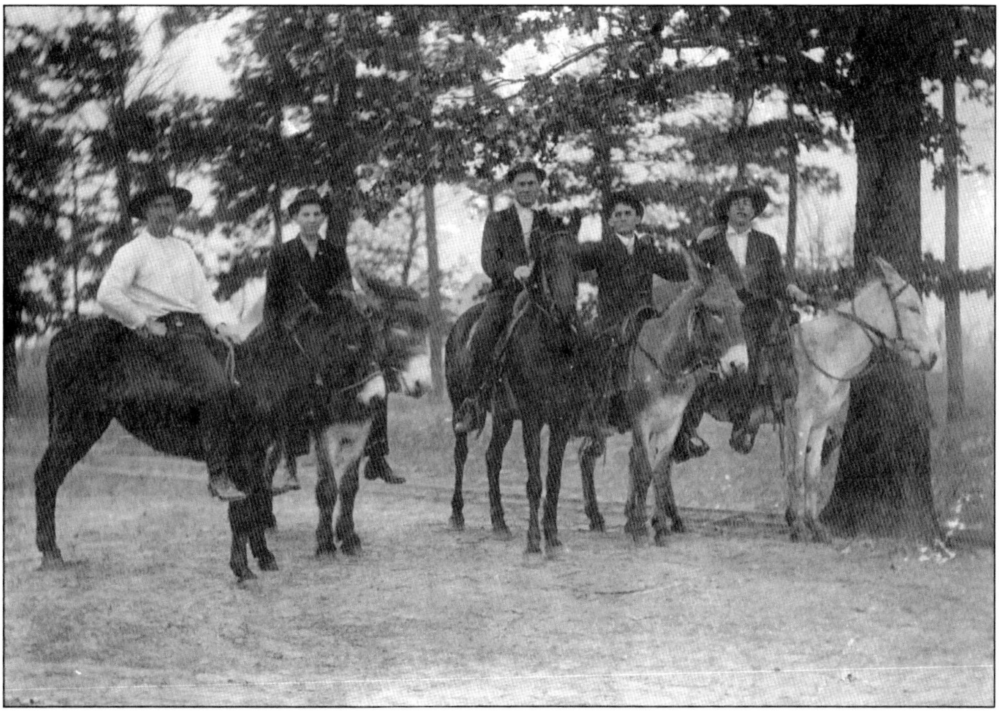

Men are sitting on their horses at the Arrow Ranch in the early 1900s. Pictured third and fourth from the left are Thomas E. White and Henry Sheppard. The ranch was located about a mile from town on Highway 77 going toward Douglasville. David V. Davis was one of the former owners. The land, now private property, is owned by descendents of the Davis family. (Courtesy of Mark and Julia Mays.)

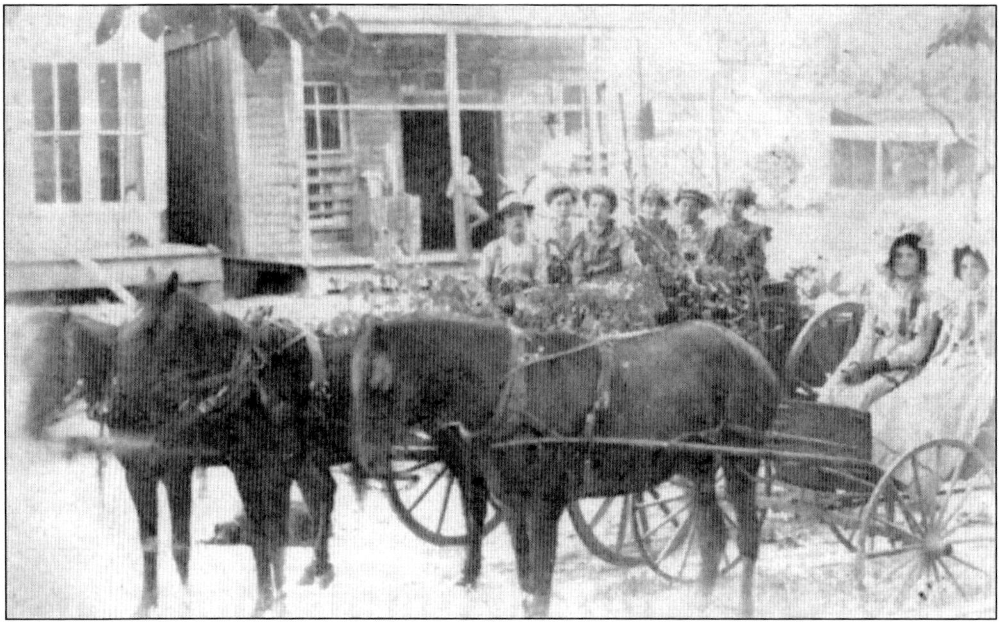

Shown is a group of Atlantans in 1912 about to depart for an afternoon in the country. Pictured in the left buggy are, from left to right, Tom Ford, Clifford Robertson, Mrs. Hub Northern, Mrs. C.H. Oden, Oscar Gibson, and Mrs. M.J. Brooks. In the buggy on the right are chaperones Mrs. Powell (left) and Estelle Ford White. (Courtesy of Pearl Brown.)

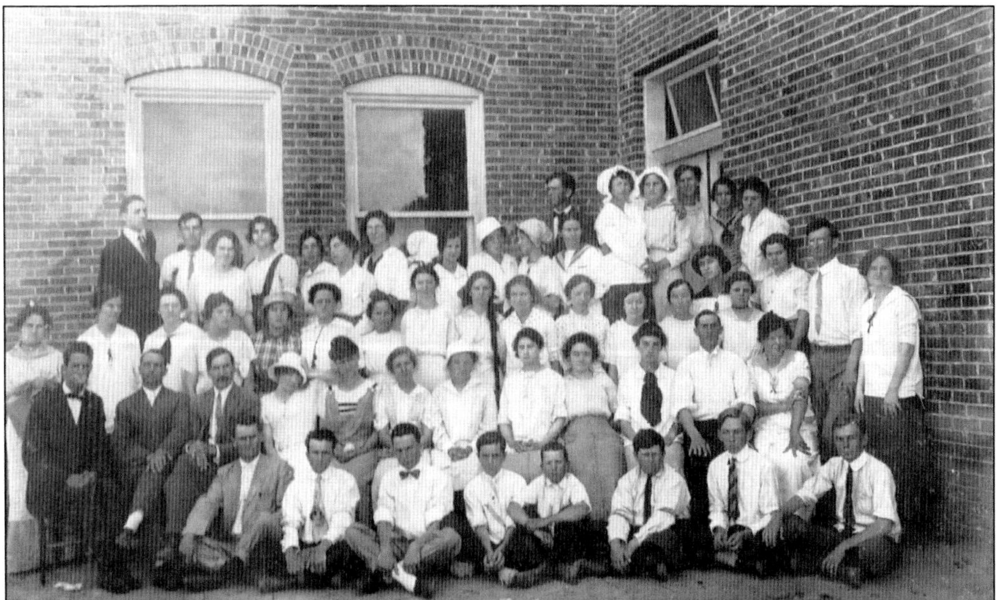

This photograph shows the Bethsaida Y Baptist Church Youth Singing School from around 1914. Several familiar faces can be identified, from left to right, as follows: (first row) first, Alb(?) Bullard; second, Raymond Clark; fourth, Boyd M.; and seventh, John D. Golsby; (second row) fifth, Bea Pitts; (fourth row) first, Reed Fannin and seventh, Ollie Henderson. (Courtesy of Mark and Julia Mays.)

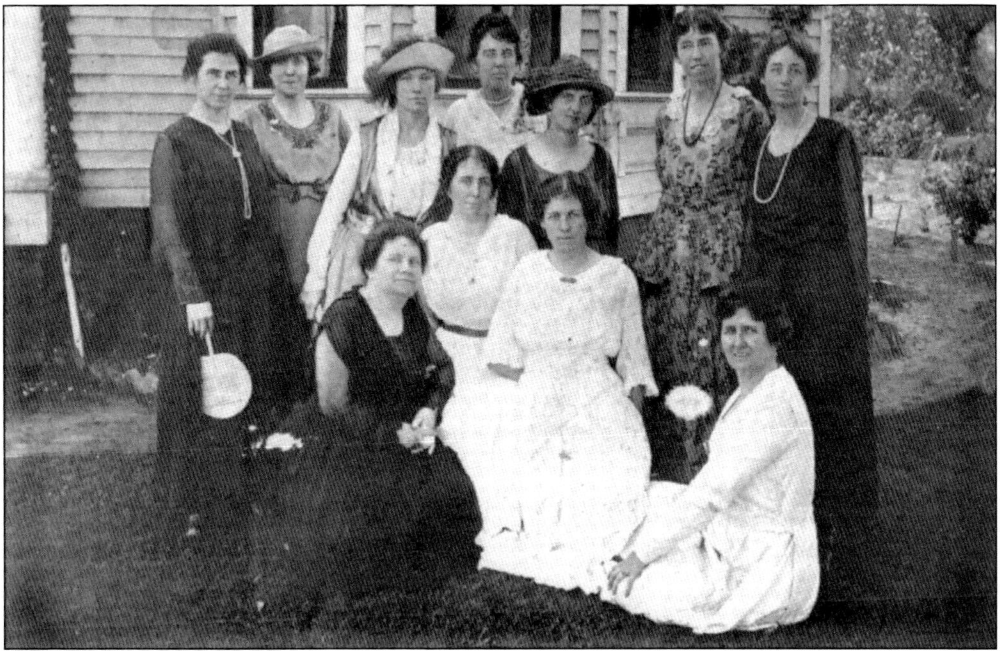

These women, attending a progressive house party in 1914, are at the home of Eva L. Miles. The Miles home once stood where Brook's Hospital used to be located. At a progressive party, the ladies socialized at one person's house for a while and then traveled to another person's house, and so on. Appearing in the photograph are, from left to right, (first row) Eula Nipper, Pauline Hortig, Bess Hoyt, and Mrs. O'Neal; (second row) Mrs. Hopkins, Daisy McClung, Prudie Willis, Mary Coke, Rosa Foreman, Lilly Miles, and Mattie Johnson. (Courtesy of Pearl Brown.)

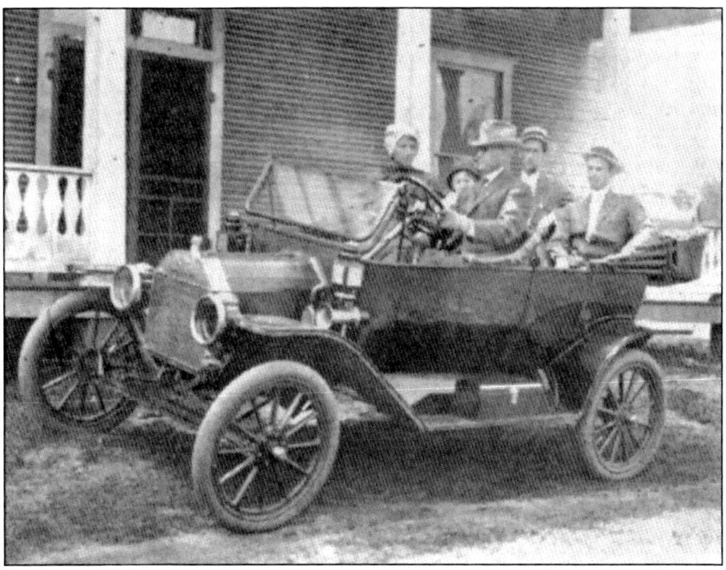

This photograph of an old Model T Ford touring car was made in 1915. The car is driven by Claude Traylor, uncle of Mrs. H.N. Hanner. Beside Taylor are his wife, Maude, and his son Eugene; they were residents of Hughes Springs. Seated in the back seat are Roy Kasling from Hughes Springs (left), and Hicks Harvey of Atlanta. (Courtesy of Pearl Brown.)

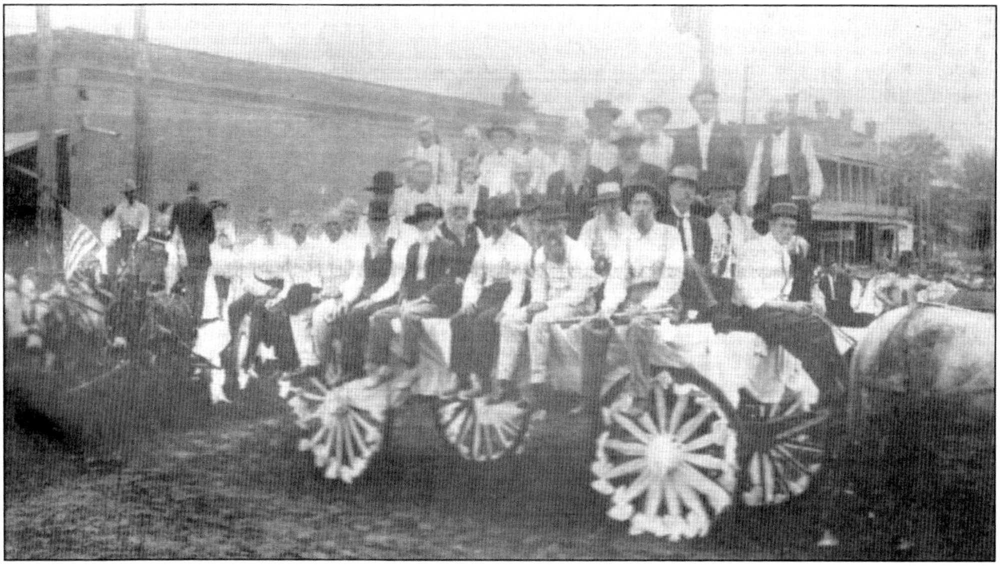

This photograph of a confederate veteran's parade dates to around 1916 and shows a group of Cass County confederate veterans. Driving the decorated wagon is Guy Hughes Sr. The picture was taken at the intersection of Hiram and Williams Streets looking south. In the background to the right is the old *Citizens Journal* office. (Courtesy of Pearl Brown.)

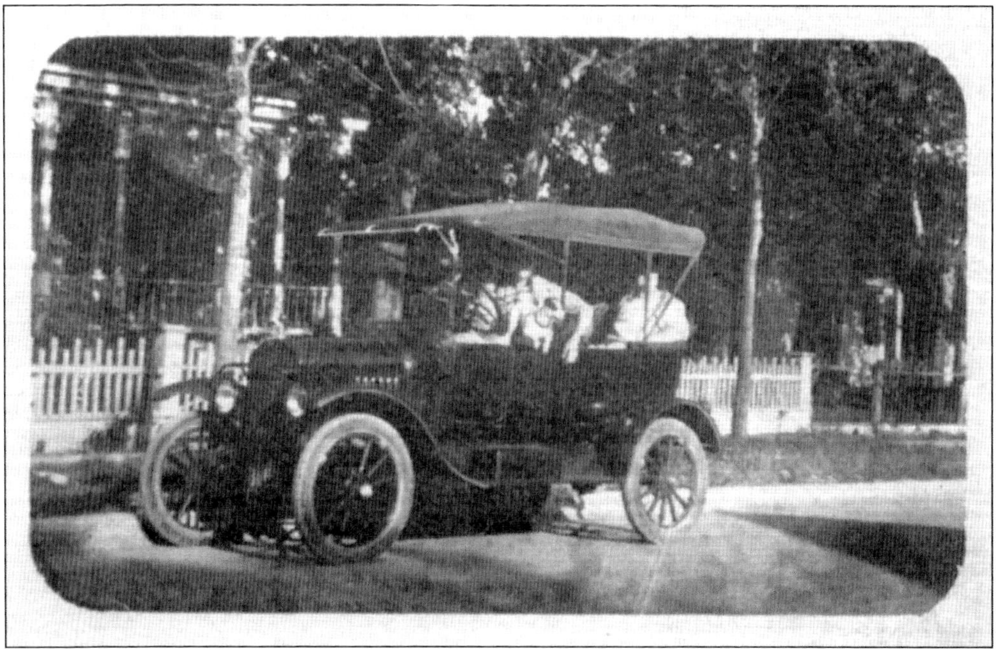

This photograph, taken around 1920, shows a group of people ready to go for a ride. Notice the dog sitting on the driver's lap. (Courtesy of Cass County Genealogical Society.)

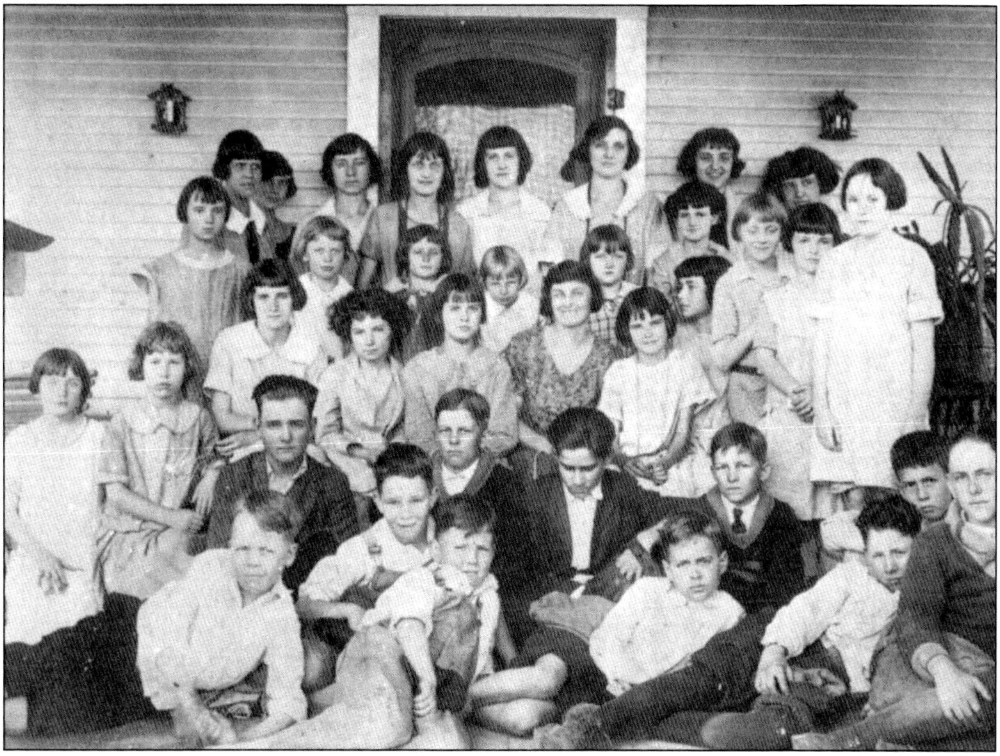

This 1925-era group is an expression class taught by Mrs. Tilford Hughes. The class was taught in conjunction with the school system and performed several plays a year. The students are, from left to right, (first row) Ferrell Ellington, M.D. Bell, Donald Bell, Paul J. Arnold, Andrew Oden, and Oma Sheppard; (second row) Earl Henderson, William Howe, Kelley Arnold, Lillian Howe, and unidentified; (third row) Virginia Holbert, Christine Harrell (Rutherford), Halcyon Porter, Edith Kidwell, Merle Harrington, Mrs. Hughes, Juanita Henderson, Kathryn Galloway, Ruth Hughes (Arnold), Annie D. Smith (Oden), and Crystal Sheppard; (fourth row) Marcelle Harrington, Kathryn L. McClung, Kathryn Henderson, Edna Gail Hanner (Walls), and Dorothy Smith (Carney); (fifth row) Evelyn Hoyt (Harper), Crystal Walker (Kennedy), Alice Clements (VanArsdale), Annie Alice Ellington, Evelyn Callicoate, Mildred Mays (McClung), Adine Pepper, and Willie Willis. (Courtesy of Pearl Brown.)

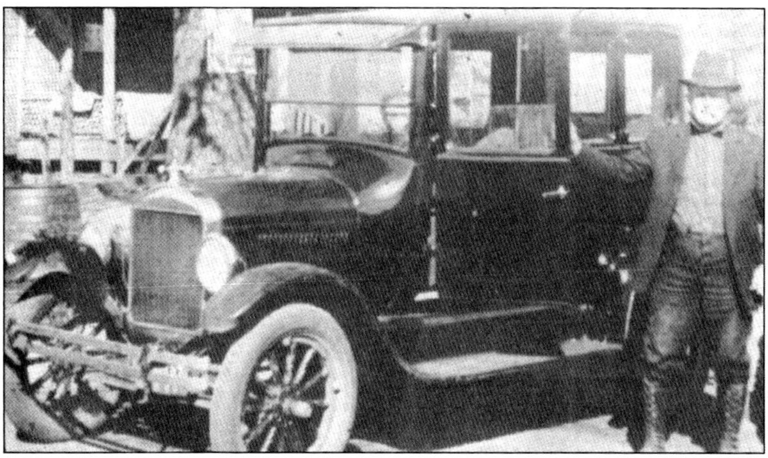

W.S. Thomas is shown with his car around 1925. He was an early resident of Atlanta, as were his parents, John and Susan Frances Meadows Thomas. (Courtesy of Pearl Brown.)

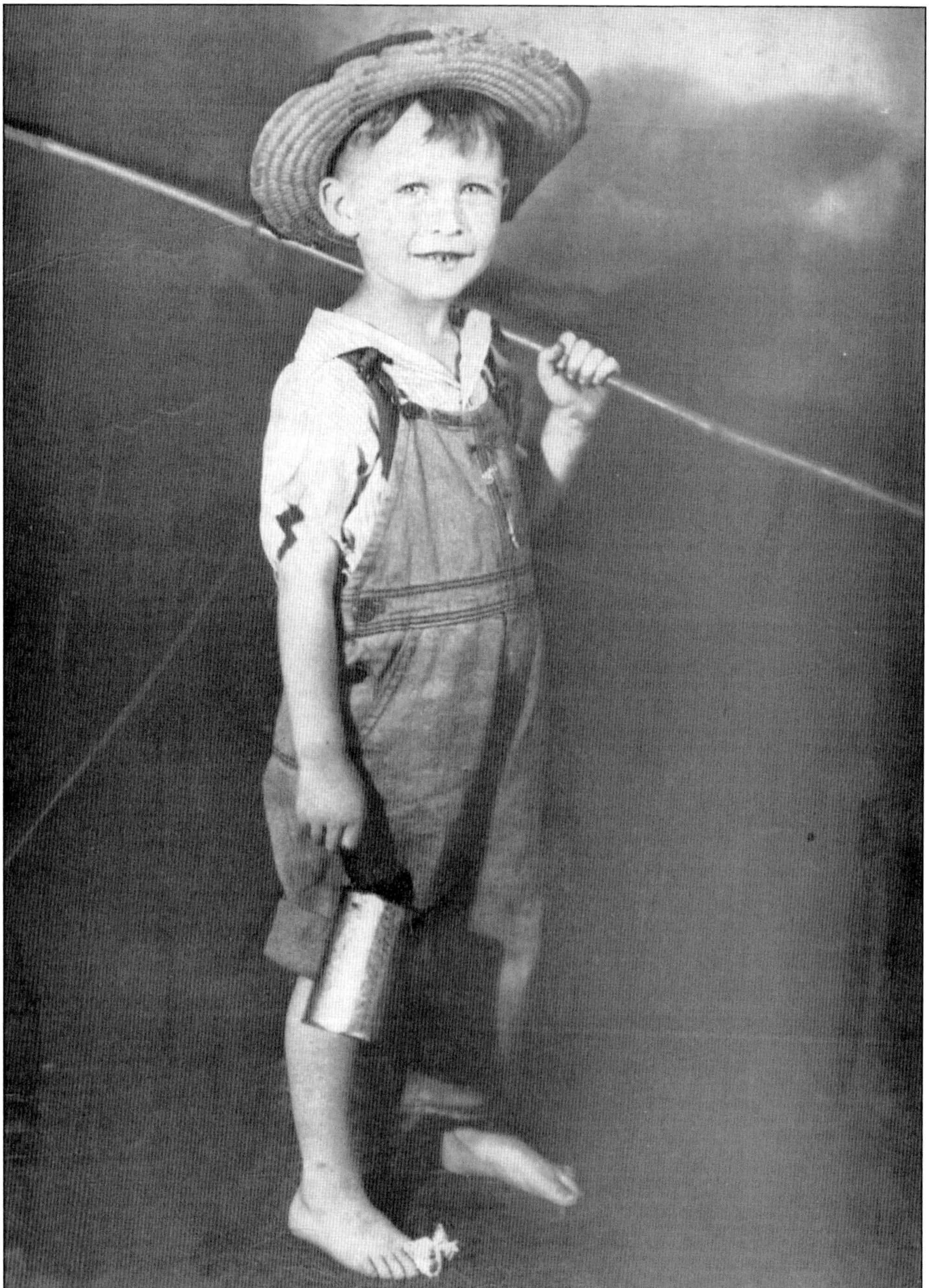

John D. "Bubba" Davis is posing on the front cover of *Field and Stream Magazine* around 1928. He was the son of David V. and Aurelia H. Davis. (Courtesy of Mark and Julia Mays.)

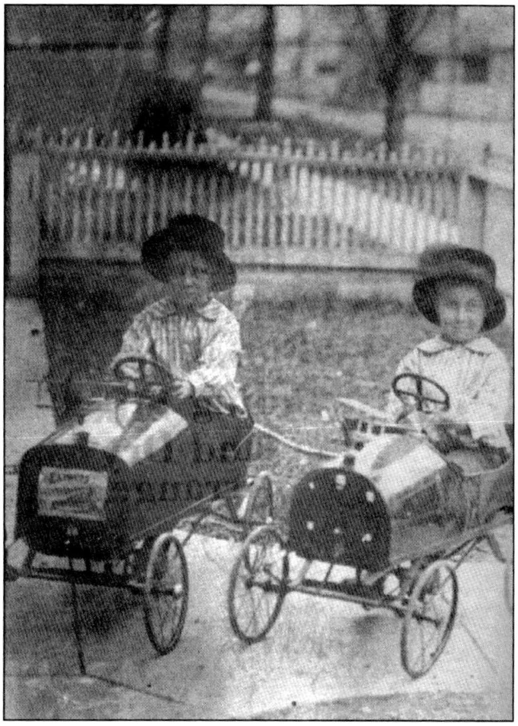

Two young boys show off their new toy cars in this photograph from 1920s. (Courtesy of Cass County Genealogical Society.)

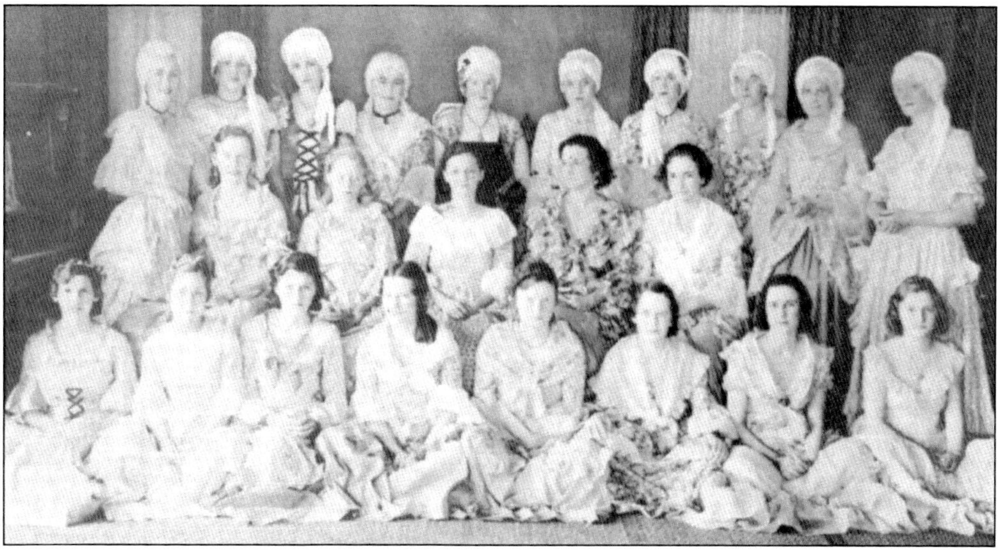

Members of the Atlanta Women's Club and a junior organization known as the Progressive Club are pictured here in costumes they wore at a George Washington birthday tea, given in February 1932 at the home of Annie Edwards. Pictured are, from left to right, (first row) Mrs. W.M. Kennedy, Christine Rutherford, Bernice O'Kelley Baker, Mrs. Calvin Dickinson, Ruth McClung, Mrs. Houston Edwards, Mrs. Archie Olds, and Edna Gail Hanner Walls; (second row) Mrs. J.C. Keller, Mrs. Kelley Arnold, Mrs. James Alexander, Mrs. Horace Coulter, and Mrs. Abb Brabham; (third row) Mrs. V.A. Richey, Mrs. Vasco Brabham, Mrs. L.L. Dalrymple, Mrs. Henry A. King, Mrs. Ben F. Ellington, Mrs. Wade Aday, Mrs. Ransome Hardy, Mrs. F.P. Ellis, Mrs. Hershel Hanner, and Mrs. Clyde Sypert. (Courtesy of Pearl Brown.)

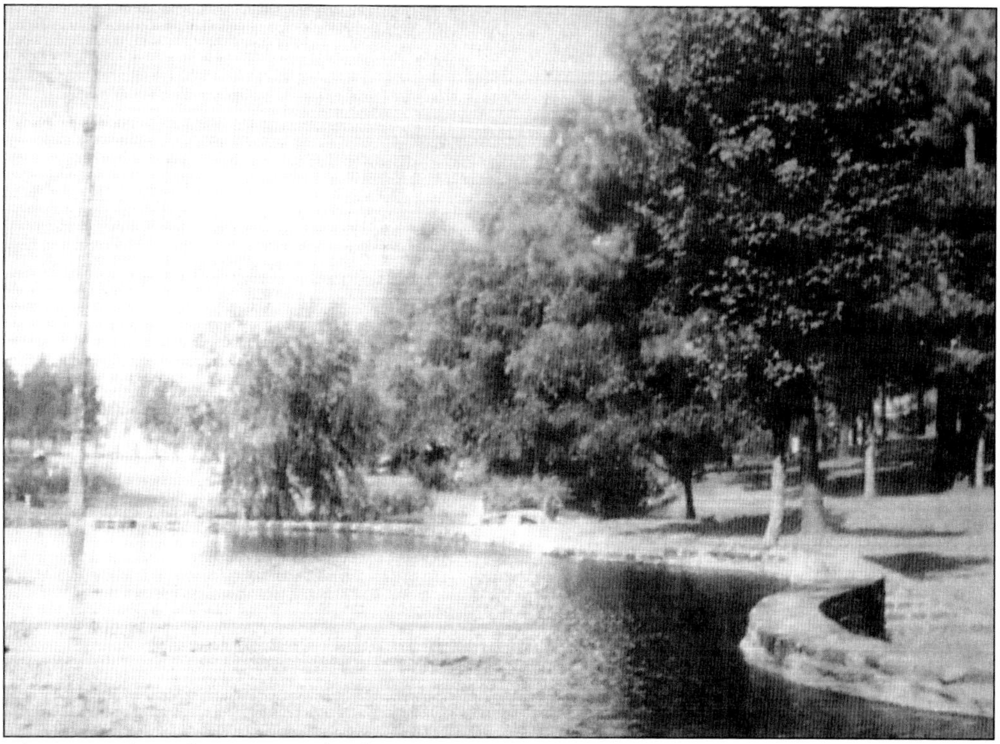

The city park on the eastern side of town is pictured sometime before 1932. The public spot held this goldfish pond. The view in this photograph appears to be looking from the northeast to the southwest. The Atlanta district office of the Texas Highway Department would later occupy this same location. (Courtesy of Cass County Genealogical Society.)

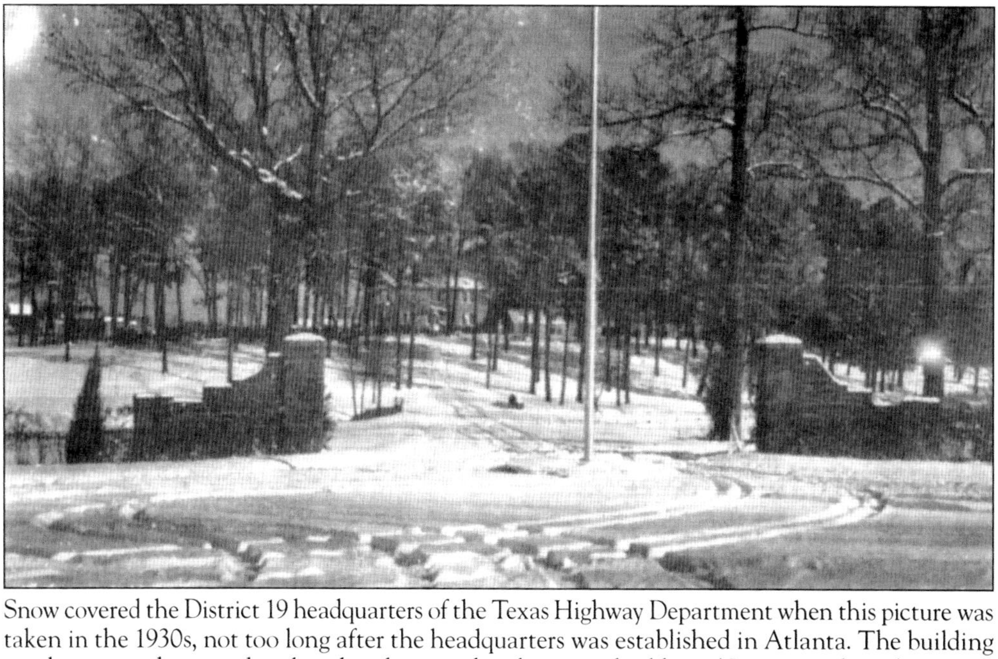

Snow covered the District 19 headquarters of the Texas Highway Department when this picture was taken in the 1930s, not too long after the headquarters was established in Atlanta. The building was later torn down and replaced with a new headquarters building. (Courtesy of Pearl Brown.)

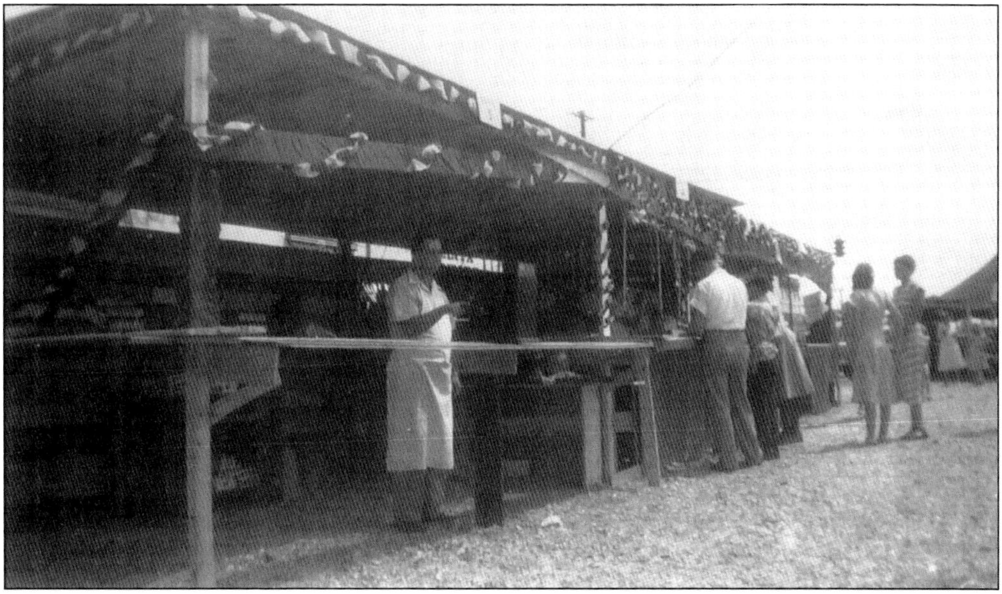

This photograph shows a view of the hotdog stand at the Atlanta Watermelon Festival in 1949. (Courtesy of Cass County Genealogical Society.)

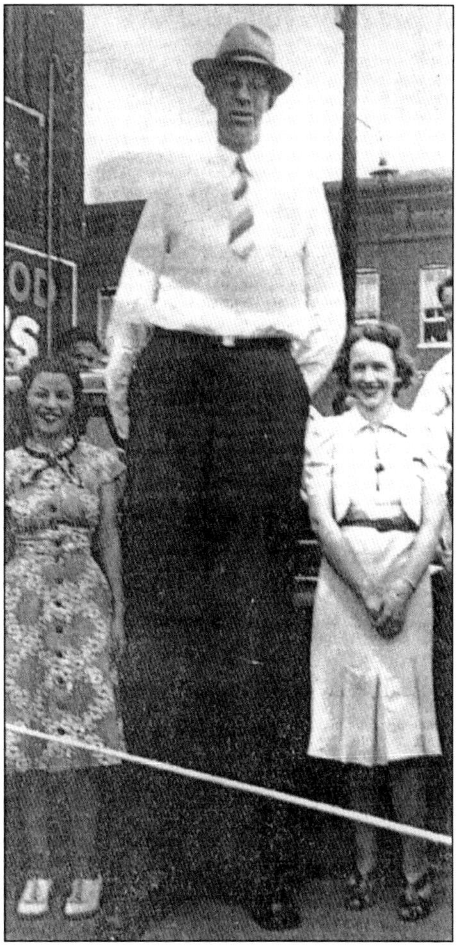

The world's tallest man, Robert Wadlow, visited Atlanta around 1938. To the left of Wadlow is Beth Davis (Mays), the daughter of David V. and Aurelia H. Davis, and to the right is Rosalie Price (Nichols). The building in the background is where Mile's Drug Store would be located. (Courtesy of Mark and Julia Mays.)

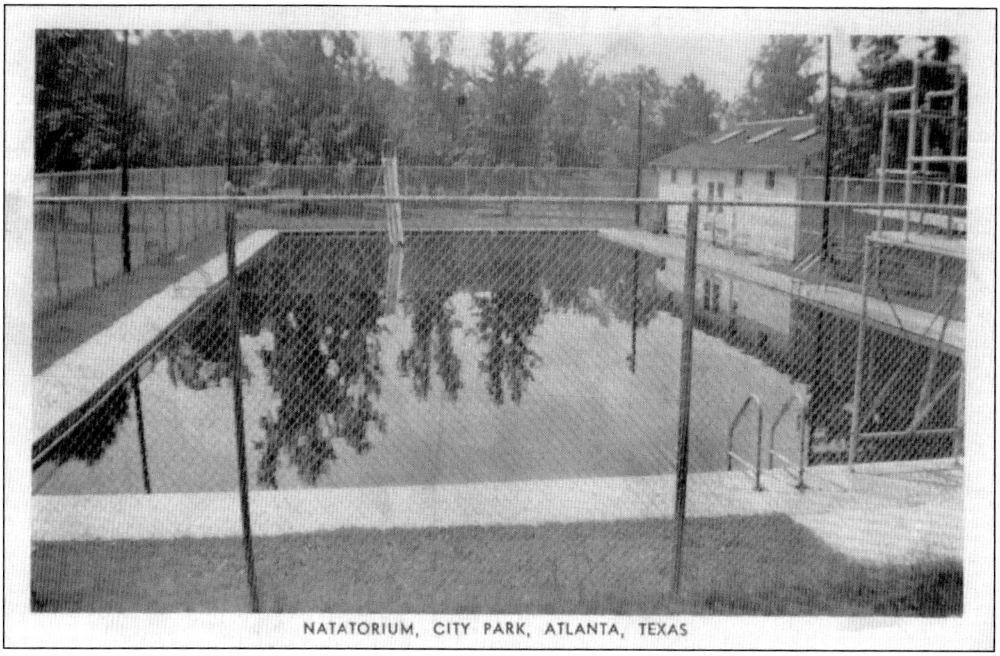

This is a 1941 postcard view of Atlanta's old city swimming pool, which used to be located in the city park just off North Louise Street. The back view of the postcard is still very readable. It was purchased at Walker's Drug Store in Atlanta. (Courtesy of Heather Ridpath Pilcher.)

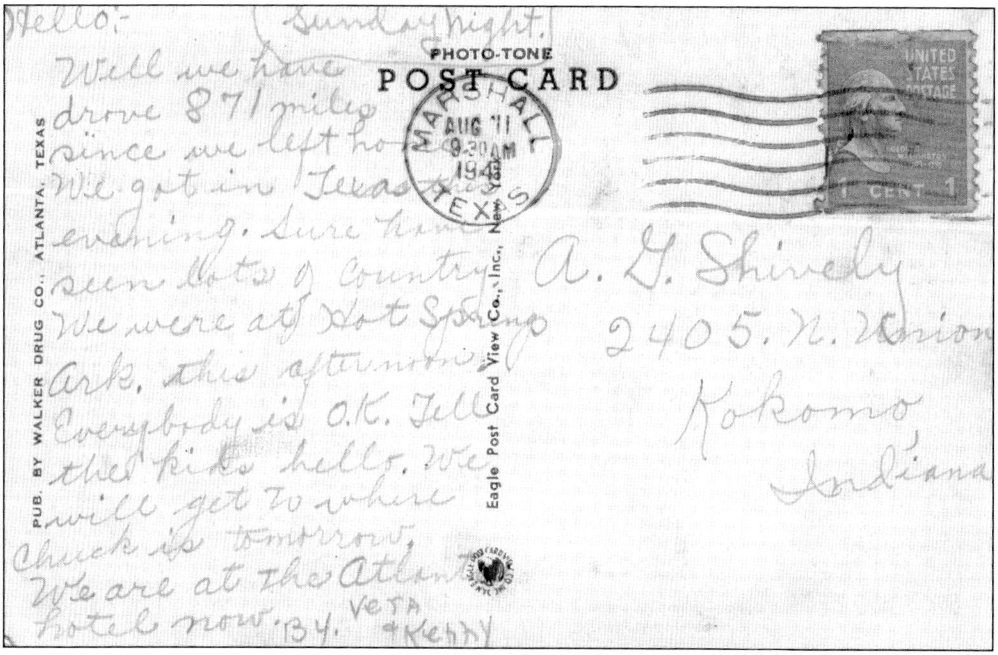

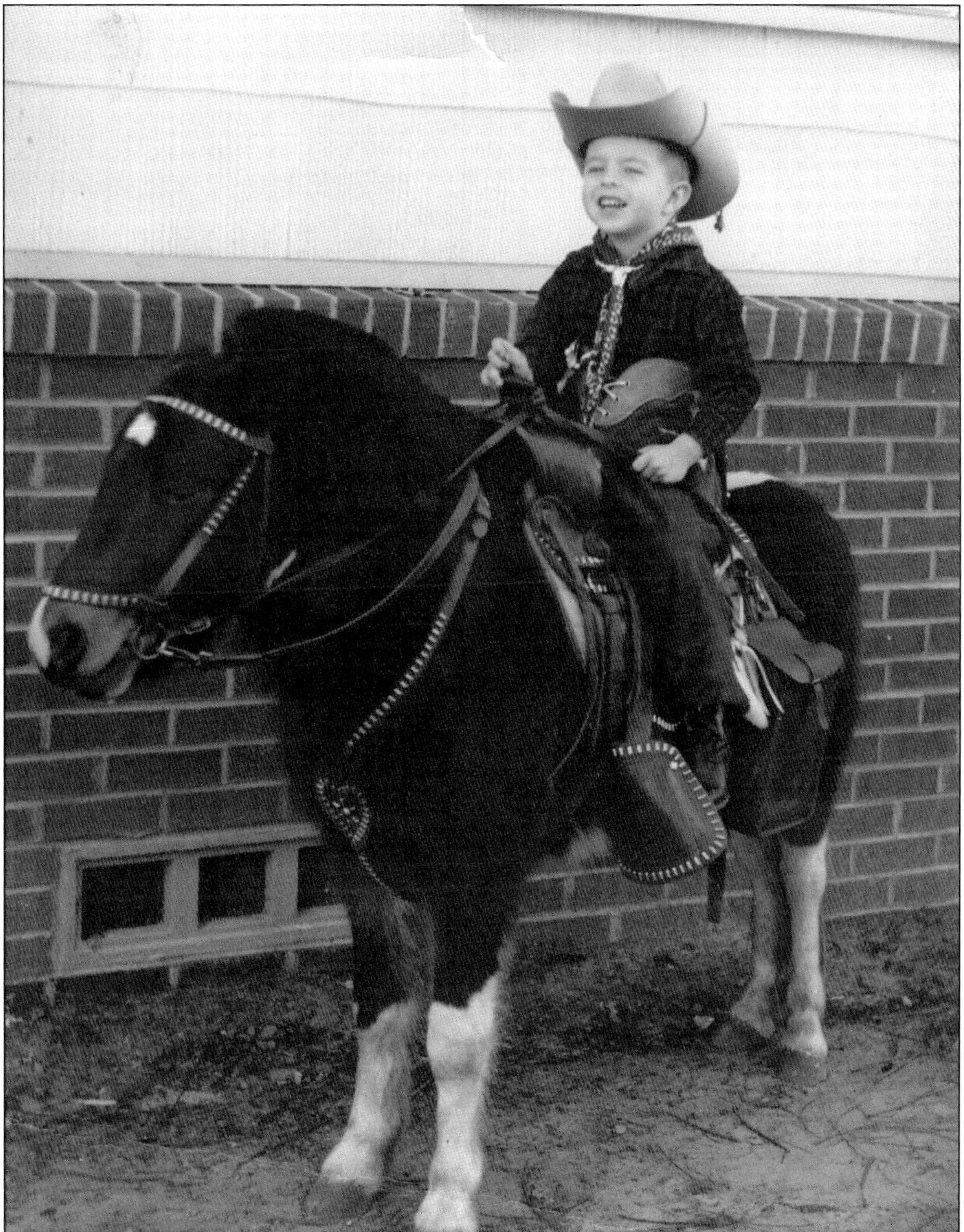

This photograph of Mark Mays was taken around 1954 at the family's home on Polk Street. Mark is the son of Beth Davis Mays and grandson of David V. and Aurelia H. Davis, who owned the Arrow Ranch. (Courtesy of Mark and Julia Mays.)

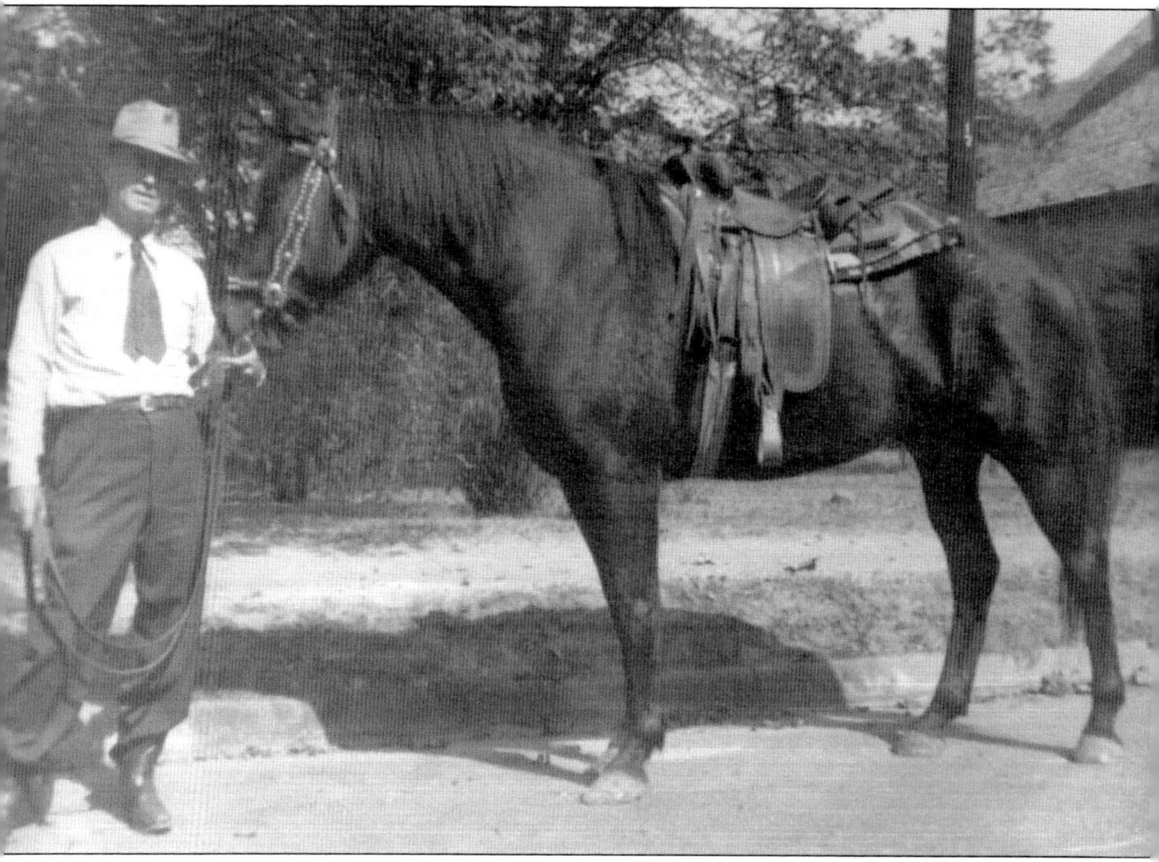

David V. Davis is standing with a horse at his Arrow Ranch during the 1950s. Although the ranch is no longer open, the property is still held by descendants of Davis. (Courtesy of Mark and Julia Mays.)

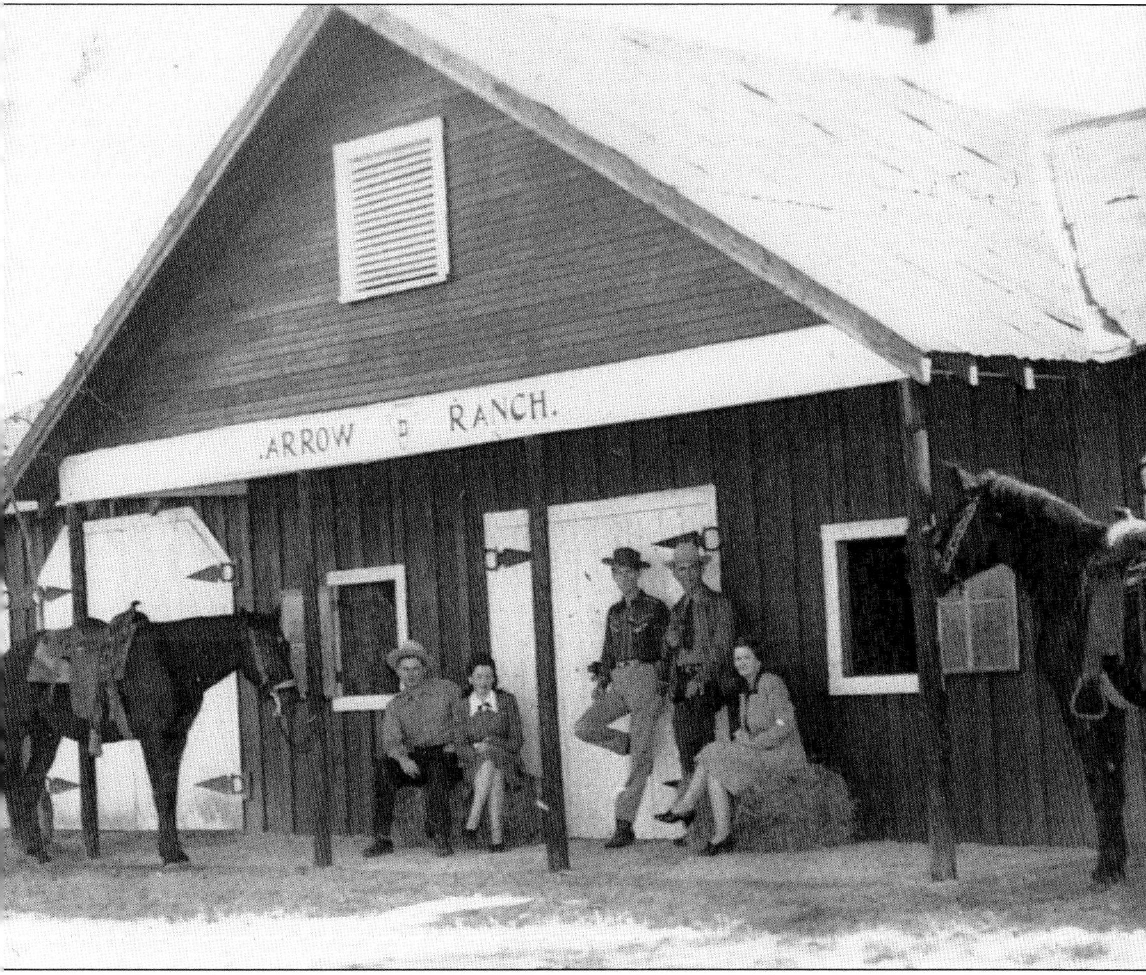

This photograph of the Arrow Ranch was taken in the 1940s. Then-owner David V. Davis used to teach riding lessons at the ranch. The ranch, a part of the community since the early 1900s, was located on Highway 77 about a mile outside of town on the way to Douglasville. (Courtesy of Mark and Julia Mays.)

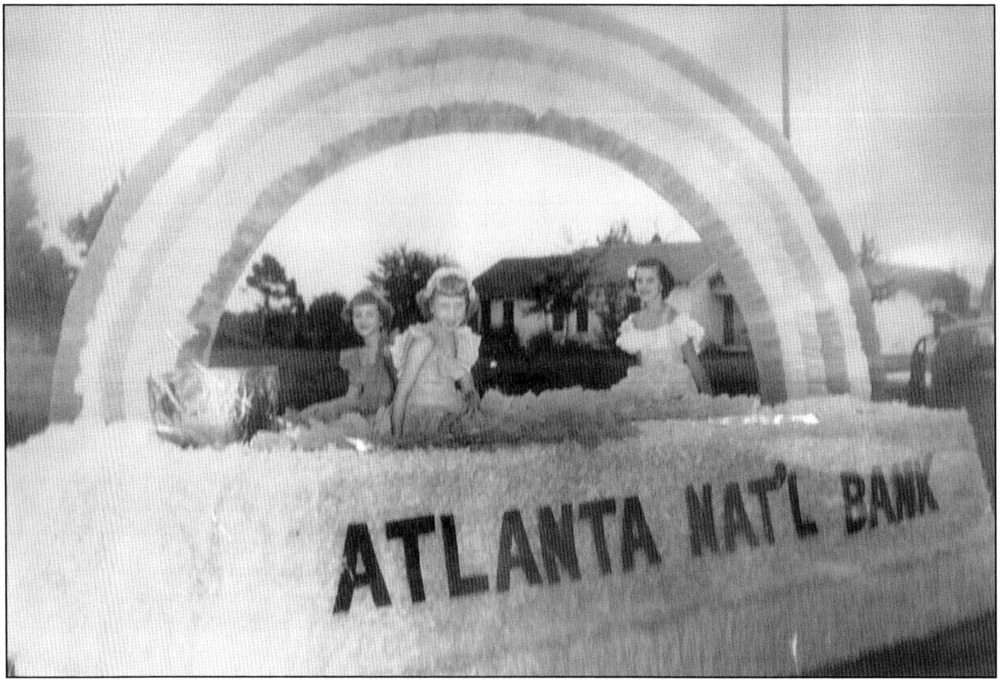

The Atlanta National Bank entered this float in a parade for the Atlanta Forest Festival. The photograph was taken around 1950. (Courtesy of Cass County Genealogical Society.)

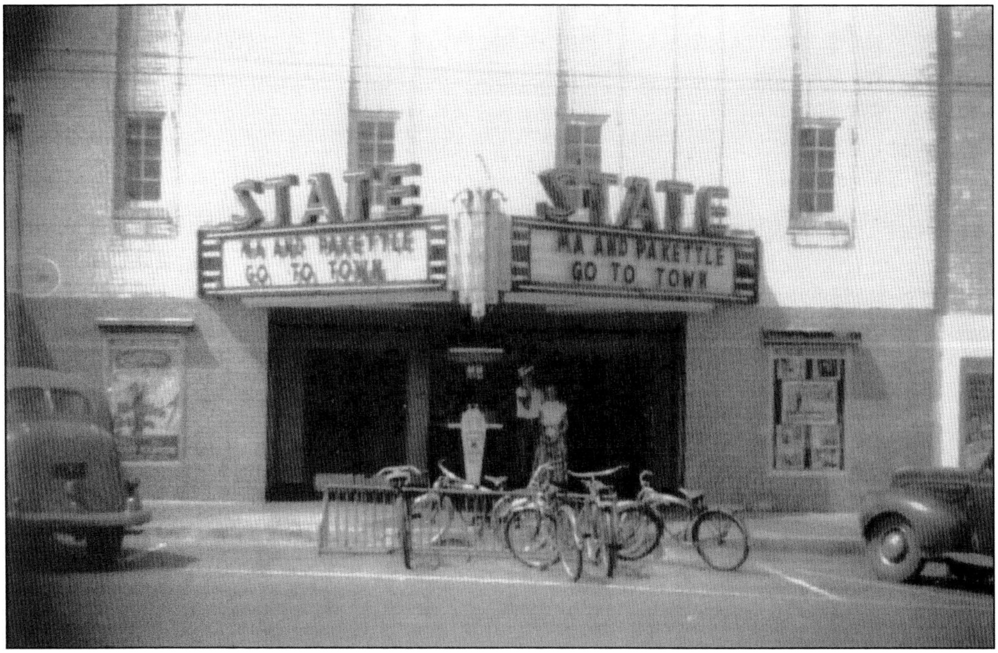

This is how the old State Theatre on Main Street looked during the 1950s. The featured picture at the time was *Ma and Pa Kettle Go to Town*, starring Marjorie Main, Percy Kilbride, and Richard Long. The second-story windows were covered during a renovation of the building, and the Star Theatre is now closed. A segregated theater for African Americans was located next door on the right. (Courtesy of Cass County Genealogical Society.)

Six

The Old Home Place

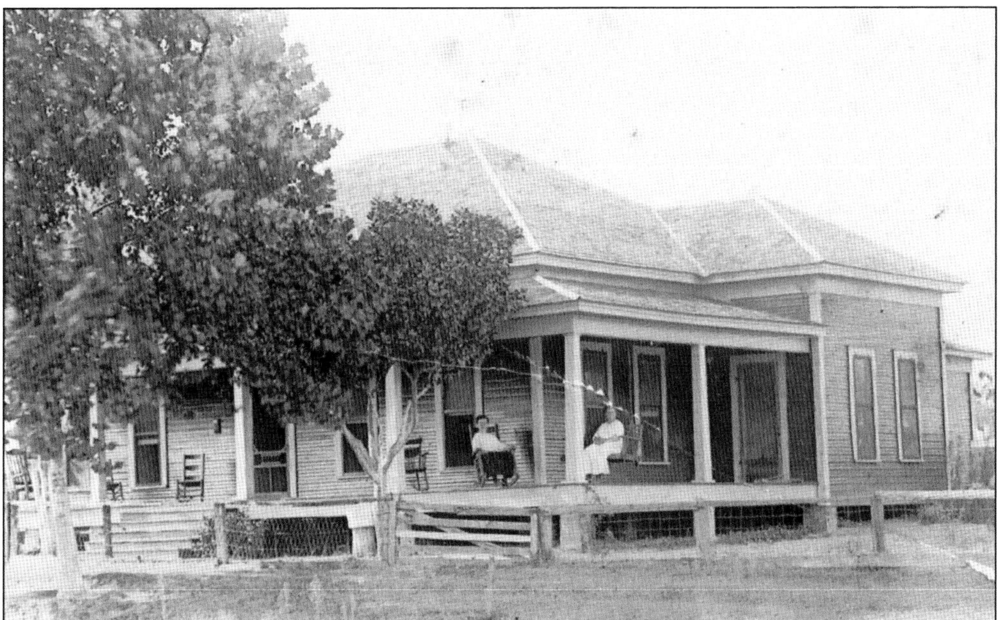

This is a 1920s view of the Perdue home at 411 Tipton Street. Reverend Perdue is sitting in the porch swing, and Mary Bartlett is in the rocker. The house burned around 1938. (Courtesy of Cass County Genealogical Society.)

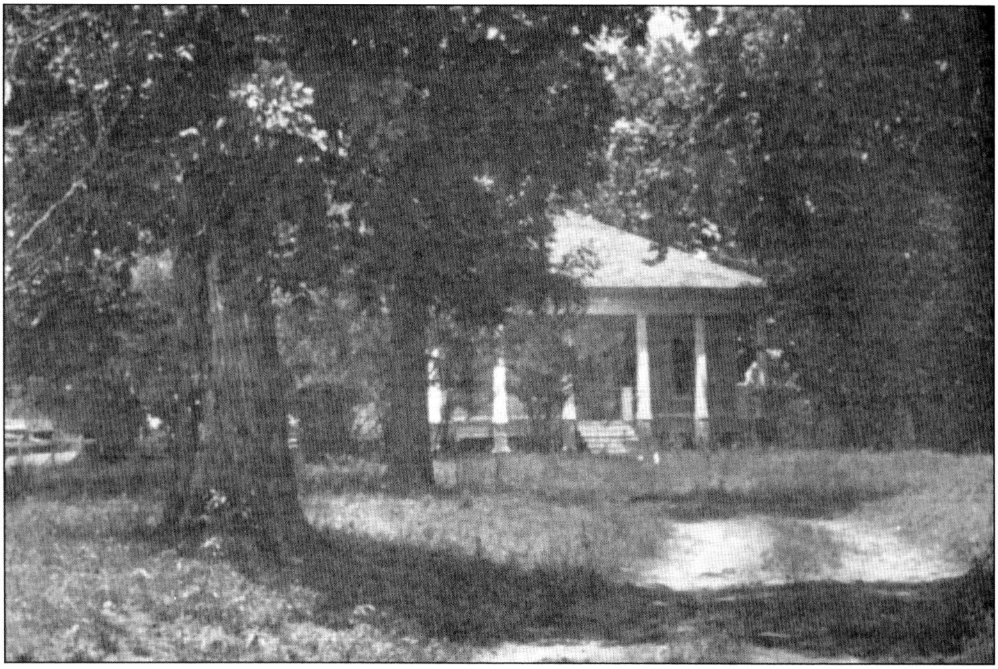

This is all that is left to mark the site of Old Atlanta. Rev. Jesse Dodd built this house around 1862. The town sprang up around it in anticipation of the coming of the T&P railroad, but when the railroad went through Capt. P.R. Scott's farm instead, the townspeople moved to what is called Lanark Crossing and started another town. When they failed to get a clear title for this land, they moved again and started Queen City. Dodd's grandsons are the Brooks brothers, James and Jesse, both doctors. (Courtesy of Cass County Genealogical Society.)

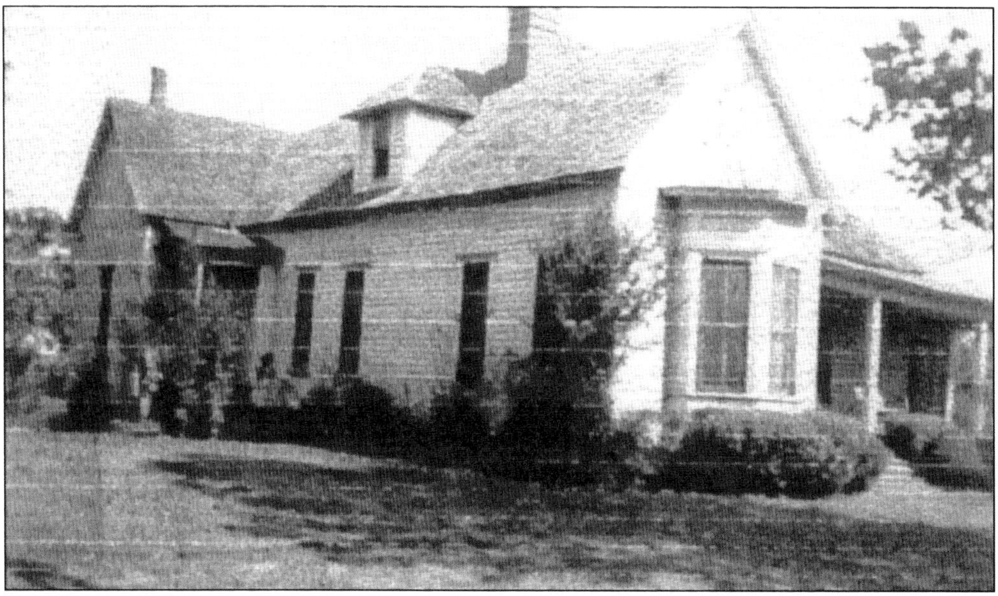

Writing above the picture states, "John and Claude Hughes home on Hiram Street across from the First Methodist Church parking lot. The Davis home was next door on the corner of Hiram and Louise Streets." (Courtesy of Cass County Genealogical Society.)

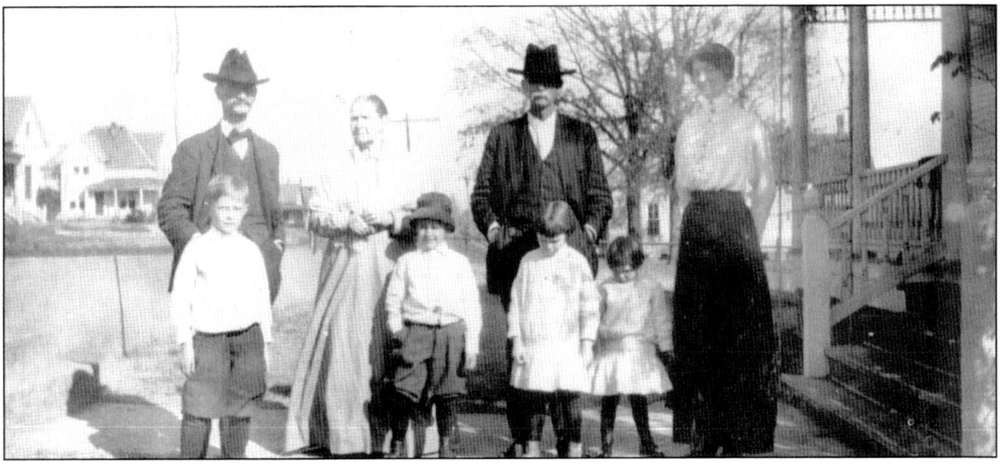

Several members of W.D. "Pa Bill" Lanier's family pose in front of the early T.R. Richey home on North Louise Street. The children standing in the first row are thought to be Thomas Lanier Richey (left), son of T.R. and Mattie who owned the home on North Louise, and three children from Crossely family. In the second row from left to right are Dr. Andrew Crossely, Pa Bill's son-in-law who served as a state representative in Austin; Paulina Frances Lemmon Lanier, daughter of Felix Grundy Lanier, a citizen of the Texas Republic; Pa Bill Lanier, who served in the Confederate army and two terms in the Texas Legislature in 1915 and 1917; and Dr. Crossely's wife. It is unclear whether Crossely's first or second wife is pictured. Crossely's first wife was a Lanier, but she died when she was fairly young. Dr. Crossely and Paulina Lanier are buried at Pine Crest Cemetery, and Grundy Lanier is buried in the Mt. Zion Cemetery. (Courtesy of Cass County Genealogical Society.)

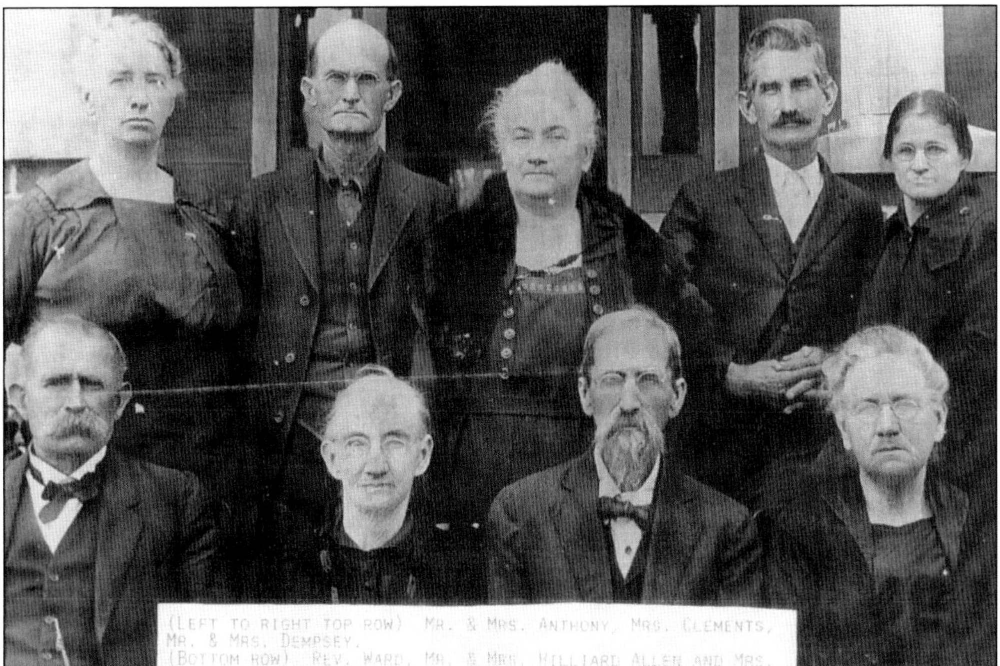

Standing in front of a home in Atlanta are, from left to right, (first row) Reverend Ward, Mr. and Mrs. Hilliard Allen, and Docia Davis; (second row) Mr. and Mrs. Anthony, Mrs. Clements, and Mr. and Mrs. Dempsey. (Courtesy of Cass County Genealogical Society.)

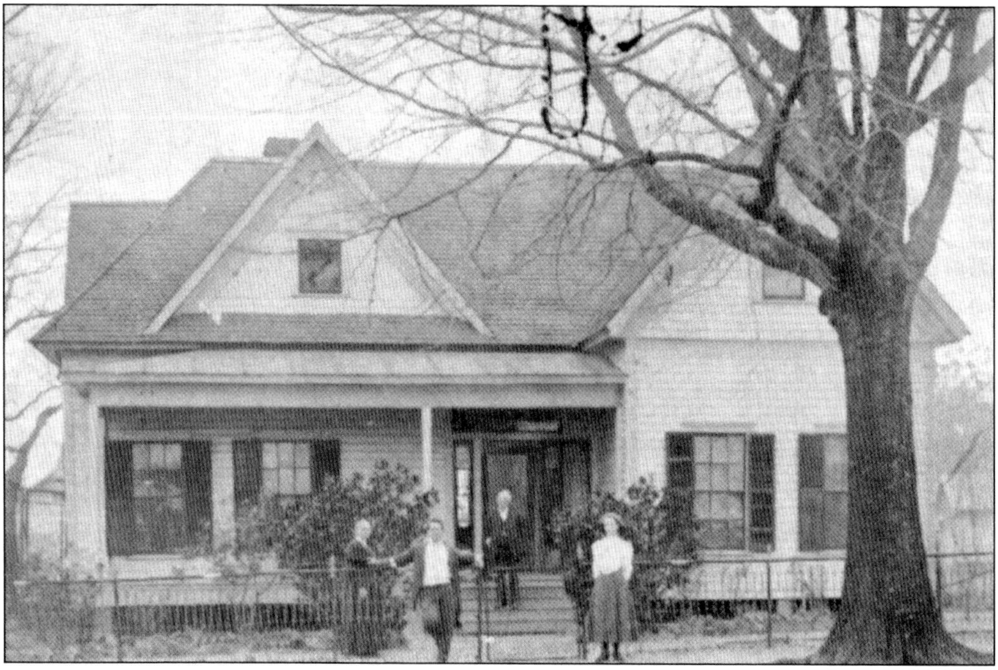

One of the early homes in Atlanta was the Johnson home. J.D. Johnson was a merchant in Atlanta. This house was on Hiram Street where the Atlanta National Bank used to be located. Pictured in front of the house around 1910 are, from left to right, Mr. and Mrs. Johnson, Crossley Johnson, and Mrs. Guy Hughes Sr. (Courtesy of Pearl Brown.)

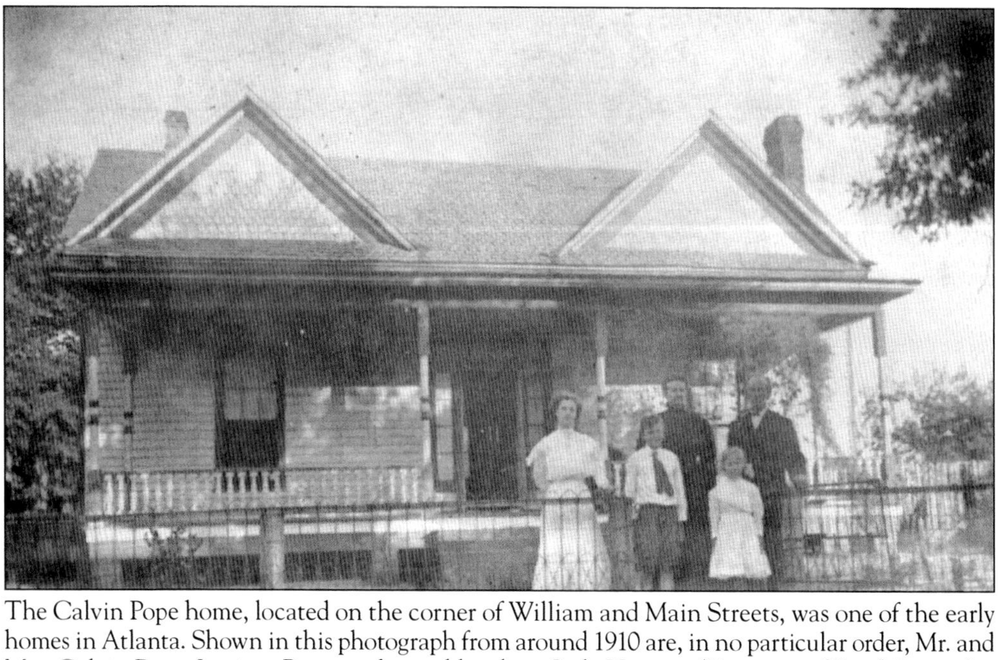

The Calvin Pope home, located on the corner of William and Main Streets, was one of the early homes in Atlanta. Shown in this photograph from around 1910 are, in no particular order, Mr. and Mrs. Calvin Pope, Lucious Pope, and granddaughter Sada Haynes. (Courtesy of Pearl Brown.)

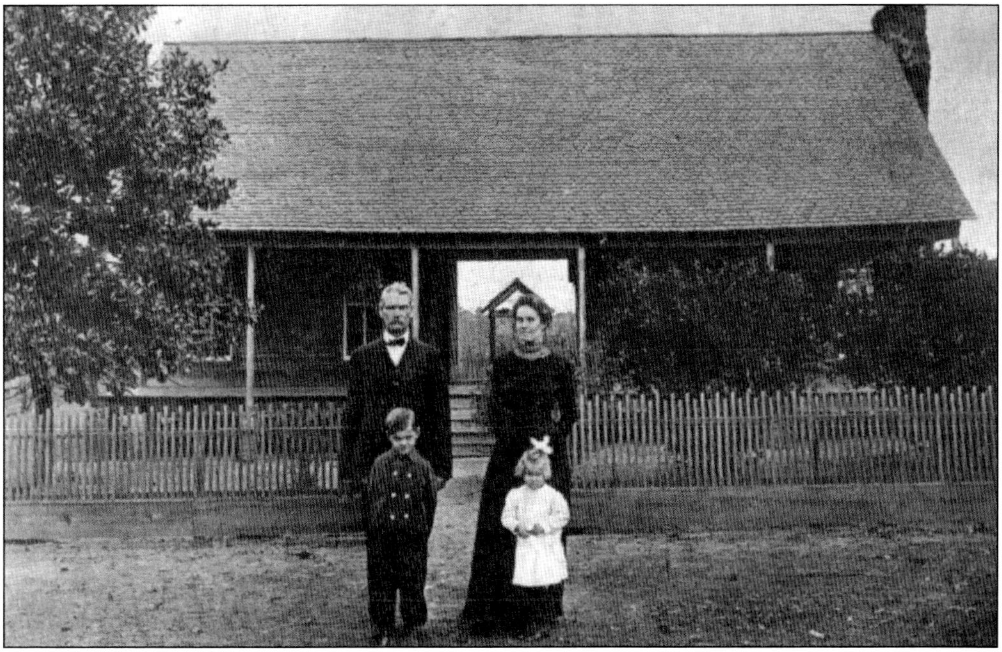

Shown is the John A. Haynes family standing in front of their home located near Atlanta going towards Douglasville in the early 1900s. Mr. Haynes is pictured with his wife, Ellie, and children, Horace and Mabel. (Courtesy of Pearl Brown.)

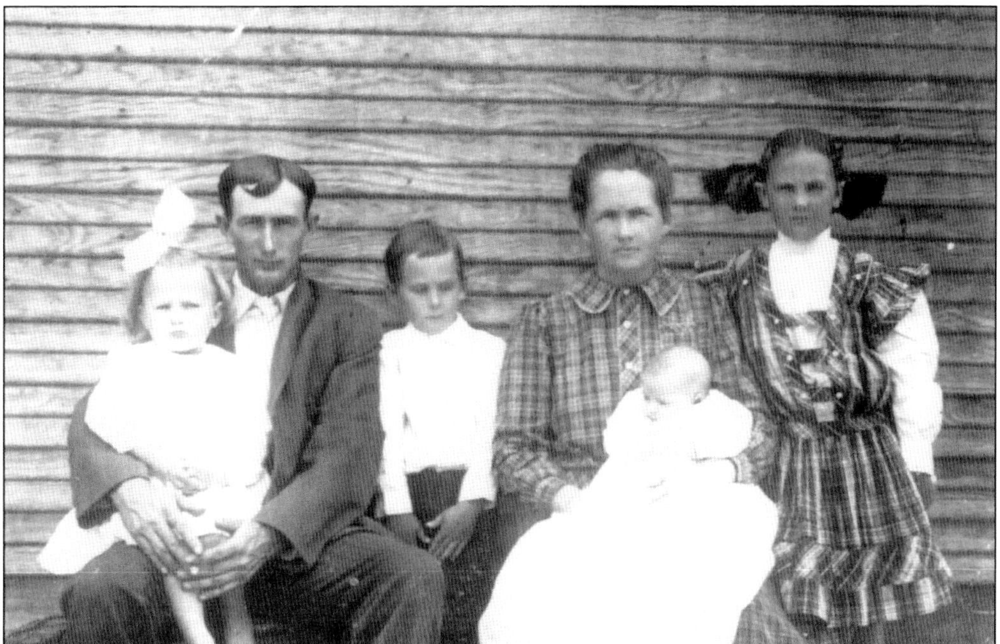

The Watkins family is posing for a photograph taken around 1913. From left to right are Lela Mae Watkins (Parker), Lonnie Watkins, Paul A. Watkins, Lula Watkins (Watson), baby Elizabeth Watkins (Shelton), and Bessie Watkins (McDonald). (Courtesy of Cass County Genealogical Society.)

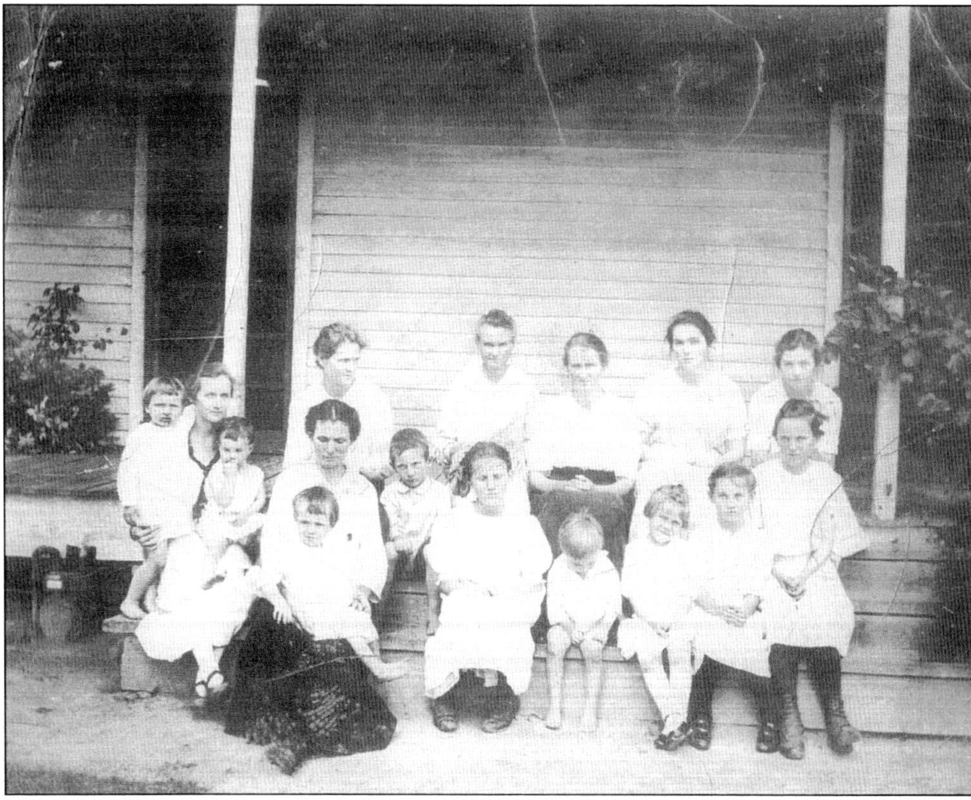

Grandmother Emma Prator is sitting on the front porch of her home with her girls around 1915. (Courtesy of Cass County Genealogical Society.)

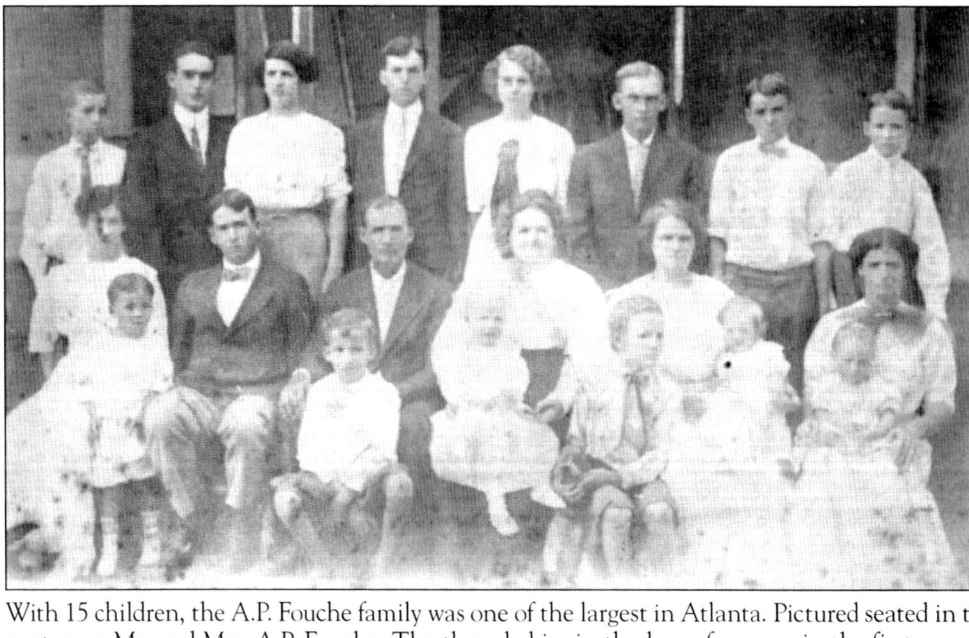

With 15 children, the A.P. Fouche family was one of the largest in Atlanta. Pictured seated in the center are Mr. and Mrs. A.P. Fouche. The three babies in the laps of women in the first row are grandchildren. The remaining 15 are all the children of the Fouches. (Courtesy of Pearl Brown.)

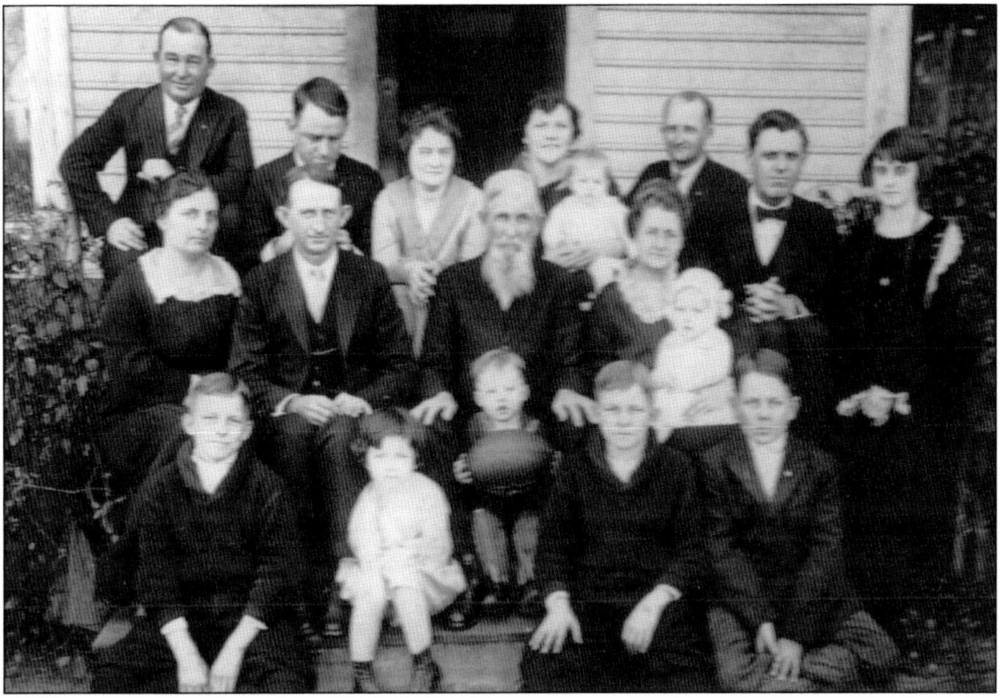

Pictured in 1923, the W.A. Howe family included, from left to right, (first row) W.C. Howe, son of Thomas A. and Mattie Sue Howe; Rina Beth Davis (Mays), daughter of David V. and Aurelia H. Davis; Billy Bob Howe, son of Robert and Marie Howe; Lillian A. Howe, son of T.A. and Mattie Sue Howe; and Emmett H. Florence, son of R.E. and Margaret Florence; (second row) Martha S. Howe, Thomas A. Howe, William A. Howe Sr., Margaret Howe Florence, baby Robert J. Florence, Robert E. Florence, and Lily Florence Warren, daughter of R.E. and Margaret Florence; (third row) William A. Howe Jr., David V. Davis, Aurelia Howe Davis, Marie Starkey Howe, baby Carolyn Howe (Jones), and Robert A. Howe. (Courtesy of Cass County Genealogical Society.)

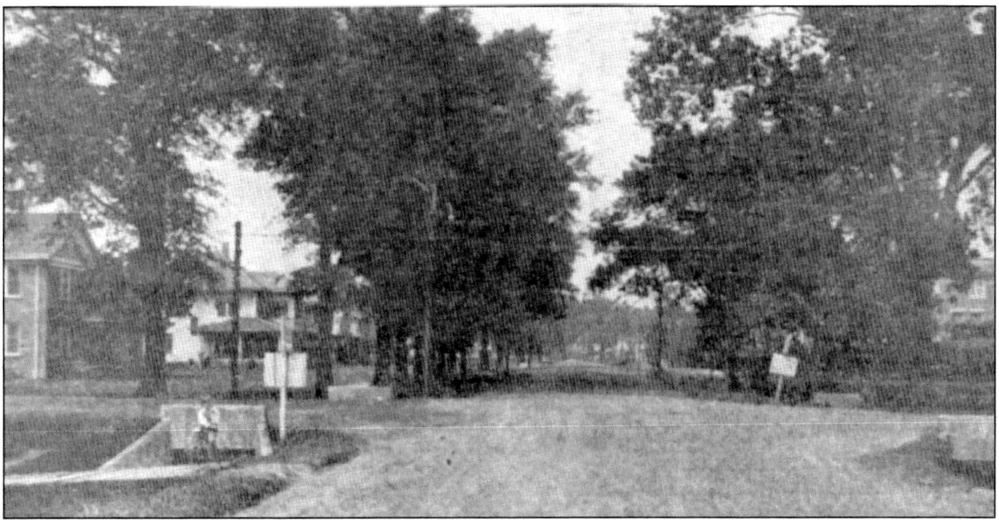

This is a view of Louise Street looking north from Main Street in 1929. The Lanier family built a home on North Louise Street in the early days of Atlanta. (Courtesy of Cass County Genealogical Society.)

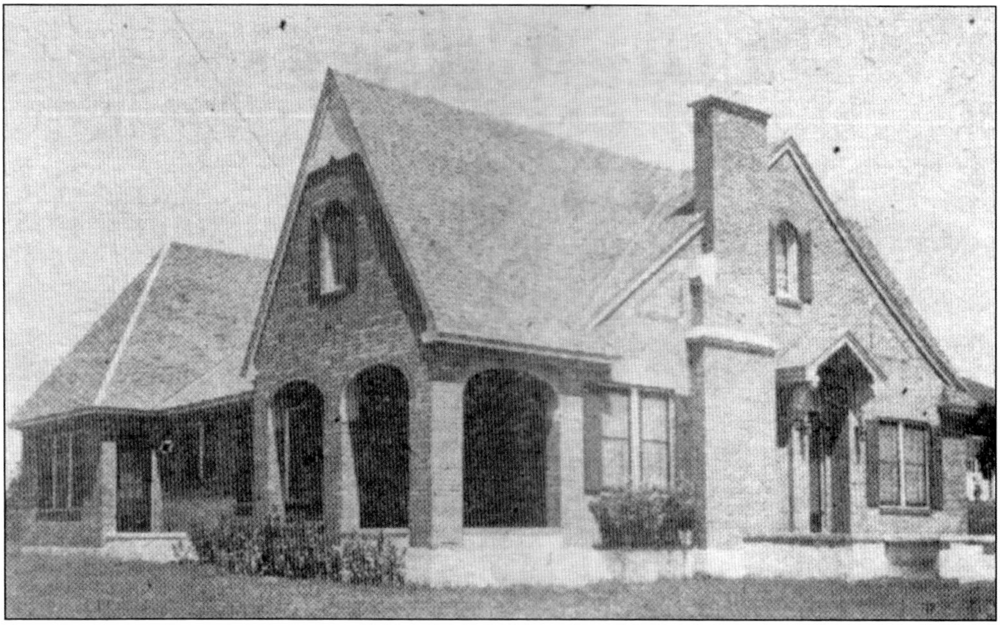

The Henry R. King residence is photographed here in 1929. Mrs. King was a member of the Atlanta Women's Club and appears on page 81 in a photograph from 1932. (Courtesy of Cass County Genealogical Society.)

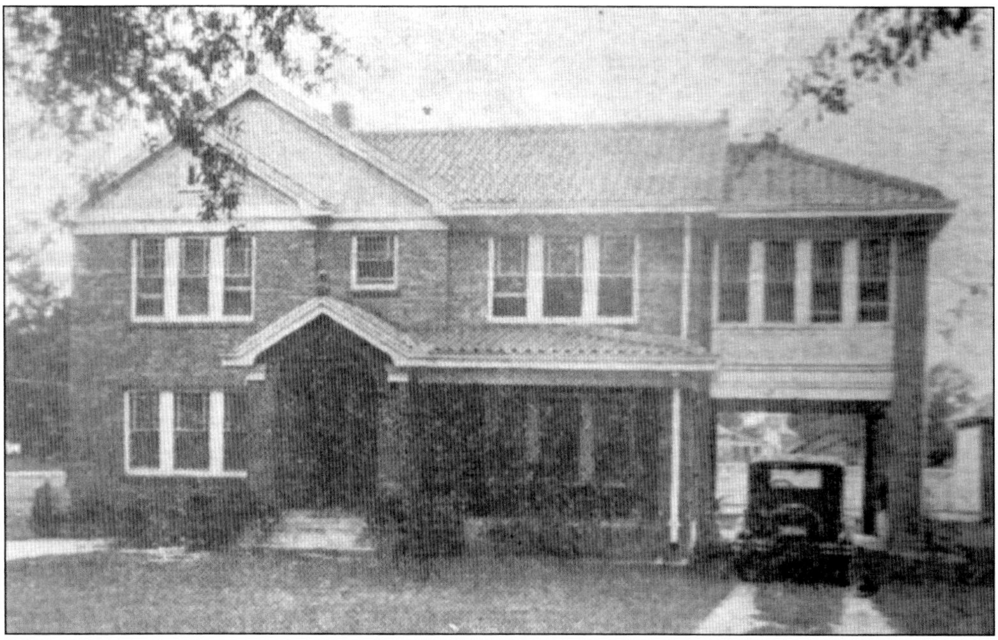

This photograph of Mrs. A.A. Edwards's residence was also taken in 1929. The home's garage shows that it was built after the automobile replaced the horses on the streets of Atlanta. (Courtesy of Cass County Genealogical Society.)

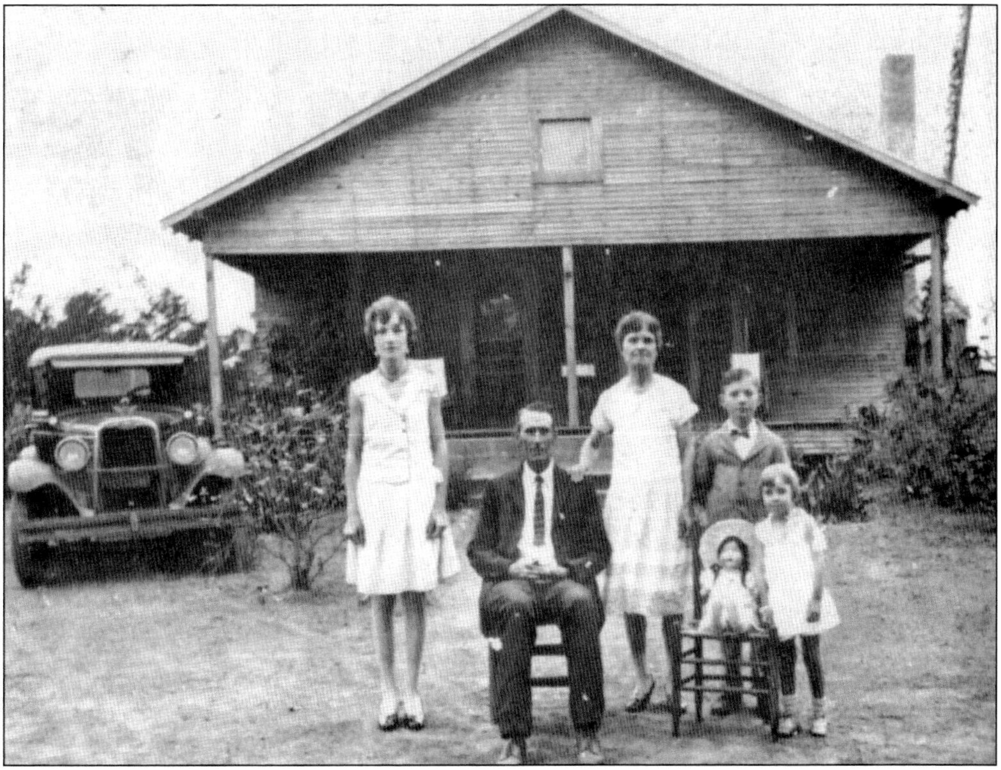

The R.W. Carter family sat for this photograph in 1929. The Carter family is one of the early Atlanta families. The oldest Carter daughter (far left) married Ennis Steger. The boy is A.W. Carter, and the small girl married Kenneth L. Thompson. The home was located one mile north of Queen City. (Courtesy of Pearl Brown.)

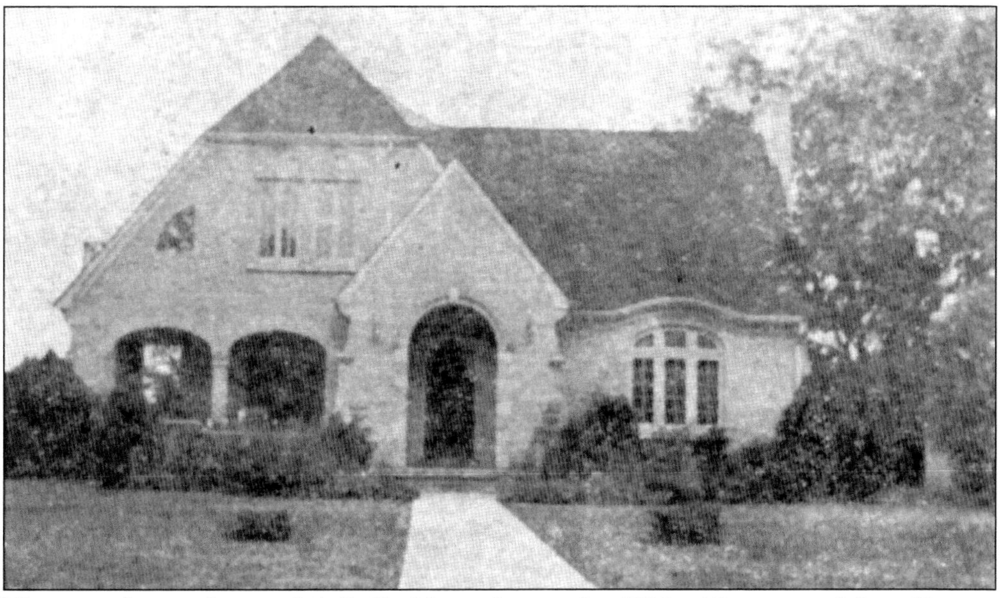

This was the residence of A.O. Brabham during the 1930s. (Courtesy of Cass County Genealogical Society.)

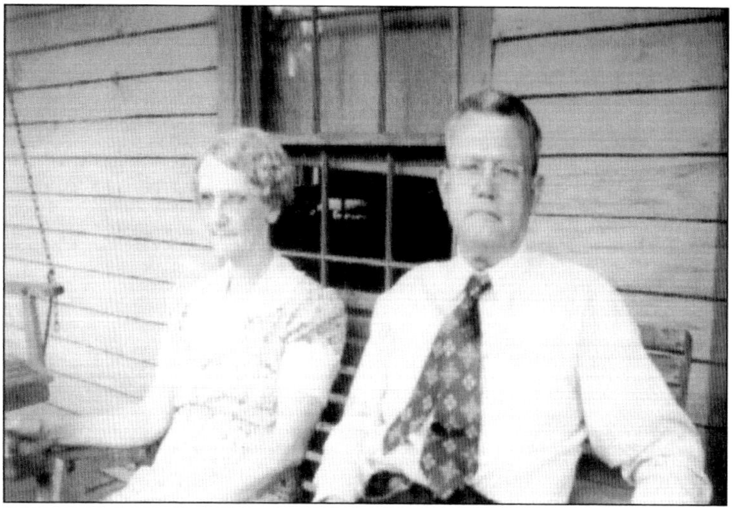

Ada Carlton Bryan is sitting on a porch swing with brother John T. Carlton in 1940. (Courtesy of Cass County Genealogical Society.)

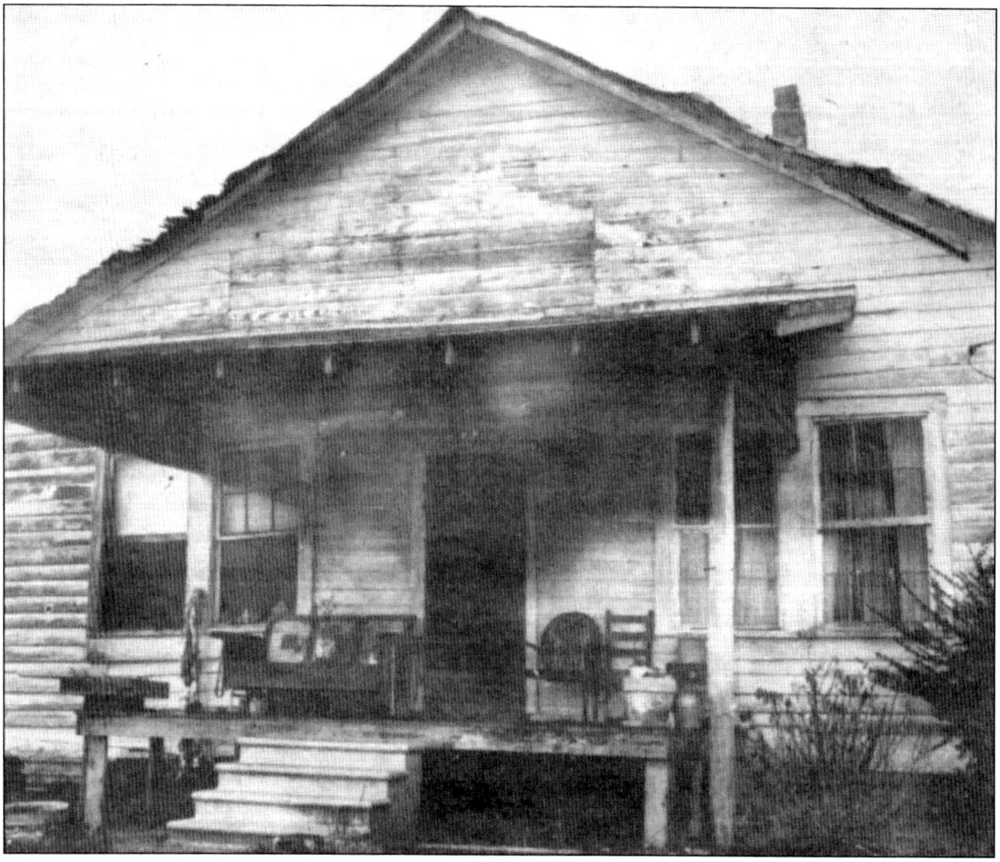

Sylvester Young lived in this house when the *Citizens Journal* photographed it for a 1979 article entitled, "Birthplace of the Journal." This home was, at one time, the plantation dwelling for Colonel Sledge, who came to Cass County from Georgia. It was here that 20 men held an organizational meeting for the *Journal* in 1879. Sylvester's father bought the property from Curtright heirs, took off the top story, and changed the entrance to the side of the original home. (Courtesy of Cass County Genealogical Society.)

Seven

Family and Friends

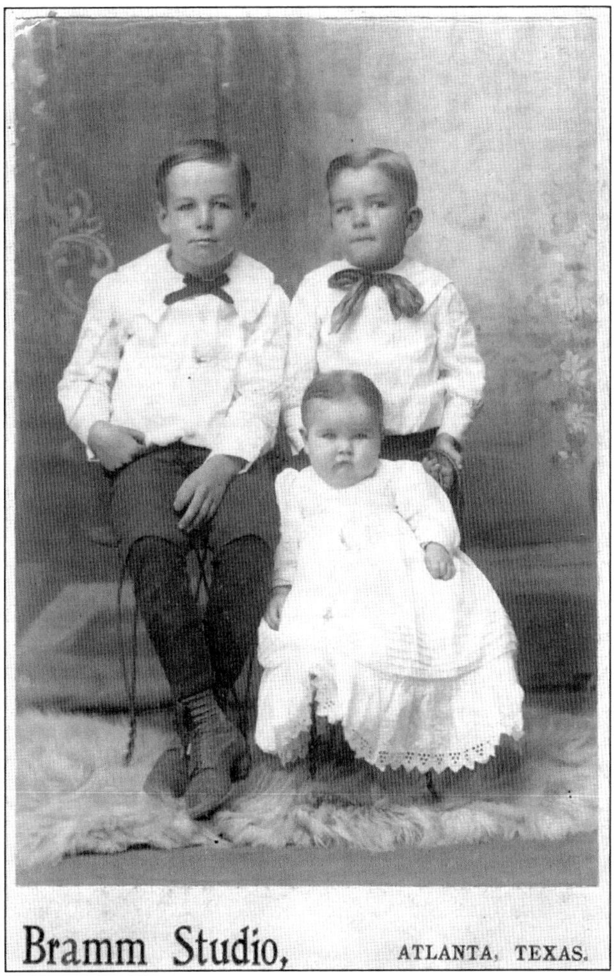

Posing for a portrait from the 1890s are, from left to right, siblings Shelly, Ouida, and John Clark. The picture was taken at Bramm Studio located on Hiram Street. (Courtesy of Mark and Julia Mays.)

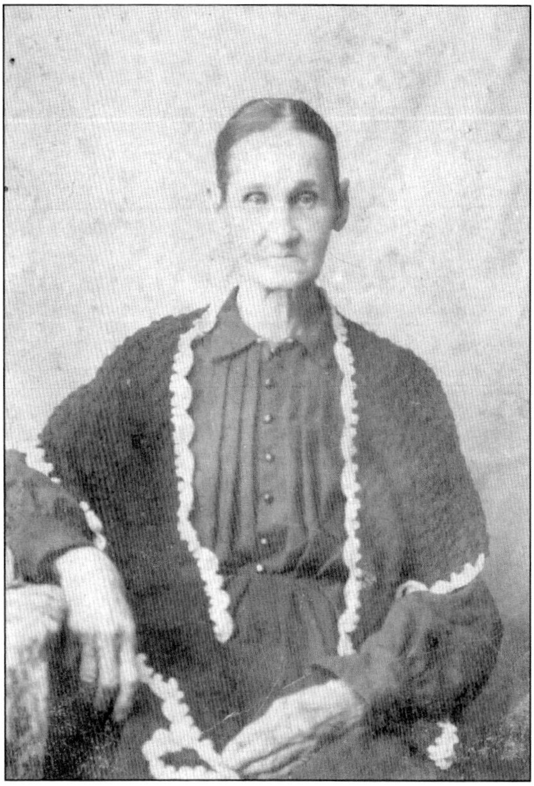

Mary Jane Stephens White was the wife of William V. White and the mother of Charles C. White. This photograph dates from around 1870. (Courtesy of Mark and Julia Mays.)

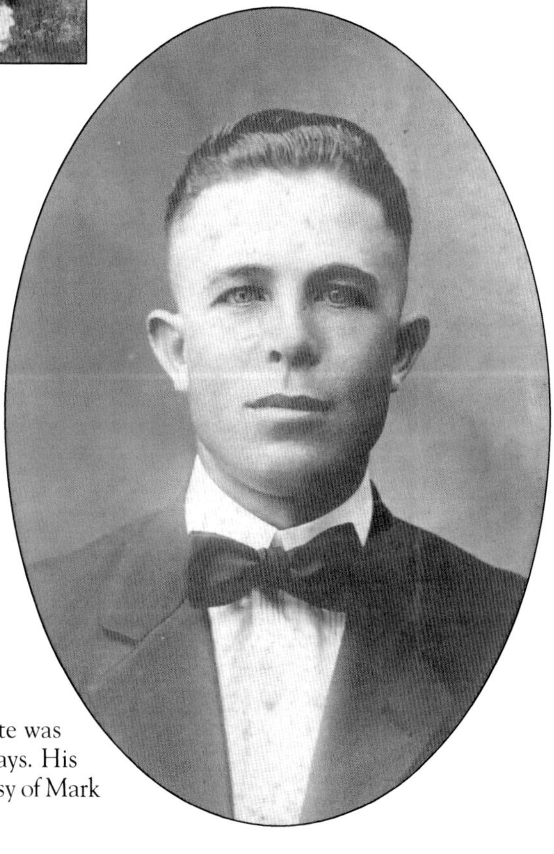

Shown here around 1895, Charles C. White was the great-grandfather of Julia Stephens Mays. His home was located on Hiram Street. (Courtesy of Mark and Julia Mays.)

David M. Pyle was born in Walton, Georgia, in 1820. He moved to Cass County before the Civil War with his wife, Nancy. David passed away in 1915, and Nancy died in 1924. The next three photographs were taken during a family reunion with his brothers in the early 1900s. (Courtesy of Patricia Pyle Ridpath.)

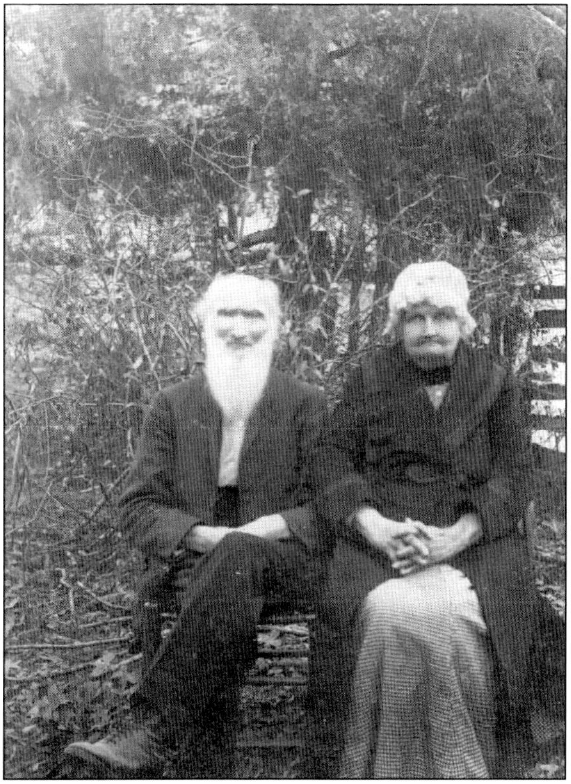

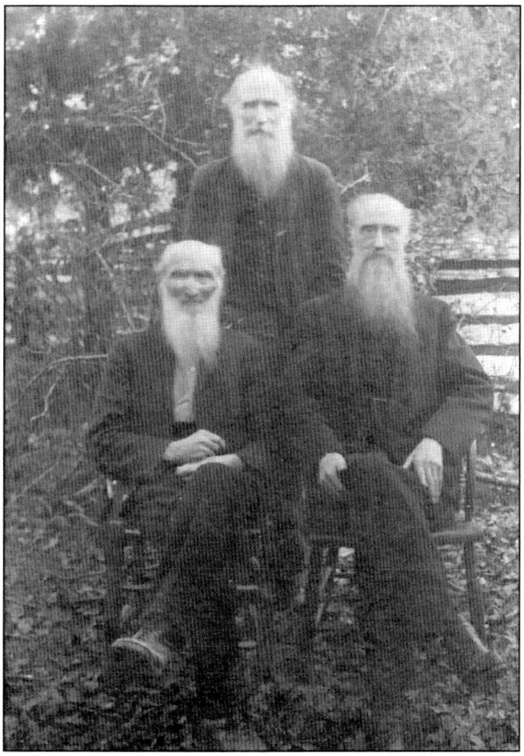

David M. Pyle (left) is sitting with brothers Elisha R. (seated, right) and James M. in front of a fence at David's home near Atlanta. Elisha was visiting from Georgia, and James was visiting from Arkansas. (Courtesy of Patricia Pyle Ridpath.)

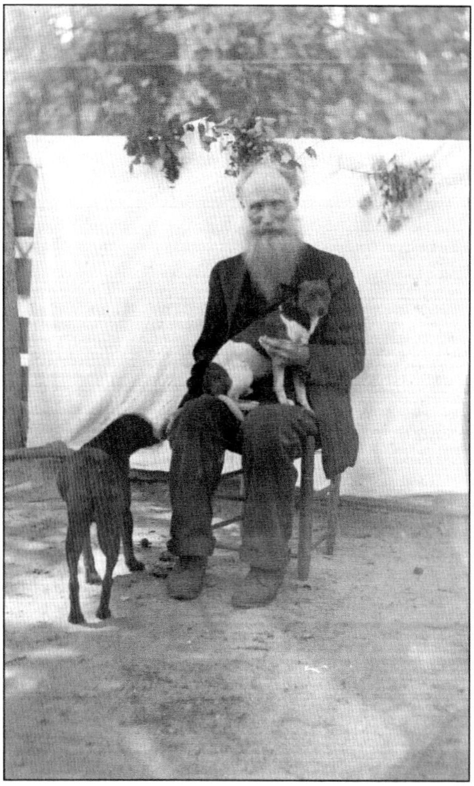

James M. Pyle is seated in front of a sheet that was being used as a background for the photograph. (Courtesy of Patricia Pyle Ridpath.)

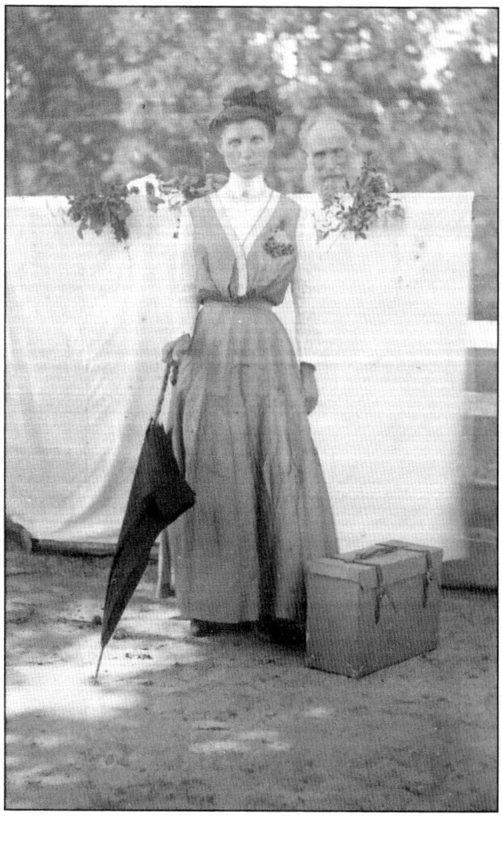

James is standing behind his wife, Martha, who is using an umbrella and a traveling case as props. (Courtesy of Patricia Pyle Ridpath.)

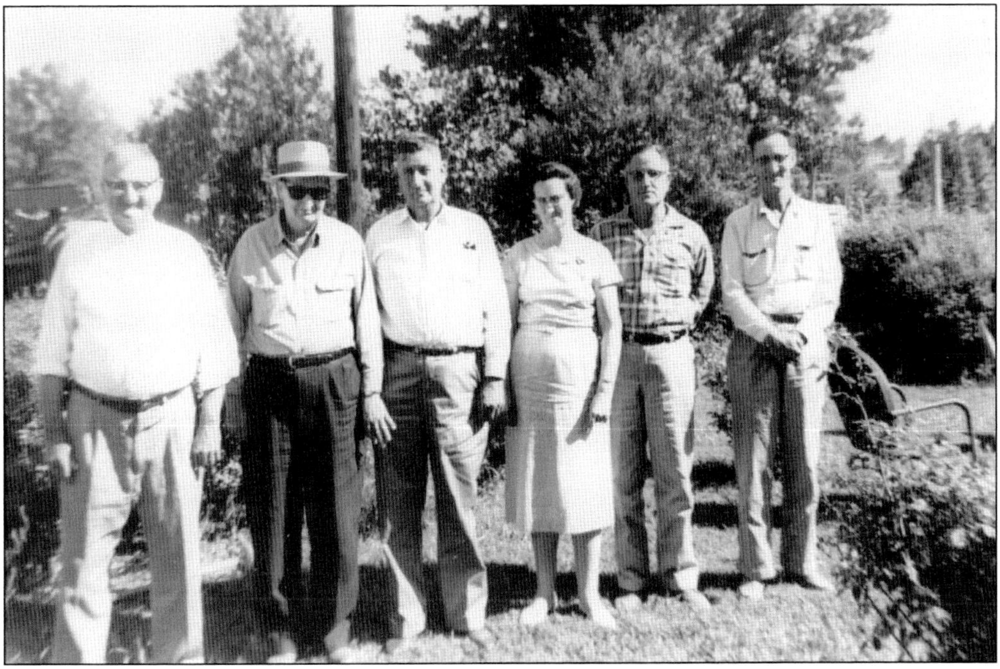

The grandchildren of David M. Pyle, posing for this 1960s photograph are, from left to right, Alton Pyle, Hershell Pyle, Horrace Pyle, Faye Pyle Harvin, Carroll Pyle, and Grady Pyle. (Courtesy of Patricia Pyle Ridpath.)

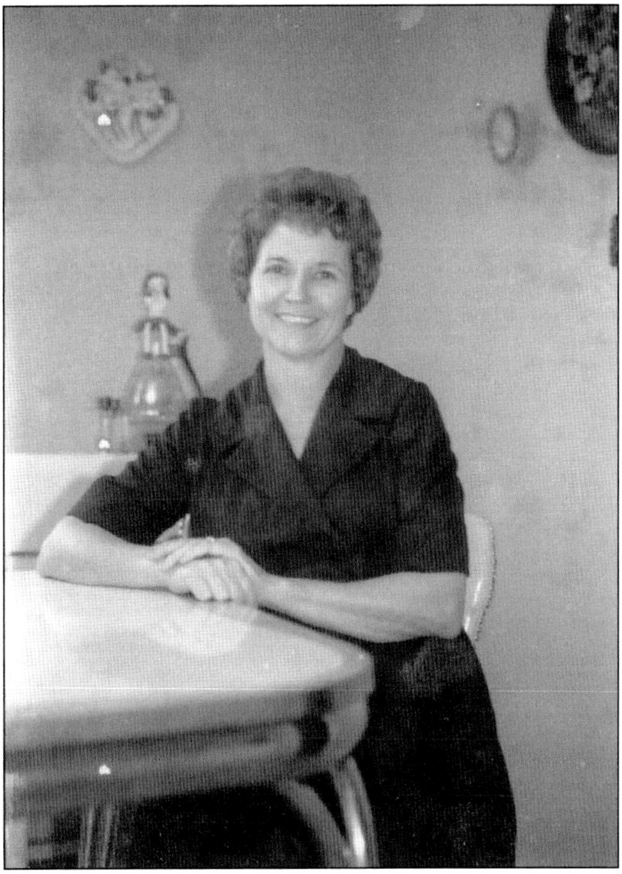

Pearl Brown, wife of Oliver E. Brown, is sitting in her home on East Main Street around 1955. The Atlanta Church of God began services in 1951 in the Brown home. The Browns owned the Atlanta Tire Shop, and their children grew up in Atlanta. (Courtesy of Pearl Brown.)

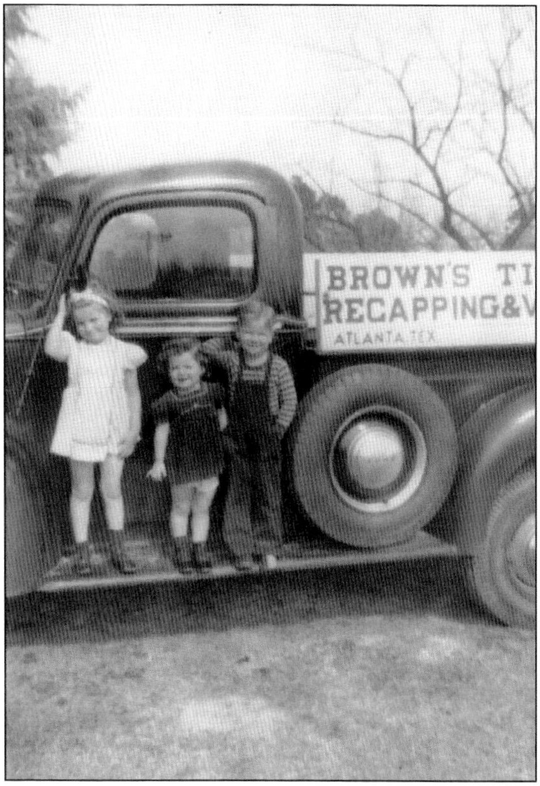

In this photograph from 1946, Louise (left), Sondra (center), and Rodney Brown, the children of Oliver E. and Pearl Brown, stand on the running board of their father's work truck. (Courtesy of Pearl Brown.)

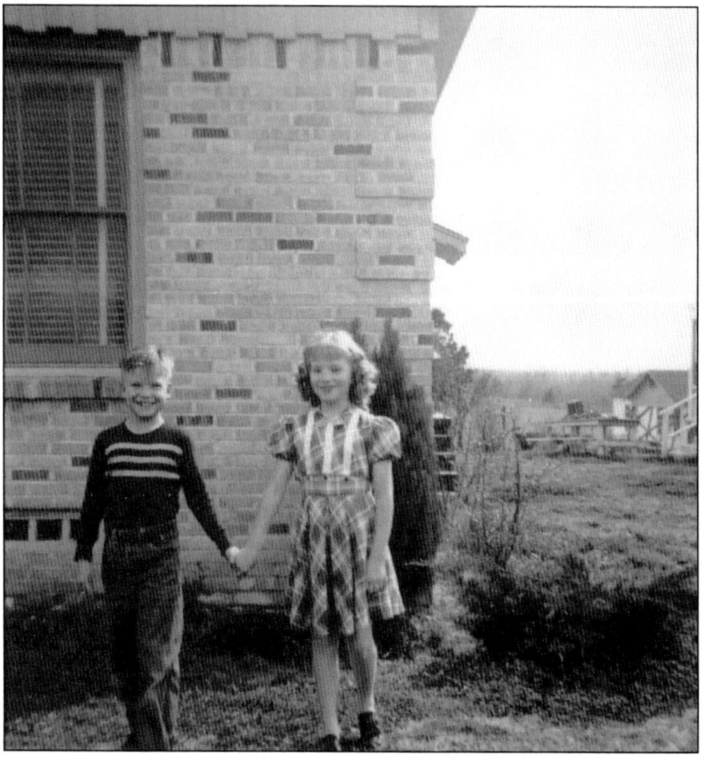

An older Louise and Rodney Brown stand in front of their East Main Street home around 1950. (Courtesy of Pearl Brown.)

This portrait of Irene Bradley was taken around 1955. Bradley is a longtime resident of Atlanta. J.T. Bradley, her brother, worked for the Atlanta Police Department for many years. Local teenagers considered Bradley a kind man for telling them where the other police officers were sitting so they could avoid trouble. J.T. Bradley passed away from a heart attack in the late 1980s. (Courtesy of Irene Bradley.)

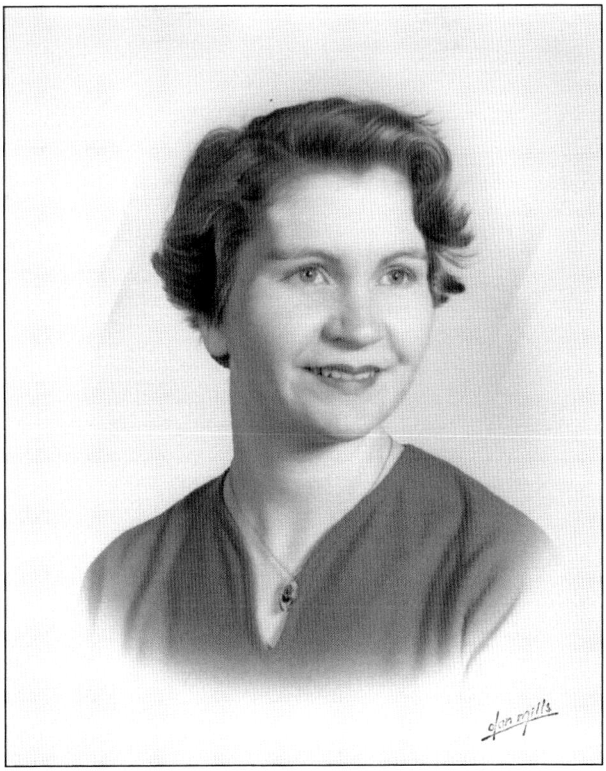

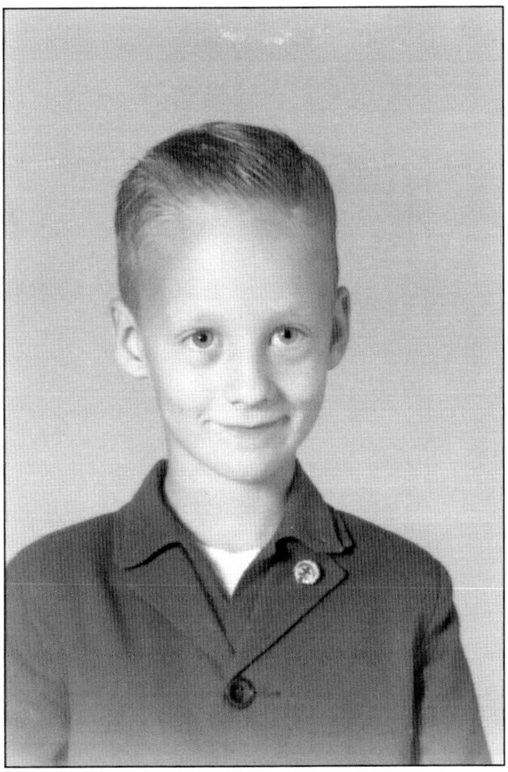

Keith Cherry is the nephew of Irene Bradley. He was five years old in 1965 when this kindergarten photograph was taken. Cherry still resides in Atlanta. (Courtesy of Irene Bradley.)

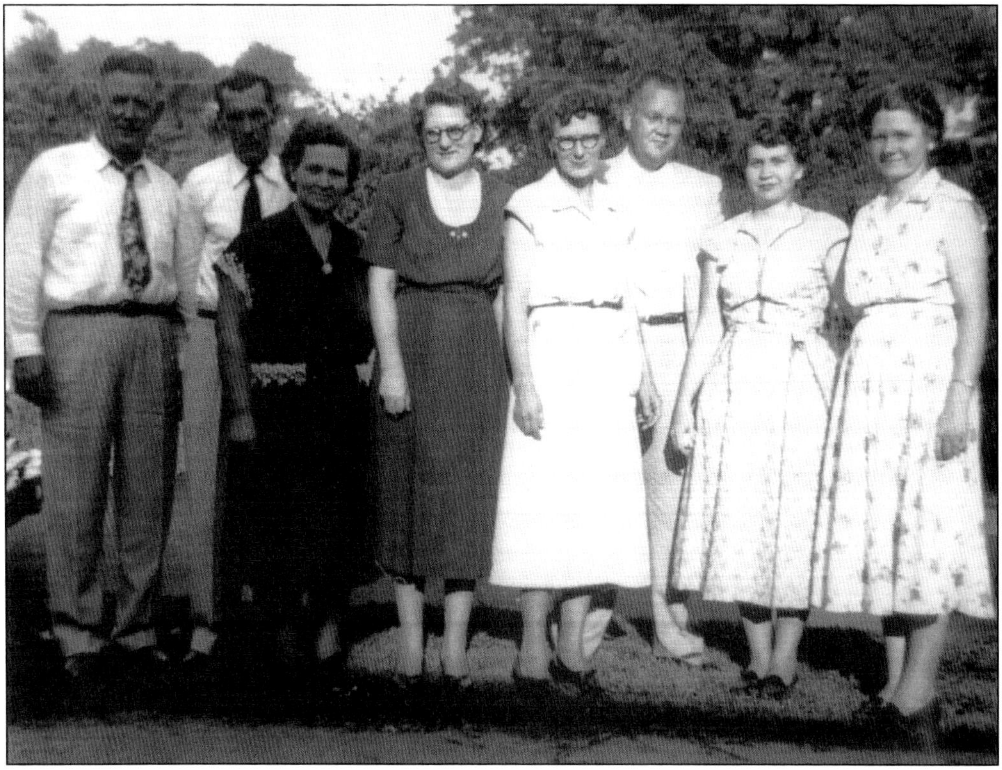

Family and friends are pictured with J.T. and Irene Bradley after their father's funeral in Atlanta, around 1953. Standing here after the funeral are, from left to right, Charlie Carey, Walter Carey, Edna Hartsell, Nettie Cherry, Pearl Jones, J.T. Bradley, Irene Bradley, and Nellie Presley. (Courtesy of Irene Bradley.)

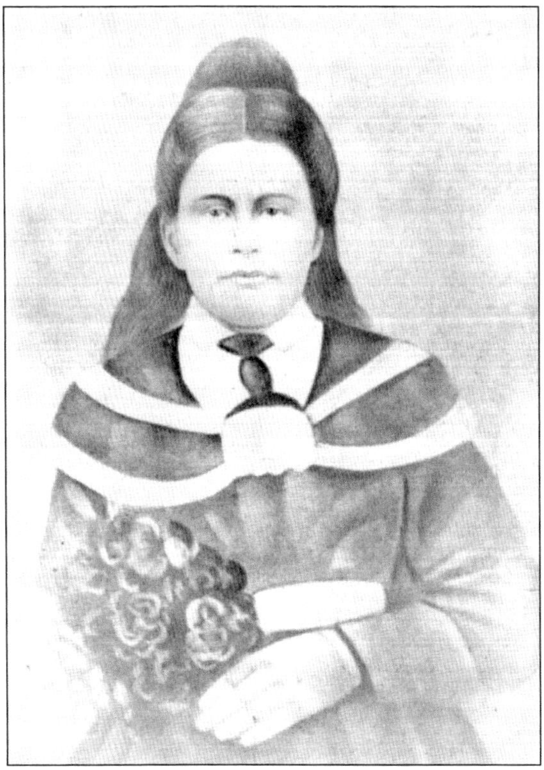

Susan Frances Meadows, wife of John Thomas, was an early resident of Atlanta. She and her husband owned the property just west of Atlanta where the Beverly Hills subdivision is now located. Susan died at the age of 36 and is buried at Laws Chapel. (Courtesy of Pearl Brown.)

This photograph of Mamie and Robert P. Miles was taken around 1886. Their father, T.A. Miles, established Miles Drug Store in 1897. (Courtesy of Cass County Genealogical Society.)

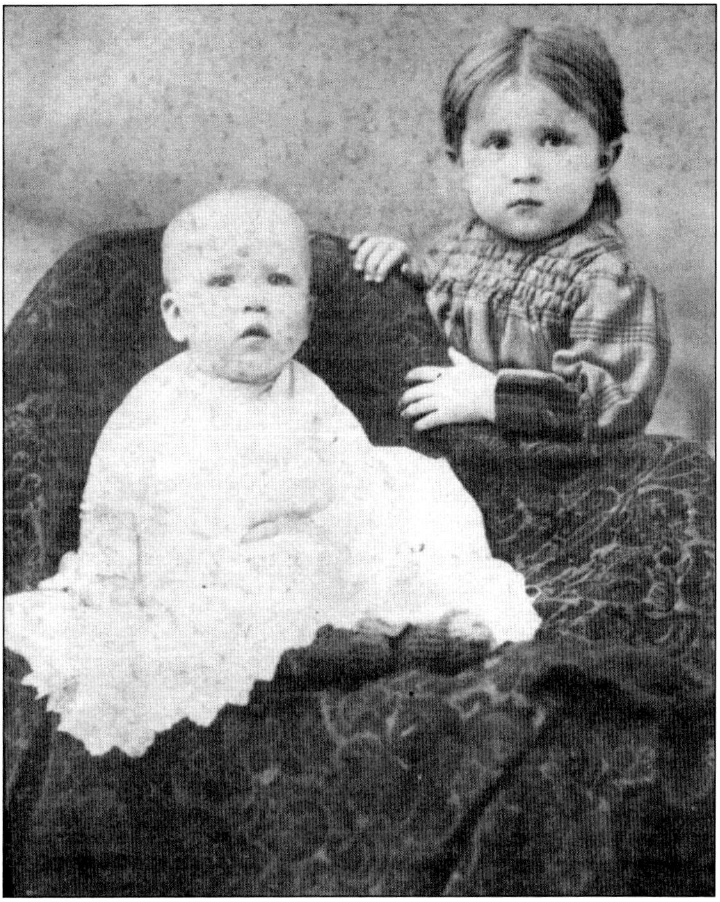

Mary Jane Prator Dupree is the only known person in this photograph from the 1890s. She is standing in the second row to the far right, just behind the man. (Courtesy of Cass County Genealogical Society.)

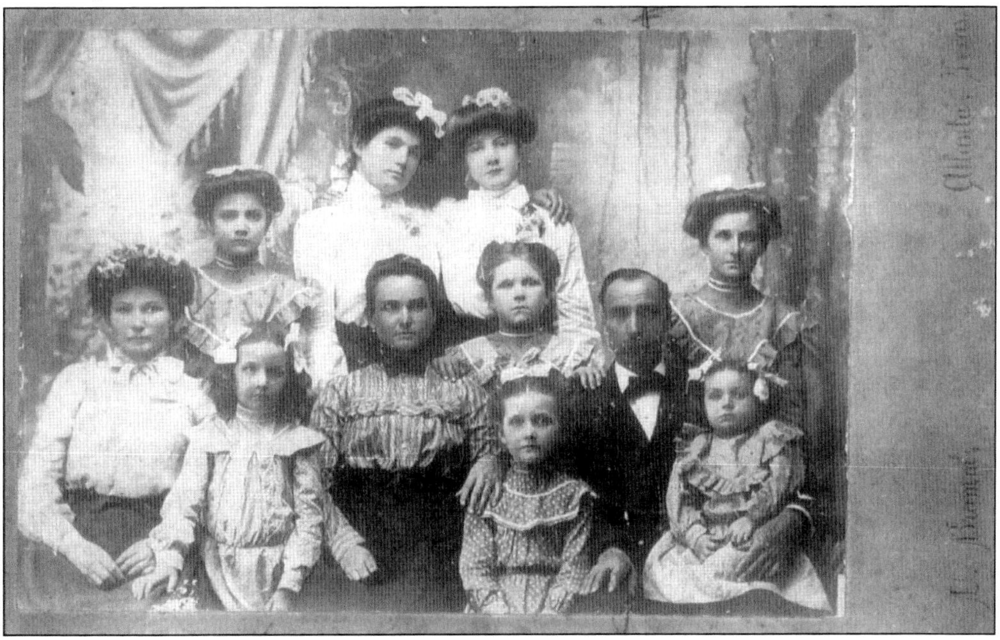

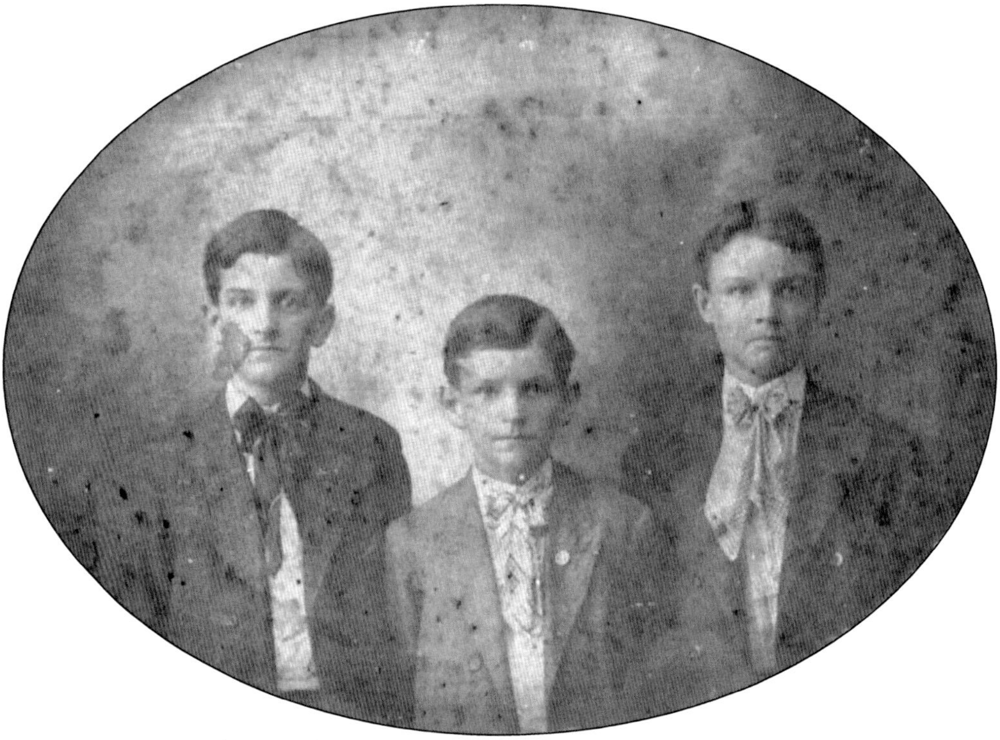

Posing in this 1890s photograph are, from left to right, Allen Perdue, Clifford ? , and unidentified. Perdue was accidentally killed in July 1910 at J.G. Hughes and Company. (Courtesy of Cass County Genealogical Society.)

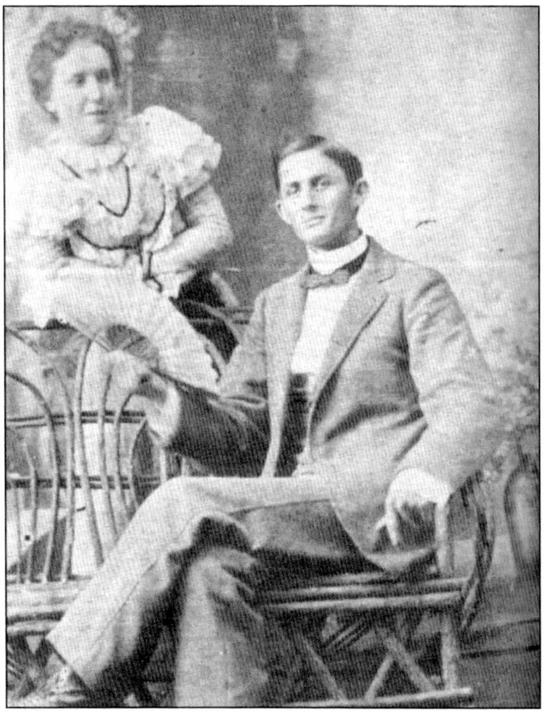

Daisy and Wright McClung pose in an 1890 photograph. Daisy was a schoolteacher, and she knew plenty about the newspaper business. She was the daughter of John M. Fletcher, the *Citizens Journal's* first publisher. (Courtesy of Cass County Genealogical Society.)

This photograph, taken in 1904, shows Mr. and Mrs. J.R. Griffin and their son Howard. Mr. Griffin is the son of George Griffin, an early Atlanta settler and restaurant owner. In his later years, J.R. resided at 113 Miller Street in Atlanta. (Courtesy of Pearl Brown.)

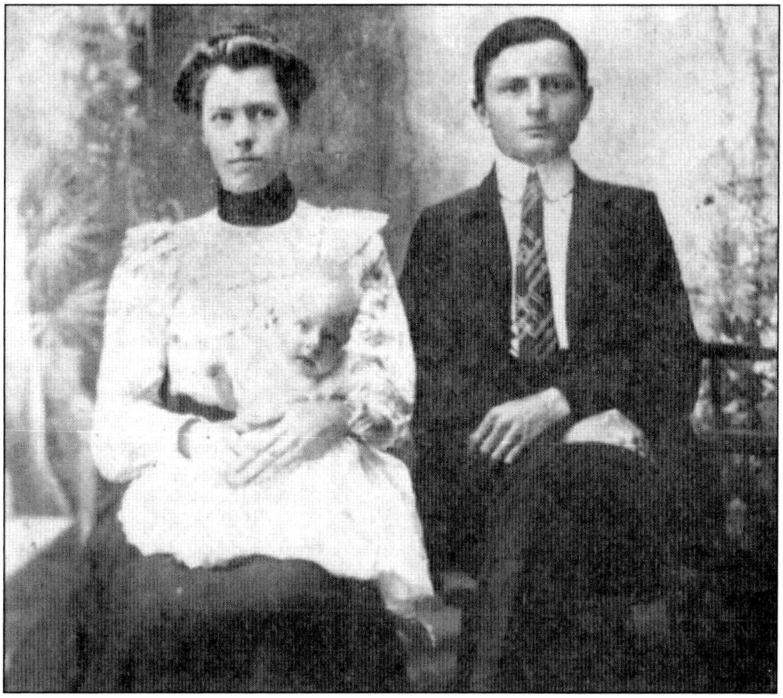

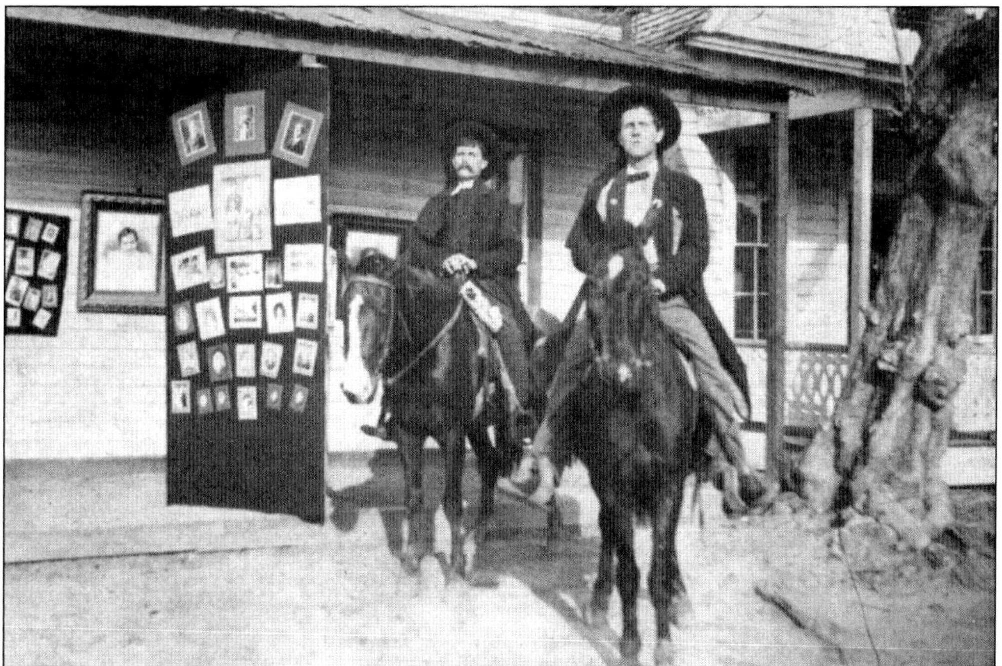

Pictured in front of Bramm's Studio on Hiram Street in 1910 are W.H. Brown (left) and his brother-in-law Sam Tyson. Brown was born in Cass County and came to Atlanta with this family in 1872 when he was one year old. His father, Hiram Brown, operated a blacksmith shop in the early days of Atlanta. (Courtesy of Pearl Brown.)

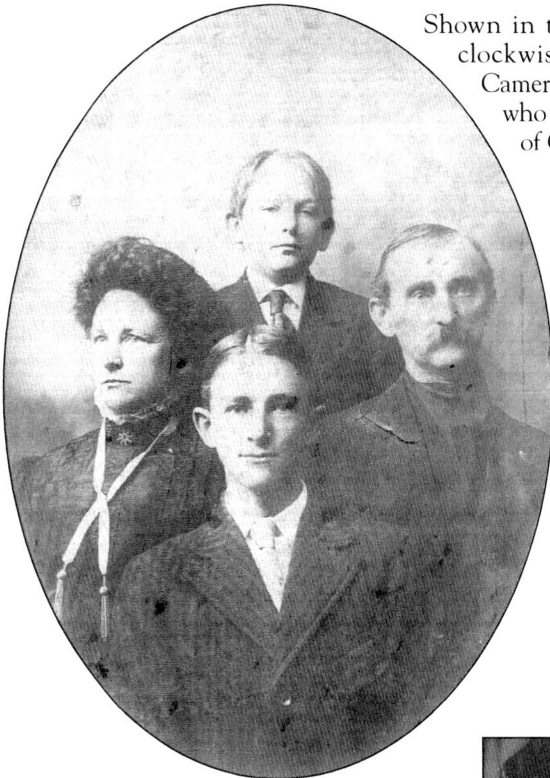

Shown in this photograph from around 1890 are, clockwise from the left, Mollie Cameron, Don Cameron, William F. Cameron, and R.P. Cameron, who was the father of Fred Cameron. (Courtesy of Cass County Genealogical Society.)

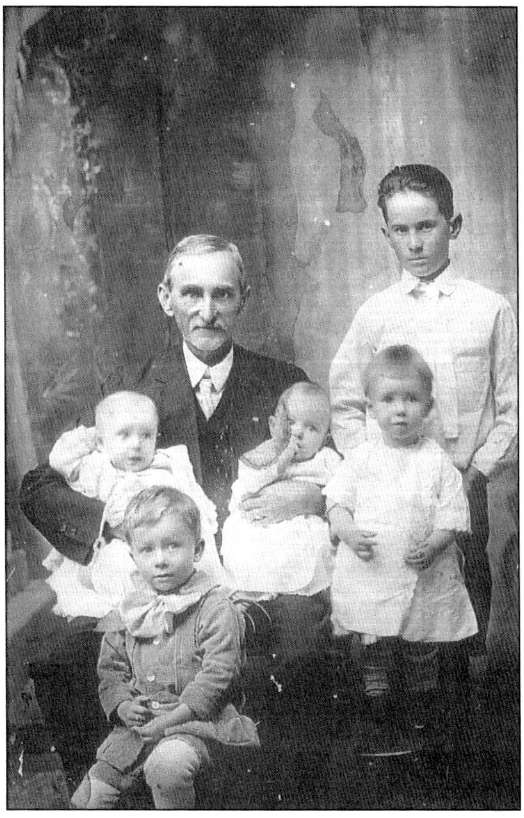

William F. Cameron poses for a c. 1900 photograph with his grandchildren. Pictured are, from left to right, (first row) Cameron Glass; (second row) Rob Cameron, William F. Cameron, William C. Cameron, and Bob McMahon; (third row) Fred Cameron. (Courtesy of Cass County Genealogical Society.)

Four generations of Camerons are shown here around 1915. They are, from left to right, Sarah Temperance Locket McCoy ("Mama Sadie"), William P. Cameron, Mary C. McCoy Cameron, and Fred Cameron. (Courtesy of Cass County Genealogical Society.)

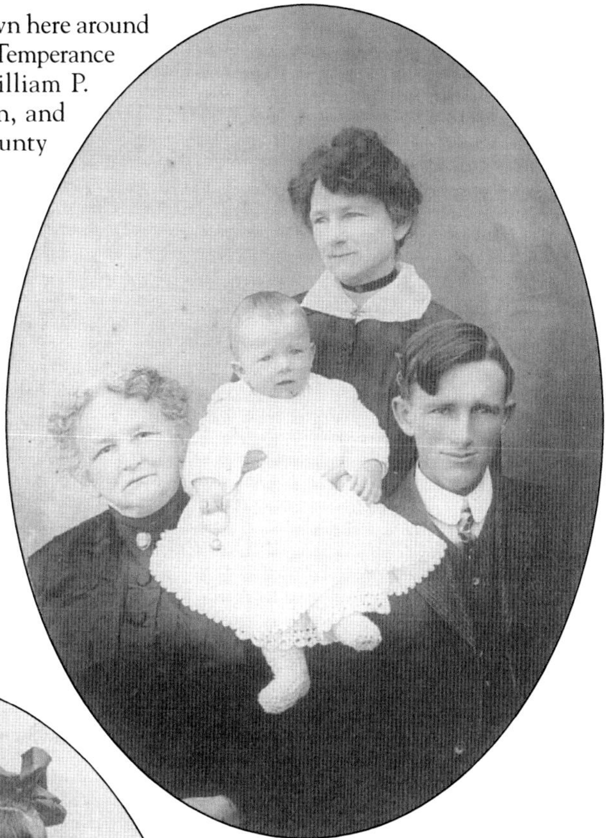

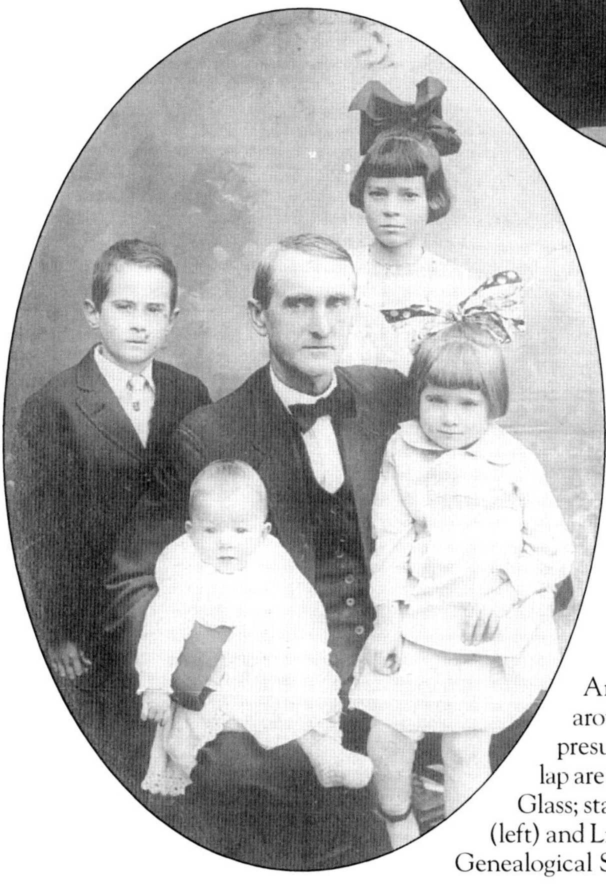

Another Cameron family portrait from around 1925 shows Fred Cameron with his presumed grandchildren. Seated on Fred's lap are baby Fred Cameron (left) and Margarie Glass; standing behind Fred are Cameron Glass (left) and Lillian Glass. (Courtesy of Cass County Genealogical Society.)

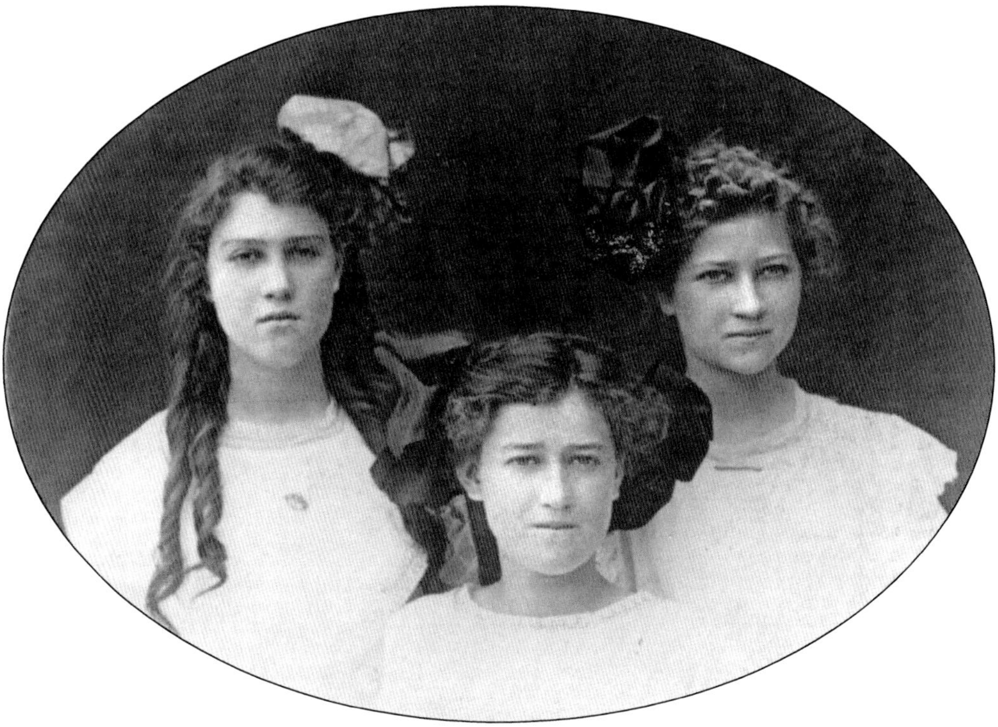

Pictured around 1910 are Walter Blackey's daughters. From left to right, they are Erma (married J.D. Fouche), Ora (married Vern Clements), and Bessie (married C.F. Perdue) Blackey. (Courtesy of Cass County Genealogical Society.)

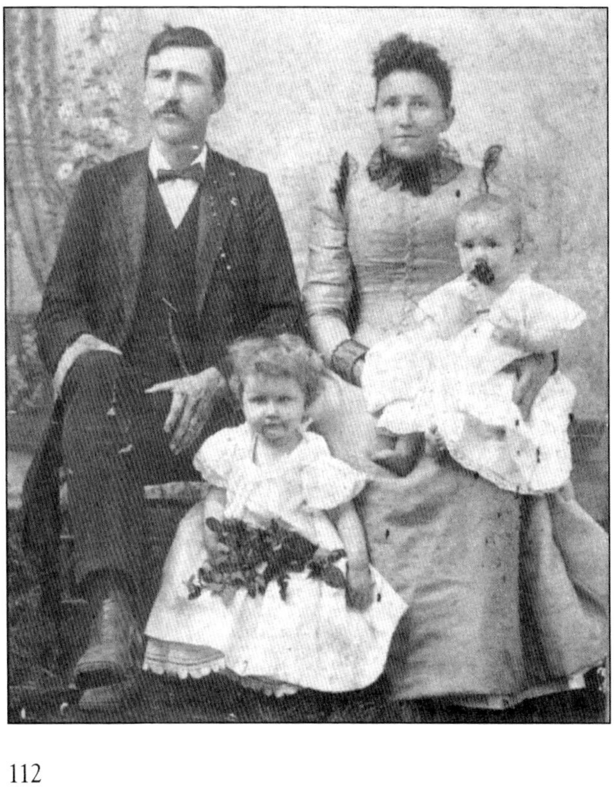

Lorn L. and Della Johnson Davis, both natives of Cass County, came to Atlanta in its early days. They were married in 1889. He served for a while as a county clerk and owned a general merchandise store. In this 1890s photograph are, from left to right, Lorn L., daughter Louise, wife Della, and son Roger. (Courtesy of Pearl Brown.)

Hershel and Marie Hanner (Ellis) are pictured here in 1912. They were the children of Mr. and Mrs. John Hanner. (Courtesy of Pearl Brown.)

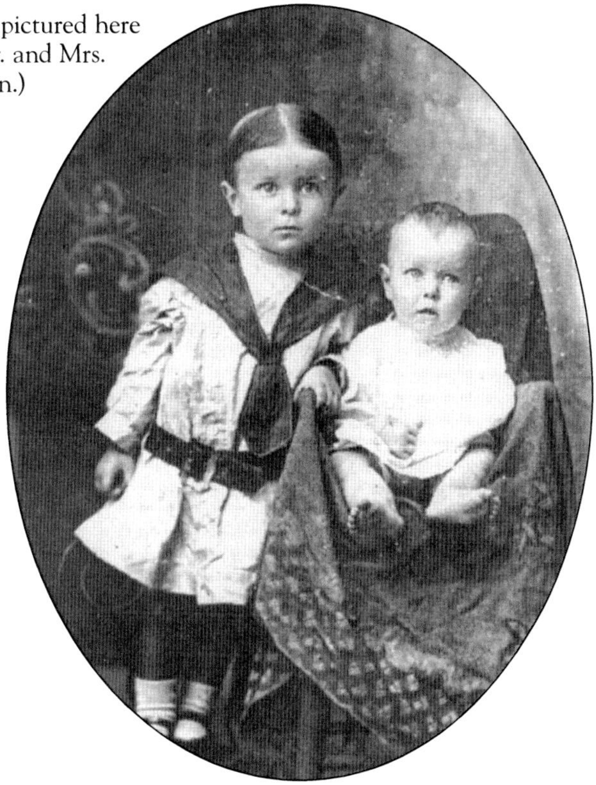

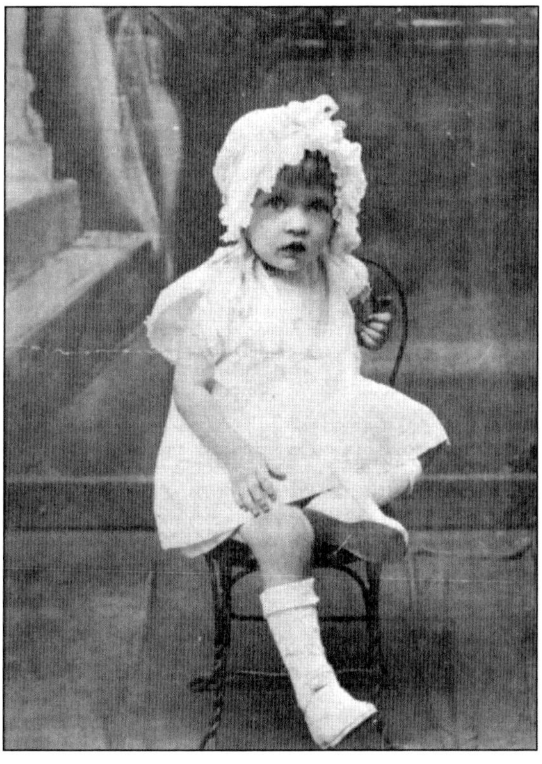

Edna Gail Hanner (Walls) is pictured here in 1918. She was the daughter of Mr. and Mrs. Nath Hanner, who were some of the founders of Hanner's Funeral Service in Atlanta. (Courtesy of Pearl Brown.)

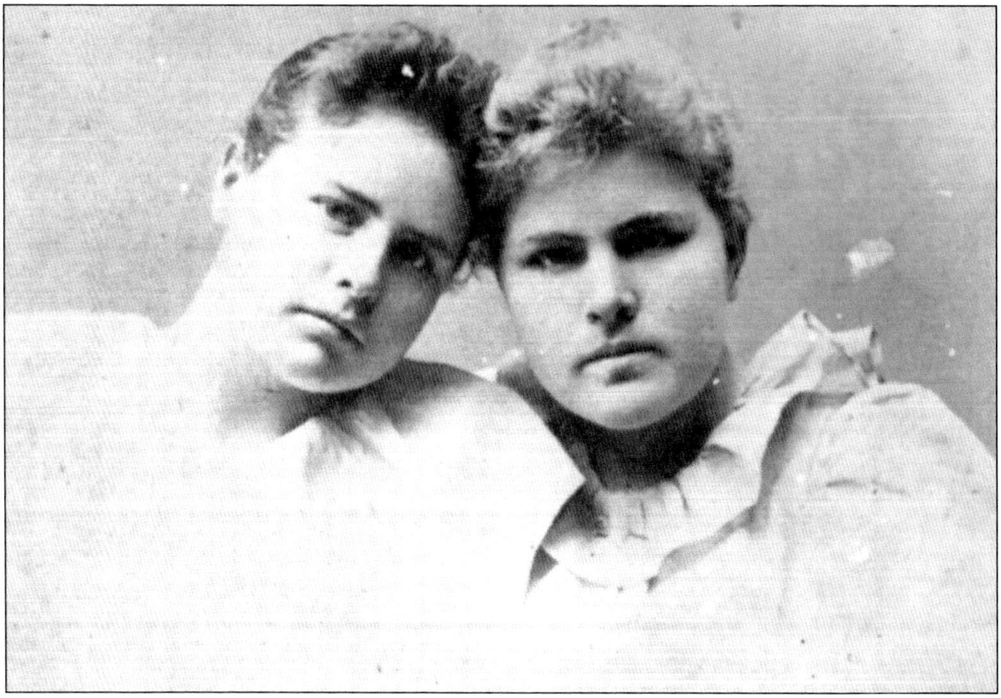

Eva Thomas Echols and Doshia Thomas Cruse were early settlers in Atlanta. They were the daughters of John and Susan Frances Meadows Thomas. (Courtesy of Pearl Brown.)

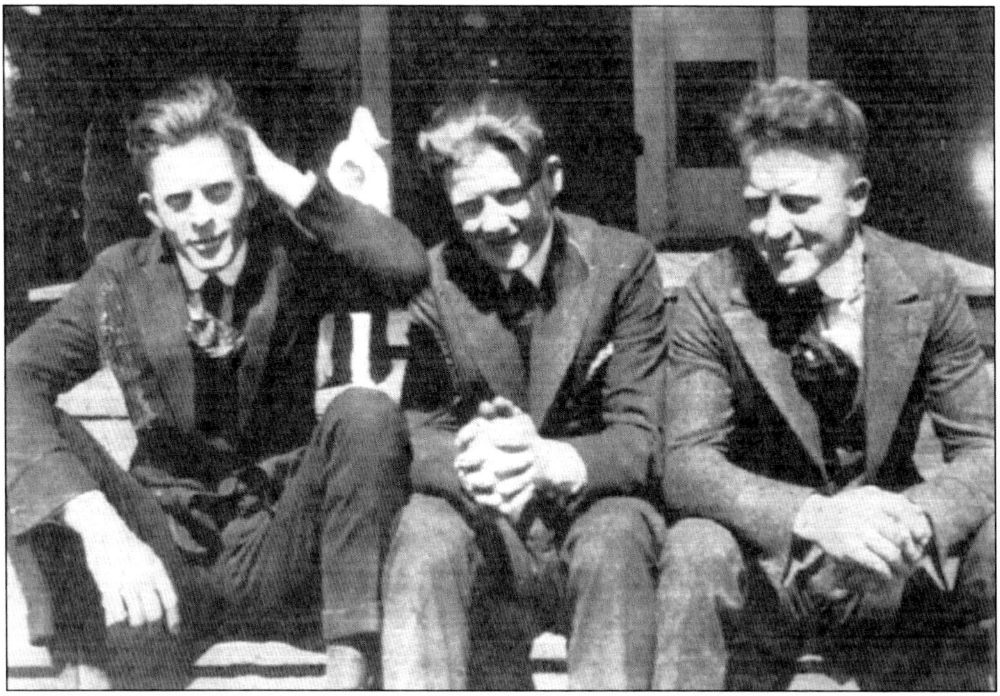

This 1920 photograph of three brothers reads, "Raymond with brothers Hope and Edd. Just back from World War I. George was still overseas in the occupation forces. 'All home, but one.' " (Courtesy of Cass County Genealogical Society.)

T.A. Miles established the first Miles Drug Store in 1897. He and his wife are shown here with their son and daughter, Robert P. and Mamie Miles, and a friend. The order of the children in this photograph was not defined. (Courtesy of Pearl Brown.)

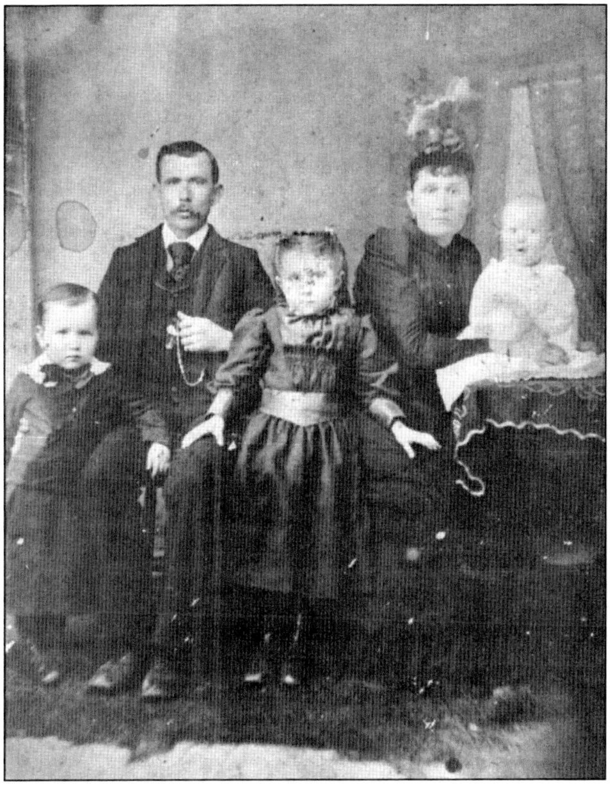

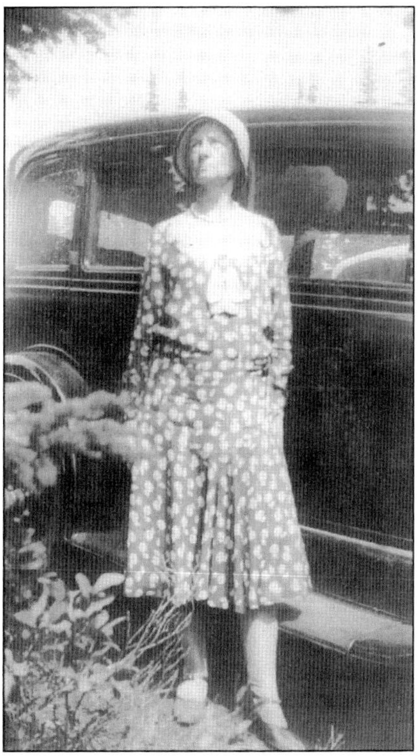

Cheelie McCoy Cameron, also known as "Miss Molly," poses in front of a car in this 1920s photograph. (Courtesy of Cass County Genealogical Society.)

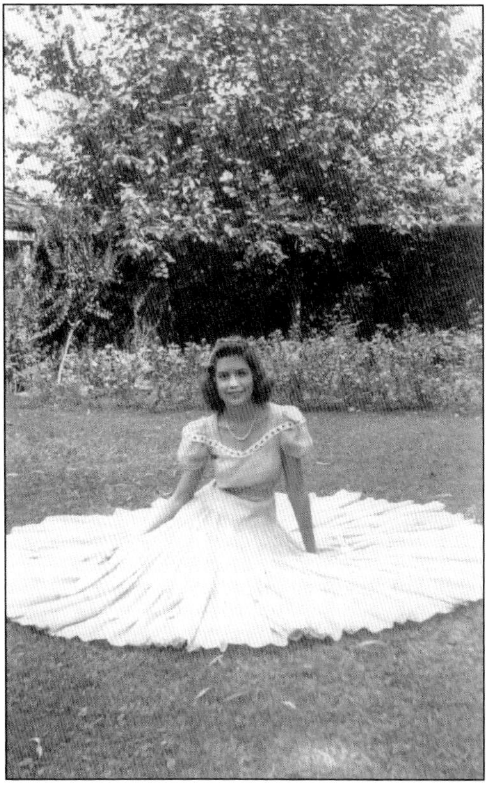

Inez Wilson poses in a long gown for this 1950s photograph. (Courtesy of Cass County Genealogical Society.)

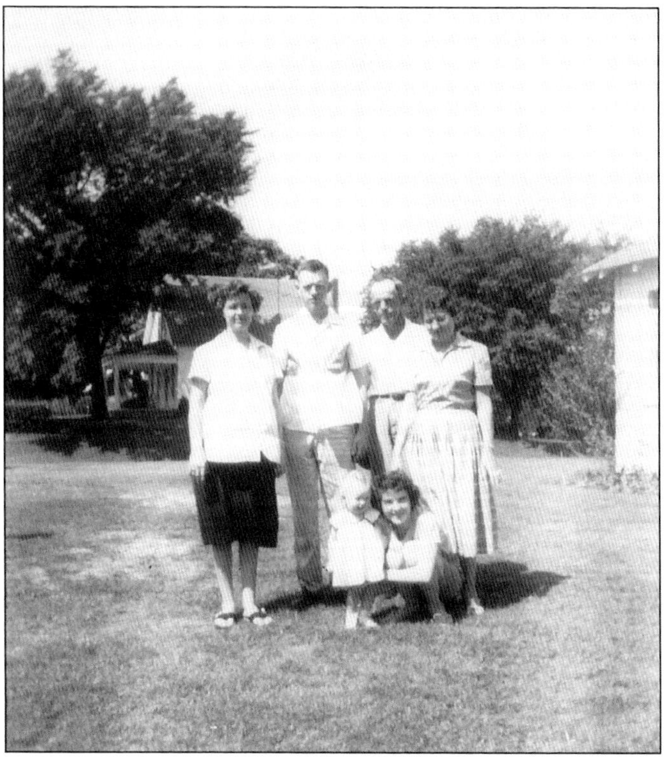

The Evans family is pictured in front of their home near Atlanta. Standing in the yard are, from left to right, (first row) Elizabeth Evans and Elaine Evans Gibbins; (second row) Lou Parker Evans, Ross Evans, M.E. "Mutt" Evans, and Clara Updegraff. (Courtesy of Cass County Genealogical Society.)

Eight

The Centennial Year of 1972

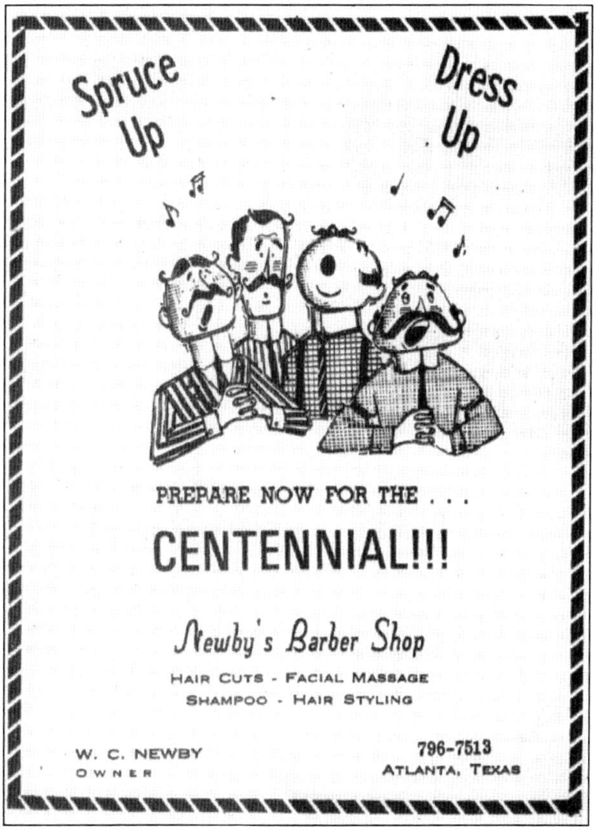

Newby's Barber Shop advertised for the centennial. The advertisement featured an old-fashioned barbershop quartet and appeared in the *Citizens Journal*. (Courtesy of Pearl Brown.)

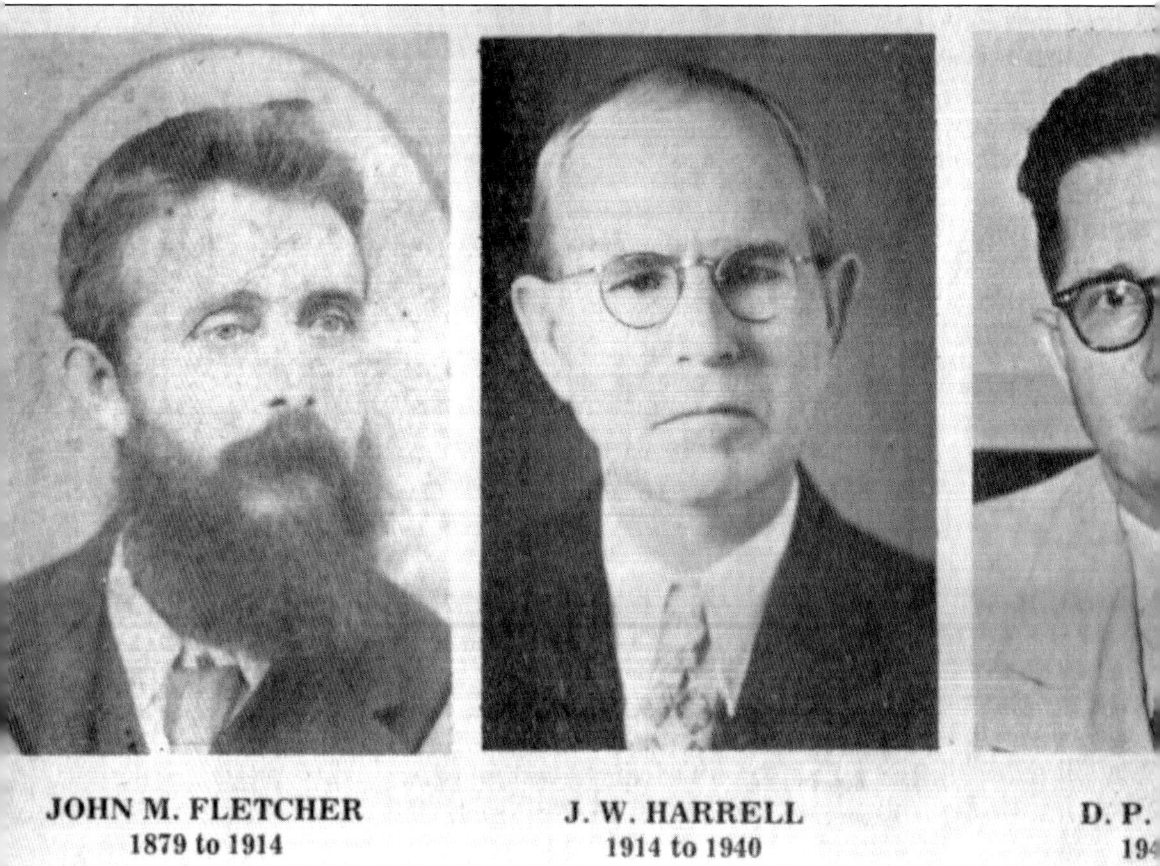

There were only five different publishers for the *Citizens Journal* between 1879 and 1972. From left to right they are John M. Fletcher (publisher from 1879 to 1914), J.W. Harrell (1914–1940),

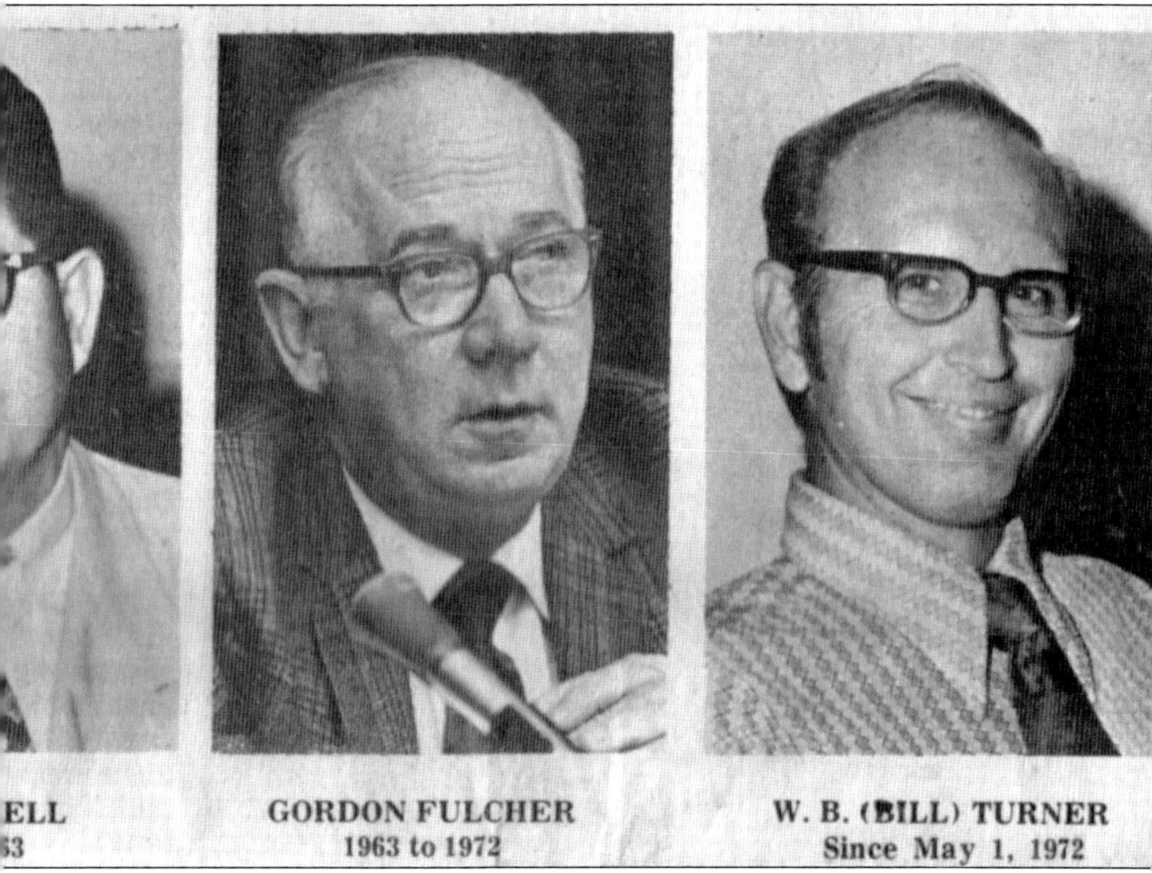

D.P. Harrell (1940–1963), Gordon Fulcher (1963–1972), and W.B. Turner (May 1, 1972–present). (Courtesy of Pearl Brown.)

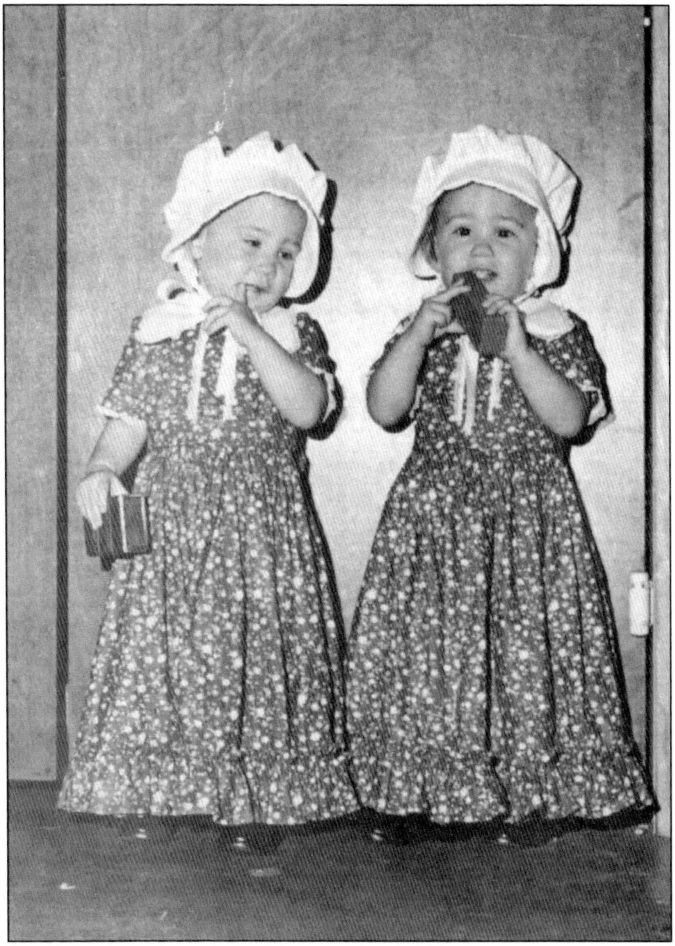

The caption under this 1972 newspaper photograph commemorating Atlanta's 100 years reads, "Centennial Cuties." Shannon and Sharon were the 15-month old daughters of Mr. and Mrs. Ronnie Hailey of Atlanta. Their dresses were made by their grandmother Mrs. Glen Petty. (Courtesy of Pearl Brown.)

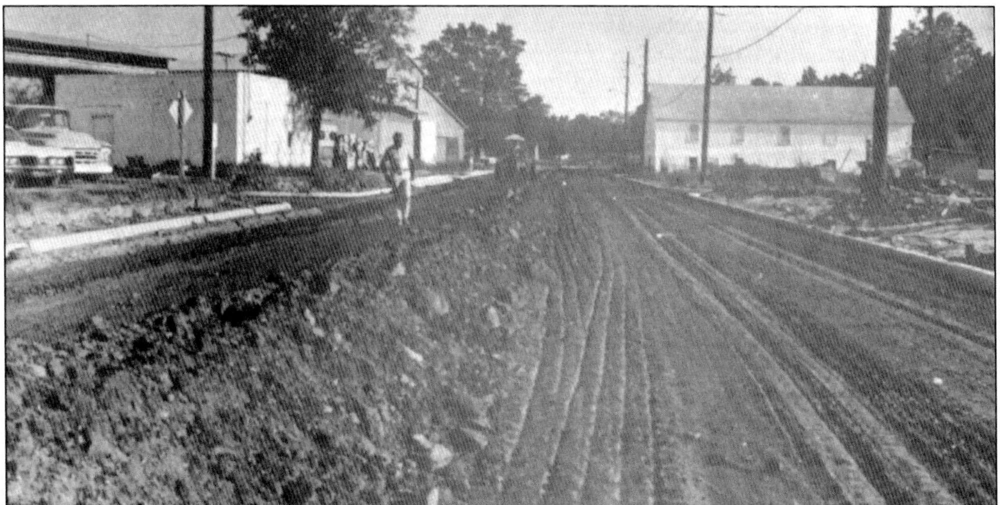

A construction project on Holly Street (then known as FM 251) in 1972 shows the street unpaved. (Courtesy of Pearl Brown.)

In 1972, the State Theatre on Main Street was showing the movie *The Cross and the Switchblade*, starring Pat Boone and Erik Estrada. This photograph appeared in the centennial issue of the *Citizens Journal*. (Courtesy of Pearl Brown.)

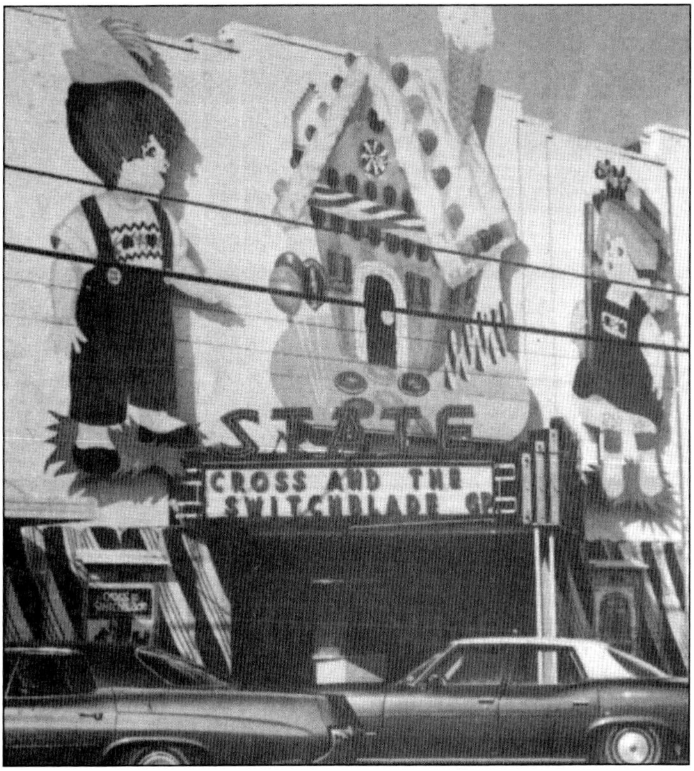

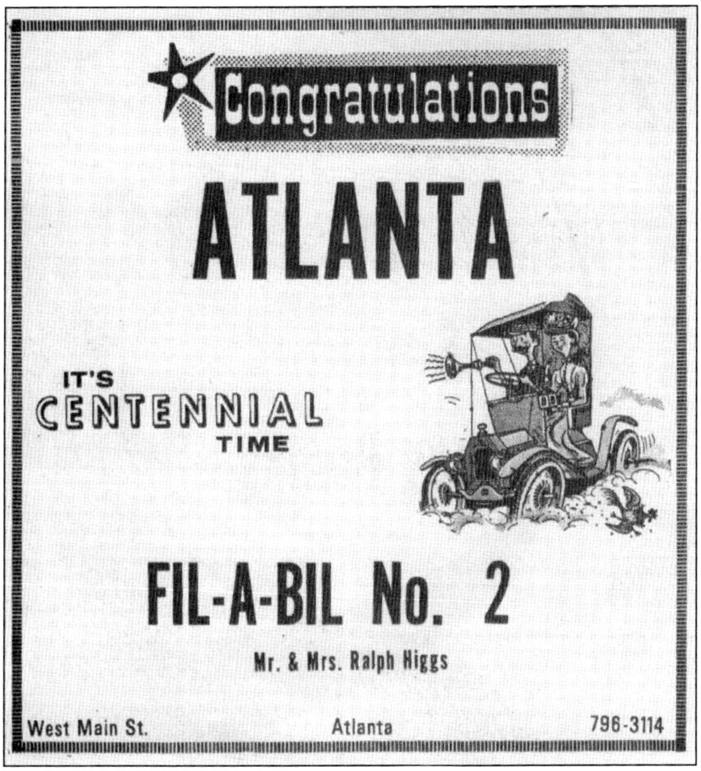

Many of these types of advertisements were shown in the *Citizens Journal* during 1972. This one was purchased by the Fil-A-Bil convenience store, which was located on West Main Street. The authors remember visiting this store often to buy candy when they were children in the 1970s. (Courtesy of Pearl Brown.)

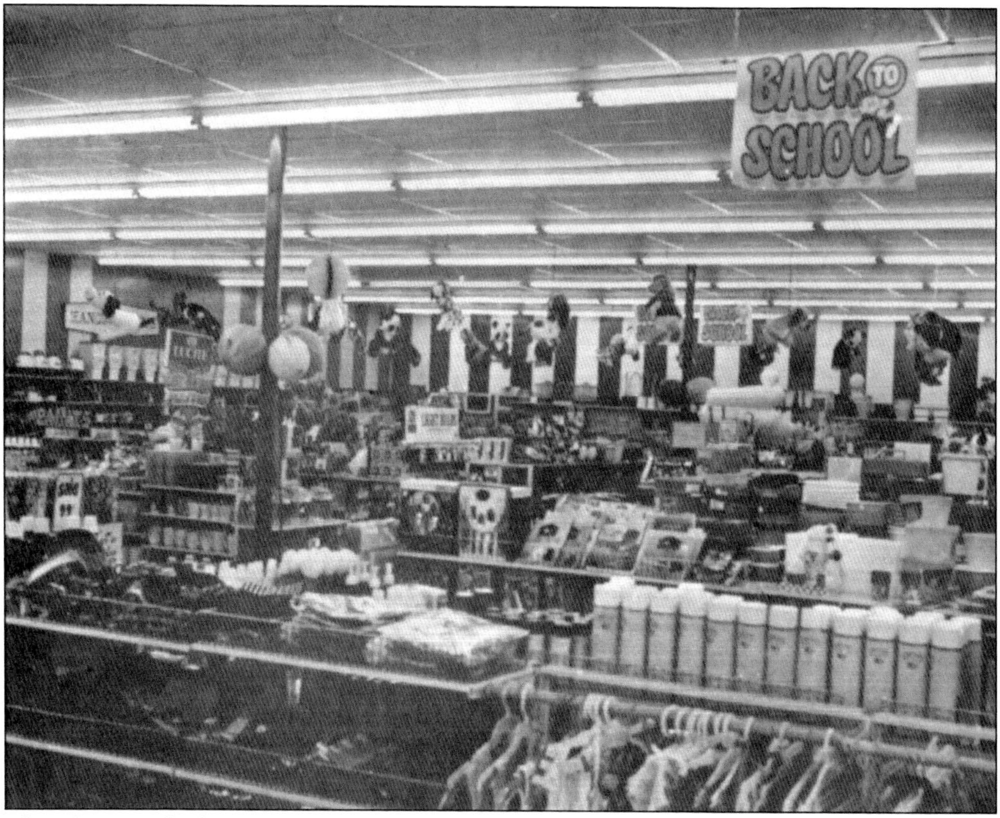

This photograph shows an inside view of Ben Franklin's, located in the Pine Acres shopping center on East Main Street. The store is getting shoppers ready for "Back to School." (Courtesy of Pearl Brown.)

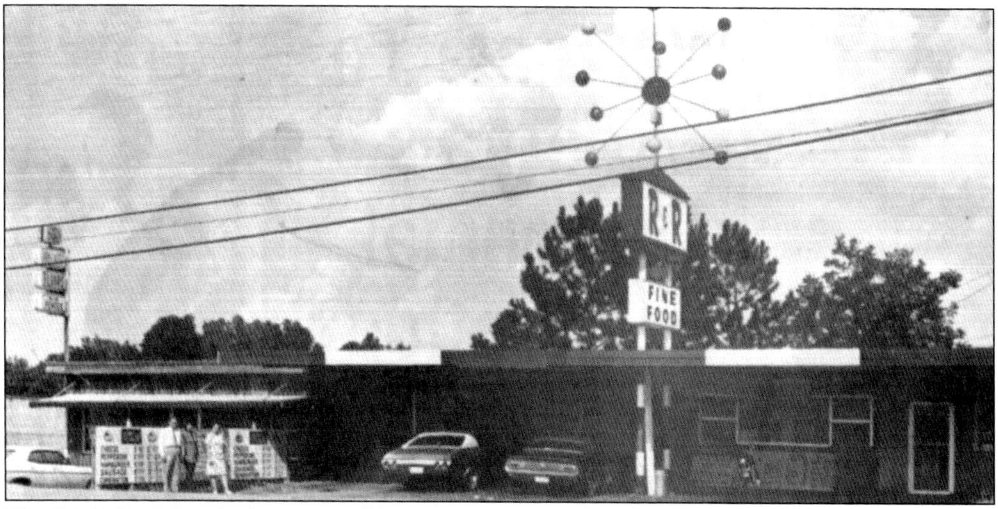

The R&R Drift Inn had a memorable sign with colorful balls that looked like balloons on top. It remained mostly vacant after the late 1970s but was quite popular in its heyday. Next door in the same complex was the R&R Fence Company. (Courtesy of Pearl Brown.)

Debbie Harrist presents a special guest invitation to Mayor Bonny Roark from the Jerry Lewis Muscular Dystrophy Telethon. (Courtesy of Pearl Brown.)

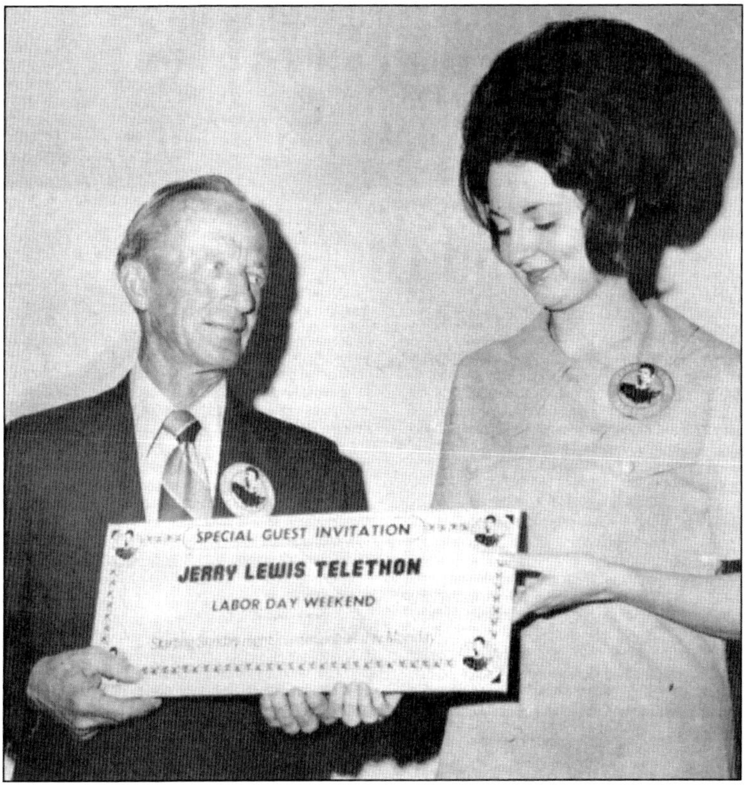

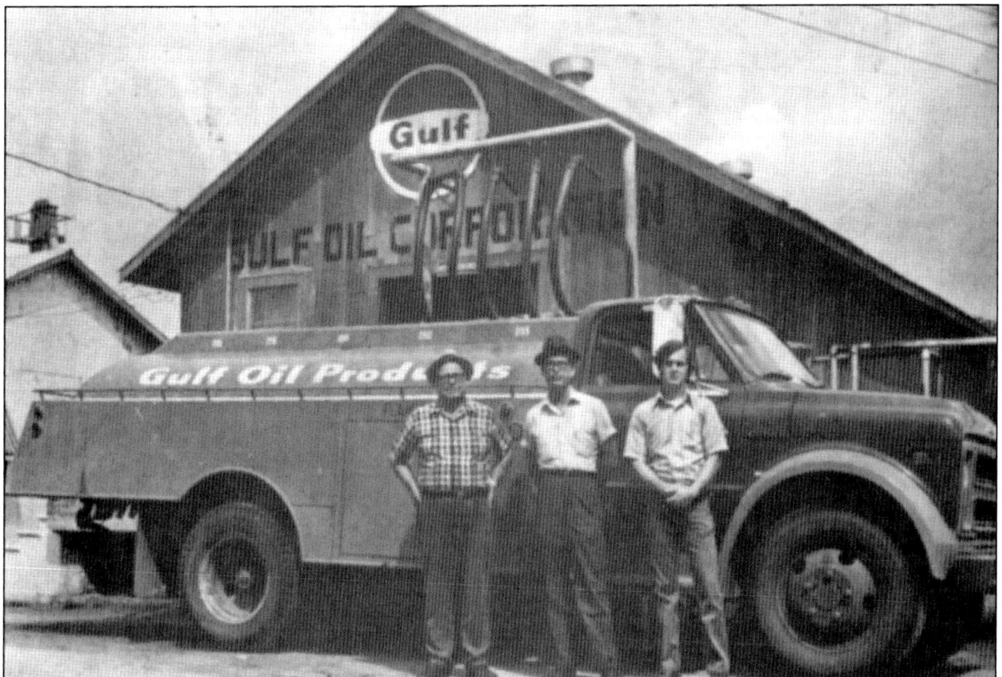

H.F. McWilliams's Gulf Oil Corporation business began in Atlanta in the 1930s on South West Street. (Courtesy of Pearl Brown.)

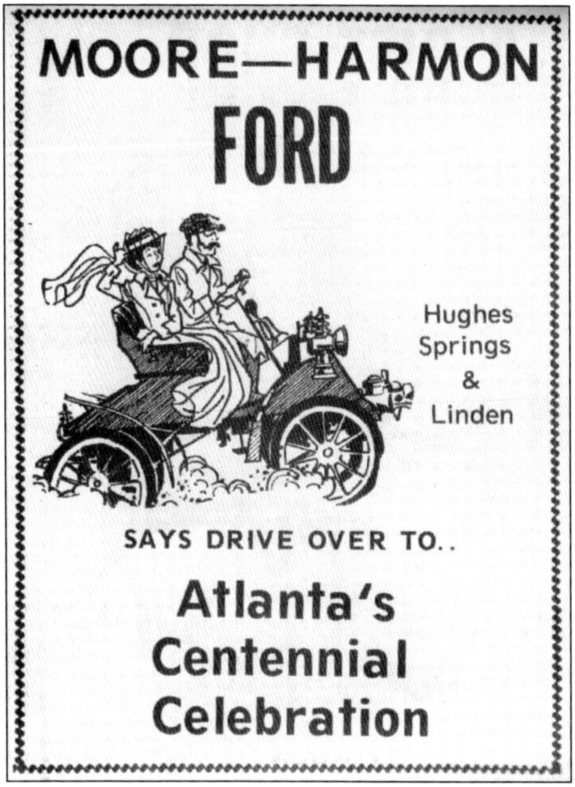

Even businesses outside Atlanta placed advertisements to commemorate the centennial year. (Courtesy of Pearl Brown.)

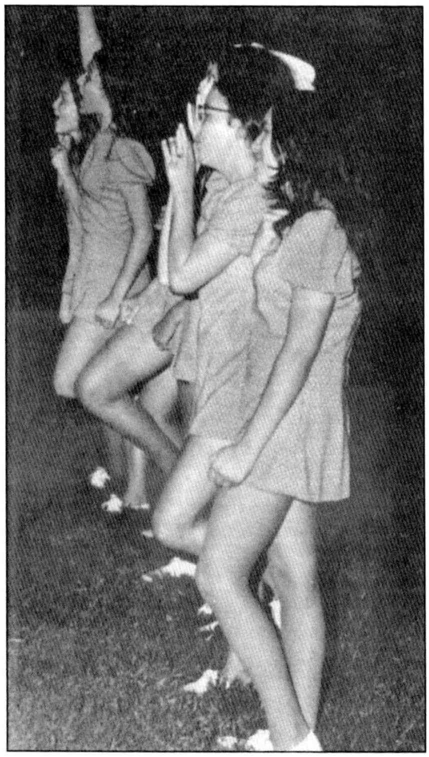

The Atlanta High School cheerleaders were out in full force for the Rabbits' first game of the 1972 season against the DeKalb High School Bears. (Courtesy of Pearl Brown.)

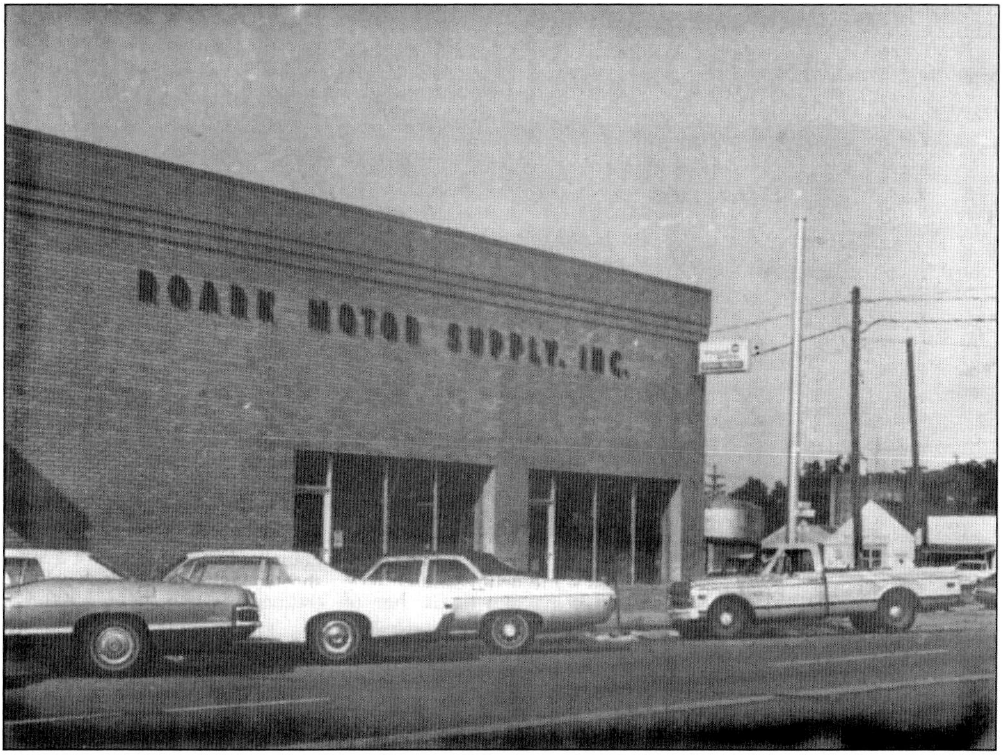

Roark Motor Supply Company, now Roark Auto Parts, is still located at 100 East Main Street. (Courtesy of Pearl Brown.)

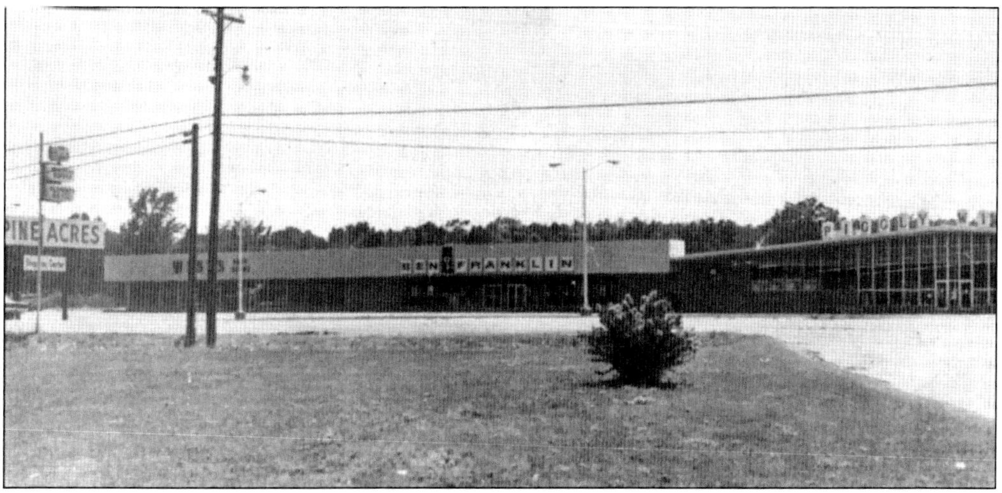

A view of Pine Acres Shopping Center in 1972 shows West's Department Store, Ben Franklin, and the Piggly Wiggly. The shopping center still operates today with different businesses. The Piggly Wiggly is now Brookshire's, and the grass in the foreground was paved to add more parking. (Courtesy of Pearl Brown.)

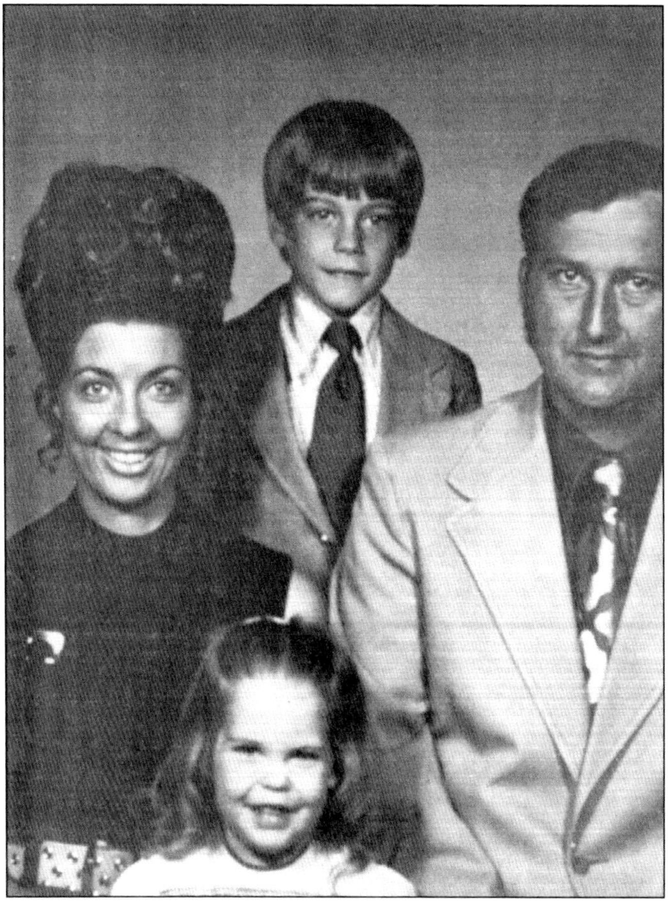

The Dick Grogan family appears in a centennial issue of the *Citizens Journal* in 1972. (Courtesy of Pearl Brown.)

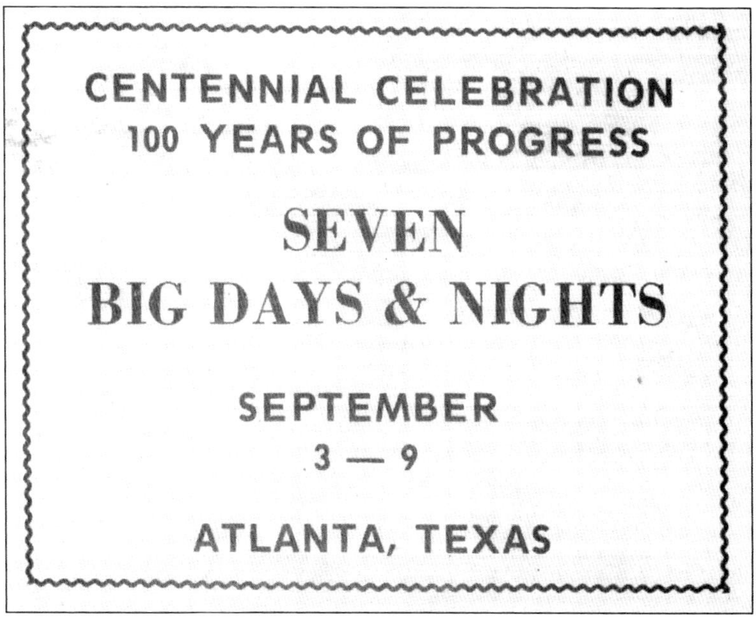

Atlanta's centennial was celebrated for an entire week, September 3–9, 1972. Printed just above this advertisement was a schedule of all the activities during the week of festivities. (Courtesy of Pearl Brown.)

INDEX